Horsemen of the Outback

Their Spurs and Their Spurmakers

Revised Edition

Dedication

Dedicated to
Edna Zigenbine Jessop, Boss Drover
and
Mick Bower, Ringer

Mick Bower, Manbulloo, Northern Territory, 1963

Edna Zigenbine, Windorah, Queensland, 1953

Some of us are fortunate to meet, during our lifetime, a few people for whom we develop a great respect and affection and so, with memories of droving and ringing days in the Territory in the 1950s, I have dedicated this book to Edna and Mick.

Horsemen of the Outback

Their Spurs and Their Spurmakers

Revised Edition

•

Don J Corcoran

First published in 2003 by Central Queensland University Press

Second published in 2012 by Boolarong Press, Salisbury, Brisbane, Australia.

National Library of Australia Cataloguing-in-Publication entry

Author:	Corcoran, Don (John Edward), 1936-
Title:	Horsemen of the outback / Don J. Corcoran.
ISBN:	9781921920530 (pbk.)
Subjects:	Spurs--Australia.
	Blacksmithing--Australia.
	Horsemen and horsewomen--Clothing--Australia.
	Horsemanship--Australia--Equipment and supplies.
Dewey Number:	682.0994

Typeset by Watson Ferguson & Company

Cover design by Jane Dorrington

Front cover painting: Ron Bostock

Back cover photo: Rodney Watson, Diamantina River, late 1940s

Printed and bound by Watson Ferguson & Company, Salisbury, Brisbane, Australia.

Author's Note - Revised Edition

SINCE 'HORSEMEN OF THE OUTBACK' was first published in 2003, I have received numerous letters and photographs from former ringers and drovers and am pleased to be able to include their stories in this revised edition.

Sadly, many I wrote about then have since passed on, and those I know of are listed here.

Edna Zigenbine Jessop died in Mount Isa in 2007. Also gone are R. M. Williams of Toowoomba, Ken Martin of Winton, Clargie Saltmere of Camooweal and, more recently, Bill Hamill of Yelarbon.

In N.S.W. Annie Adams, one of the Darcy family and widow of blacksmith Deal Adams, died in Newcastle , and Frank Clark, a former N.S.W. Mounted Police Trooper, and father of Tony Clark, died in Parkes aged 102 years. As Tony said, 'He had a good run'.

Mick Bower's partner, Nida Lowe, passed on in Katherine in December 2009. A couple of years earlier Buck Buchester, who spent more than 50 years in the Victoria River country, also died, as did John Nicolson of Halls Creek in the Kimberley.

Stan Morgan, of Port Lincoln, S.A., died in 2004 – Stan was the designer of the unique Morgan Rigid Spur in 1945. I was fortunate in late 2003, after many long letters and phone conversations, to finally meet Stan in Port Lincoln.

In some cases these deaths were not unexpected – I am now seventy six years of age and many of those I worked with in the 1950s were often much older. Again, I recall that Clarrie Pankhurst is quoted back in 1993 saying to his wife, Emily, – 'There's not too many of us left, love, we're a dying breed.' Kelly Dixon, in his poem about Hippy Wilson, *One of the Vanishing Breed,* also expresses similar sentiments.

On a happier note, there were also many achievements - historian Darrell Lewis, who assisted so much in the first edition, (including very critical and constructive editing of the manuscript), was awarded a Ph.D. after his thesis, dealing with the Victoria River district, was passed with flying colours. This thesis, titled *A Wild History – Life and Death on the Victoria River Frontier*, has now been published. Other works produced by Darrell include *Beyond the Big Run*, *The Murranji Track*, *Roping in the History of Broncoing* and, with Lexie Simmons, *Kajirri The Bush Missus.*

Jill Bowen, the editor of the very popular, but now discontinued 'HOF Newspaper', through which so many readers contributed to my research, was awarded an Order of Australia Medal in 2003, in recognition of service relating to the Australian Stockman's Hall of Fame and Outback Heritage Centre,

Longreach Queensland. Congratulations Jill and Darrell!

Lloyd L. Fogarty has published *Not Without His Sons*, an account of his life on Auvergne Station in the northwest corner of the Territory. Len Hill published *Droving With Ben Taylor – Up and Down The Canning Stock Route in 1946*, and Ernie Rayner, with Anne Marie Ingham, published *Wild Cattle, Wild Country – Old Mates and Memories from the Top End.*

In 2004, along with other World War 2 veterans, Ralph G. Proctor was an honoured guest of the British and Netherlands Governments in Holland, commemorating the 1944 Battle of Arnhem and the following year Ralph published his autobiography *Aim High – Proc's Journey.*

The historical and archival value of these works is significant. As I've said before, without these efforts much valuable history would be lost forever.

My thanks to Fred Bienvenu, of Myrtleford, Victoria, who has assisted greatly with his expertise in scanning and enhancing old photographs, as well as photographing spurs. I would also like to thank Liz Flood, of the Drover's Camp, Camooweal for her help, and Rodney Watson, of Atherton, for sharing his knowledge. Darrell Lewis has again kindly edited the new content for this book.

My thanks again to Ron Bostock for his superb painting, specifically done for the front cover of *Horsemen of the Outback.*

A reminder that the words 'ringer' and 'stockman' used in the text are interchangeable, although the term 'ringer' was more generally used in the Top End.

Another word which has fallen into disuse is 'roughrider', for those who rode buckjumpers and competed in other rodeo events. These days, after we started competing in rodeos internationally and adopted the American saddle in the 1960s, the riders are called 'cowboys'.

Foreword

Over two hundred years ago the first horses arrived in Australia and ever since that time they have been a key feature of life here. Without them the settling of Australia by Europeans would have been incredibly difficult, perhaps impossible. Certainly, the whole course of Australian history would have been different.

Almost all of the explorers used horses on their expeditions. Horses enabled cattle and sheep to be overlanded ever greater distances to the new stations on the frontiers, trips that in some cases took years and covered thousands of miles. During the great droving era they were essential to the movement of large mobs on monumental journeys from the outback to markets in the settled areas. And they were the means of personal transport for untold thousands of men and women, for well over a hundred years.

Horses are deeply embedded in Australian legend and mythology – think of Phar Lap and Carbine, the Australian Light Horse, the horses that the bushrangers used to evade the troopers or the one that the Man From Snowy River rode. Although motor vehicles have largely replaced horses today, they still play an important part in the lives of many Australians, and are still and essential tool on many farms and outback stations.

For over two hundred years people have been riding horses in Australia, so for two hundred years spurs have been an essential part of the equipment of Australian horsemen and horsewomen. Some might think a spur is a spur, and there is little more to say. In fact, Australian spurs have a unique history of their own. From the original English spurs brought to Sydney Cove, they have evolved over the years into many different forms and taken on a distinctly Australian character. Don Corcoran has traced this unique history, documenting standard spurs, unusual spurs, and the most famous of all – the Wave Hill spur that has entered Australian folklore.

And more! He tells personal stories of the men who used them, frontier bushmen, drovers, cattlemen and rodeo riders – and the men who made them. Don's book describes spurmaking in detail, from the old time blacksmiths to the craftsmen of today. For all who are interested in Australian history, for whom spurs were or are an everyday tool, for those interested in bush crafts, for all who love horses – this is a book that will find a welcome place on the book-shelf.

Darrell Lewis,
Historian
Australian Capital Territory

Acknowledgements

THIS WORK WOULD not have been possible without the dedicated support of David Cowans, of Berowra Heights, Sydney. David has given up much of his time, and contributed his awesome computer expertise, in particular with the scanning and enhancing of photographs and documents. Without his patience and knowledge I would still be struggling with the basics of Word 97. Thank you, David and Jill, for your assistance and hospitality.

Walter Stankiewicz, of Lane Cove, Sydney, a former neighbour at our remote property in the Broken Back Ranges of the Lower Hunter Region in New South Wales, solved the problems of running a laptop computer and 240-volt printer in a log cabin where there is no mains electricity.

Historian Darrell Lewis, of Evatt, Australian Capital Territory, an authority on the Victoria River District, gave freely of his extraordinary knowledge of the Northern Territory, where it seems he knows everyone, past and present. He has been very enthusiastic and helpful and has led me to many of the references and early photographs included here. Darrell's father, Laurie Lewis, by coincidence a former gun collecting colleague of many years ago, provided the 1902 Holdsworth, Macpherson & Co. catalogue, the photograph of 'the sleeping drover' and other material.

Ron Bostock, horse breaker, trainer, poet and artist of Rathdowney, Queensland, offered to paint an appropriate scene for the cover of the book and artist and former ringer Cliff Robinson of Townsville, Queensland allowed me to reproduce his 'burnings', one of which also appears on the back cover.

Mrs Roslyn Poignant of London, England searched unsuccessfully for photographs of Fred Gutte in the collection of her late husband Axel Poignant who was a filmmaker and photographer in Northern Australia during the 1940s and 1950s.

It is surprising and disappointing that to date 1 have been unable to locate a photograph of Fred Gutte taken while he was in the Territory.

My wife, Margaret, has given me constant encouragement, assisted with the editing, and regularly reminded me that I needed to work on the text every day in order to master the computer.

Much of my research was carried out by writing to former drovers, ringers and other people, over a period of four years, while we were living overseas in Portugal, Italy, Greece and Turkey. I received a very good response from these letters, although quite a number of people were at first bewildered why someone in any of these countries would be interested in Australian spurs. Margaret and I have met many of them since we returned to Australia.

My requests for information published in the Australian Stockman's Hall of Fame newspaper since 1996 have generated many leads and, I believe, stimulated interest in the blacksmith spurmakers. Jill Bowen, editor of that newspaper, has been an enthusiastic supporter of the project and an ongoing source of useful information. Peter Andrews, Chief Executive Officer of the Australian Stockman's Hall of Fame at Longreach in Queensland, has been most helpful arranging for the photographing of spurs displayed there.

The search for background material and relatives of Wave Hill blacksmith, Fred Gutte, eventually led me to his grand nephew, Geof Gutte, of Newton, South Australia. Geof was very co-operative and interested, immediately providing the Gutte family photograph and copies of references to Fred in Teresa Donnellan's book, *Tarcowie, Place of Wasbaway Water 1873-1898*. He later put me in touch with Fred's niece, Betty Burns of Cumberland Park, South Australia, and Fred's grand niece, Kay Cavanagh, of Sunbury, Victoria, who each sent a photograph of Fred.

Kimberly Sumner and other staff at IP Australia in Sydney have been very helpful with my search for records of patents relating to spurs.

My brother, Kim Corcoran, of Forestville, Sydney, has photographed numerous spurs for me and with his advice I was able to improve on my earlier, generally unsuccessful, attempts at photography. Similarly photographer Martin Brannan of Killarney Heights explained some of the techniques of taking close-up photos, how to reduce shadows, and what to use as a background.

The many phone calls, photographs, photocopies of catalogues and other material that J have received have been very helpful and contributed significantly to this work.

Many of those who have assisted have their stories included in the text and without exception were generous with their time, their knowledge and their preparedness to give me access to photographs and other material. In addition, I would like to acknowledge the following for their interest:-

In New South Wales, the late Gordon Gaffney OAM, of Tamworth, Hans van Hees of Scone for access to fine examples of American and other spur types, and copies of old catalogues, Colin Davidson of Scone for providing copies of old catalogues, Con Gavrilis of Turramurra, Jenny Hicks of Wahroonga, Warren Skewes of Bar-S-Dot, Moonbi, for making his spur collection and old catalogues available, John Swinfield of Roselands, Fay Young of Ashford, Viv Carter of Murrurundi and Ian Weily of The Rock.

Bluey Mould of Shepparton, Victoria corresponded, as did Les Coyle who sent some 1959 R. M. Williams advertisements. Thank you Les, I'm not sure which state you come from.

Rodger and Ann Handy, formerly of Howes Valley and now at Ashford gave me many early copies of *Hoofs and Horns*, some old horse equipment including Rodger's spurs, and some items once owned by James Douglas Wilton who died in 1987 aged eighty three years. J. D. Wilton was regarded at that time as Australia's greatest master horseman.

From Queensland 1 have had great assistance from retired blacksmith Bill Dinnie, of the Strathdickie Smithy in Proserpine. Bill has patiently explained the methods, tools and terminology of the blacksmith and 1 have learnt much from our lengthy phone conversations. Kerry Kendall of Middlemount, has kept up a steady stream of information, leads and photographs since 1994. Pat Stemm of the Waltzing Matilda Centre in Winton was most helpful and set me on the track of blacksmith William Stewart Arnold.

Others in Queensland include the late Rae Webster of Caboolture, L.C.Clark and Eric Vernon of Biloela, Dick Giles of Bargara, Jean Fearnside of Injune, John Menzies of Birdsville, Michele Lawler of Cloncurry, Morry Gay of Taigum, Noel and Carmel Williams of Camooweal, Wendy Tidbold of Sheldon who provided catalogues of L. Uhl & Sons and other material, John Major of Baralaba, Les Binnie of Malanda, Errol Conley of Condamine, Coral Hartley of Macgregor, Larry Murphy of Mingela, Cedric Burnett of Sadliers Crossing and Rose Wright of Mount Isa.

In the Northern Territory Ron Ball of Manyallaluk, Katherine, and lan Davis of Alice Springs contributed, as did John Blackley in the Australian Capital Territory, and in South Australia, Paul Reeve of Lobethal, Teresa Donnellan of Brooklyn Park, John Mannion, of Pekina, D. V. Gutte of Salisbury North, J. E. Gutte of Magill and Percival Charles Gutte of Ardrossan.

Many others have helped, some simply by their encouragement and interest, so to all of you I say, 'Thank you'.

Fred Gutte's Wave Hill spurs, shown as they were made to be worn on Cuban-heeled riding boots.

—Boots and spurs courtesy Blue Ellis. Photo Don Corcoran

Introduction

THIS IS A BOOK about Australian spurs, the men who made them and the drovers, ringers and bushmen who used them. Spurs were simply their tools of trade along with the hat, neckerchief, boots, leggings, stockwhip and the inevitable belt with its many pouches for watch, tobacco, matches, usually two folding knives and occasionally a handgun.

Properly used, spurs help the rider to control and motivate the horse while leaving the hands free. A good rider will only use the spurs when a quick turn of speed is necessary. The need for stockmen to wear spurs in Australia, and the world over, was born in cattle country.

Spurs have been found in ancient Greek and Middle Eastern tombs and the earliest form was the spike or prick spur, with a single straight point. This style changed little from around 700 BC until about 1100 AD when it was modified by making it more blunt, and by putting a 'stop' on the spike to prevent it from entering the horse's body too deeply. Similar spurs were used in Morocco and other Eastern nations at least until the mid 20th century.

The toothed wheel, or rowel, did not evolve until the 14th century, attaining an enormous size around the 17th century, the 'espuela grande' or 'great spur' of the conquistadors and vaqueros. Characteristic of these Spanish and Mexican styles were 'jingles', or more often today called 'jingle bobs'. These were usually two small pieces of metal, attached to the rowel pin, which create a jingling sound. Jingle bobs have never been part of the Australian outback scene, although some contemporary spurmakers in Australia now incorporate them in their design.

Australian bush poetry has many references to the use of spurs, for example, a brief study of Will Ogilvie's poems finds the spur in 'The Horseman', 'Life's Ride', 'Atra Cura', 'The Man Who Steadies the Lead', 'The Riding of the Rebel', 'White in the Eye', 'Outlaws Both', 'The Dingo of Brigalow Gap' and "A Draft from Tringadee', to name just a few.

William Henry Ogilvie died at his home 'Kirklea', in the village of Ashkirk, Scotland, in 1963 aged ninety three years. He had emigrated to Australia in 1890, working initially around Parkes, New South Wales, breaking in horses. During his eleven years in Australia, some of it spent in Queensland, he wrote many poems about the bush. Here was a poet who knew the outback and who lived the life he wrote about. A collection of his poems, titled 'Saddle For A Throne', was published by R. M. Williams in the 1950s.

After living in Europe from 1996 to 2000 my wife Margaret and I spent about twelve months travelling in Australia following up my research of the preceding four years. We met many of the people with whom I had been corresponding while living overseas, photographed their spurs and listened to their stories. These men and women have ridden thousands of kilometres across outback Australia, from the Kimberley to the eastern coast, and know the bush and its ways intimately. As former ringer and drover Kelly Dixon has said in verse, each is 'One Of The Vanishing Breed.'

There are three styles of spurs in this country which can be regarded as truly Australian in character. Two are blacksmith Fred Gutte's Wave Hill spur, developed and made in the Northern Territory from the mid 1940s to the mid 1950s, and the Willoughby spur, designed by roughrider Tom Willoughby in 1946. The Wave Hill spur was essentially a stockman's spur, while the Willoughby spur, although designed for rodeo work, was also popular with stockmen. A third unique style was the Morgan rigid spur, manufactured by R. M. Williams in the late 1940s, but little known then as it was overshadowed by the Willoughby spur.

To my knowledge no work has been published in Australia specifically on spurs and spurmakers, and it is my hope that this publication will encourage readers to record any information they may have about this topic, at the very least with their local historical society. The spurmakers of days gone by were generally the blacksmiths, on the stations and in the towns, some of them masters of their 3,000 year old craft of moulding iron. Master blacksmith Francis Whitaker, who died in Colorado, USA in 1999, at the age of 92, summed up the craft when he said:

> Iron has a strength no other material has, and yet it has a capacity for being light, graceful and beautiful. It has this capacity, but no desire. It will do nothing by itself except resist you. All the desire and all the knowledge of how to impart this desire to the iron must come from the smith.

In this book I have shown examples of spurs from other countries, including some from the American West to illustrate that Australian spurs as made by the outback blacksmiths were generally plain and practical without the ornamentation and embellishment much favoured by American horsemen to this day.

American spurs were influenced by the Spanish styles from South America which found their way north through Mexico, and it is interesting, though not surprising, that many spurmakers in Australia today are responding to a demand for more decorative spurs.

By the sixties, on the rodeo circuit, roughriders had become 'cowboys' and the Australian stock saddle had given way to the American/International saddle. So too, spur styles in Australia have been affected, and this trend is reflected in some of the examples illustrated in the chapter dealing with contemporary spurmakers.

This is a project which will never be complete, but it is at least a starting point. Even a blacksmith's name or the area or station where he worked is useful and I have listed references to spurmakers I have been told about, no matter how vague the information. With the exception of Jack Watson's spurs of the 1890s, I have not found any detail about spurs in the colonies prior to 1900. Certainly it is likely that most of our harness, buckles and spurs, came from England, provided by suppliers such as Josh Whetway and Sons, of Worsell.

I am hopeful that any reader who can enlarge on these references will do so by writing to me, care of Central Queensland University Press, or to the Australian Stockman's Hall of Fame at Longreach, Queensland, the Drovers' Camp Association at Camooweal, Queensland, the Waltzing Matilda Centre at Winton, Queensland, other similar institutions, or their local historical society. Otherwise this knowledge will be lost forever.

The spur and its parts

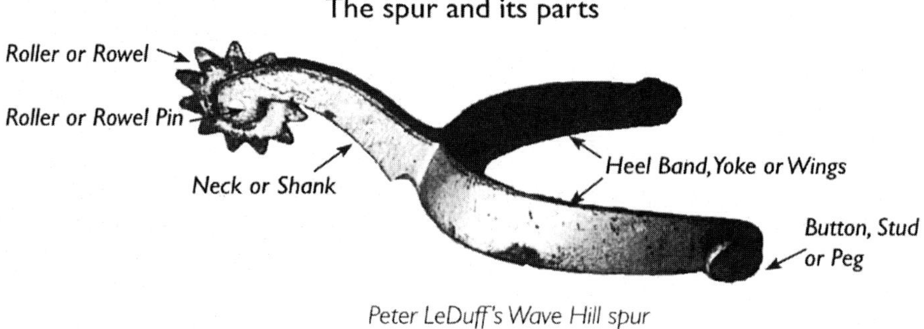

Peter LeDuff's Wave Hill spur

—Photo Megan Galvin

Imperial–Metric Conversion

Australian currency was based on the pound (£) which in 1966 was converted to the dollar at the rate of £1 equals $2.00. The pound consisted of 20 shillings (20/-) of 12 pence (12d) each. The pound was usually referred to as a 'quid' and a shilling was known as a 'bob'.

Imperial	Metric	Imperial	Metric
One inch	2.5 centimetres	One acre	0.4 hectare
One foot (12 inches)	30.4 centimetres	One gallon (8 pints)	4.55 litres
One yard (3 feet)	91.4 centimetres	One pound (16 ounces)	0.45 kilogram
One mile (1760 yards)	1.6 kilometres	One hundredweight (112 pounds)	50.8 kilograms
One square mile	2.6 square kilometres	One ton (20 hundredweights)	1016 kilograms

the horsemen

Edna Zigenbine Jessop

Mount Isa, Queensland

When Mick Bower and I arrived in Tennant Creek, Northern Territory in the early 1950s, we heard that drovers Edna and John Jessop were buying provisions at the store and were looking for men. We were promptly hired and when asked my name I replied, "John Corcoran, Mrs. Jessop." Edna said, "Well, we've already got one John in the camp, so you're Don." I have used that name ever since.

The next day we all drove up to Helen Springs and then out to No. 4 Bore where many drovers were camped waiting to take delivery of mobs, bound mostly for Dajarra, in Western Queensland.

Mick and I worked for a few weeks in the stock camp, run by Peter Sherwin, and then started on the road to Queensland with a mob of about 1250 cows.

Edna had been brought up on the road and was very knowledgeable, of course, in all matters relating to horses, droving and stock. Her knowledge and quiet demeanour commanded respect. Certainly, the two young station hands from New South Wales learnt a lot on that trip. It was a happy camp with John, Edna, the horsetailer 'Wingy' Robinson and another ringer, Jimmy Lace making up the number, and Mick and I were soon into the routine of droving.

Edna was interested in all animals and concerned for their well-being. Mick and I were very intrigued by Edna's

Top: Edna, with Pigeon, and right, with Barney Googles, at Mount Isa in the 1980s.

—Jessop Collection

pet lizard, a Thorny Devil, which she would attach by a long piece of string to a horseshoe and set it up around the camp where it could feed on ants.

It was not unusual to hear Edna call out, "Watch where you put your great feet, you ringers, careful of my lizard!"

Edna's father was drover Harry Zigenbine, originally from Charters Towers in Queensland. He was a well known and well liked character who I had heard about before I went to the Territory. Harry died in 1954 and left his droving plant to Edna.

Harry and his wife, Ruby May (nee Hammerstedt) raised eight children on the road, only two being born in the same town! In Queensland, Harry was born in Townsville, Jack in Winton, Kathleen and then Edna in Thargomindah, Joseph in Boulia and Mavis at Butru. In South Australia Eileen was born in Marree, and Andrew in Cockburn.

The family lived at Butru, a small railway siding between Duchess and Dajarra, for about eight years. Harry was away droving for much of the time and Edna and Kathleen, in their early teenage years, were breaking in any unbroken horses he left behind. They all left Butru in 1942 when Harry started droving for Vestey's first taking a mob from Wave Hill in the Northern Territory, to Morstone in Queensland.

Vestey's was an English based company, with an established trade in meat from the Argentine, and their own fleet of ships, the Blue Star Line. They leased 36,000 square miles in the Northern Territory and the North West in 1913, and Wave Hill, over 6000 square miles, was their biggest holding at that time.

This company acquired much of this land for peppercorn rents and was regarded with resentment from the start. In recent times it was revealed that they had paid no tax for fifty years and they were dubbed "the gilded tax dodgers". Their holdings eventually included Margaret River, Flora Valley, Gordon Downs, Nicholson, Sturt Creek,

Top: A thorny devil.
—Photo courtesy David McPhee

Left: A sketch of Harry by James Wieneke in 1937.
—Jessop Collection

Spring Creek, Turner River and Ord River in the Kimberley, and Mistake Creek, Limbunya, Kirkimbie, Waterloo, Birrundudu, Wave Hill, Delamere, Willeroo, Manbulloo, Helen Springs, Glencoe, Burnside, Mount Litchfield and Marrakai in the Territory and Morstone and other stations in Queensland.

In 1946, when Edna was not on the road with her father, she worked for Clarrie Pankhurst, bringing a mob from Wave Hill over to Dajarra.

Anne Marie Ingham, in her book, *The Boss Drover and his Mates,* says of that trip:

> As he was preparing for the next trip, Clarrie was approached by young Edna Zigenbine who was not working for her father, Harry, for that year. She was looking for a job and asked if Clarrie could employ her as one of his ringers or as the horse tailer. He couldn't believe his luck! Edna, about 17 at the time, had grown up in the droving tradition, learning her lessons from her famous father, and was as capable as anyone in the industry. "I'll do better than that," said Clarrie. "You take charge of the mob and I'll do the cooking." The deal was struck. "It was no skin off my nose. Edna could do it just as well as I could. She'd handled mobs on her own before and I was bloody glad to have her. I could have found plenty worse, but none better." Neither had any problems pertaining to sexual discrimination. As far as they were concerned it didn't exist. They would be on the road for five months with 1500 bullocks, and getting them to their destination in the best possible condition was the important issue. Their vision was far too broad to cavil about who did what job.
>
> Unlike her massively built father, Edna was slight, no more than five feet two inches, with exquisite features. No one could deny her beauty or her ability and she never lacked for admirers, but having grown up in a world of men, she learnt from a very early age to keep them in order.

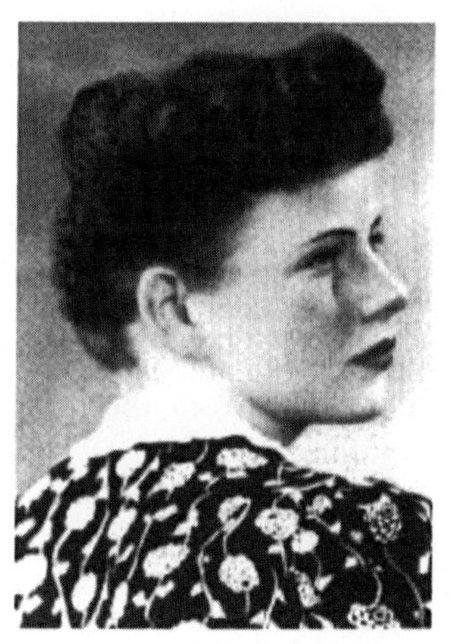

After that trip Edna then went to Tennant Creek and worked in a local cafe: "For the first two weeks, until I got my first pay, I worked in riding clothes as I owned not one dress!" After a while Edna got a job in the local hospital where she worked until 1950.

During that time Edna's mother came over to Tennant Creek and they rented a house there. They were later joined by Edna's brother Joe and sister Mavis. As

Edna at Tennant Creek, Northern Territory, about 1950.

—Jessop Collection

Edna said, "It was good to have family with me again and I thoroughly enjoyed my work and mates at the hospital. I must say that these were some of the happiest days of my life, though very different to what I was used to."

In 1950 Harry was to take a mob of bullocks from Tom Quilty at Bedford in Western Australia, for delivery to Dajarra, West Queensland. This is a trip of about 2000 kilometres and six months on the road. Harry's health was failing at the time and when he asked Edna to come and help him and the boys she gave up her job, took the bus to Darwin, flew to Halls Creek in the West and was soon back in the saddle.

Harry became very ill on the Murranji Track in the Territory, and handed the mob over to Edna to take into Queensland. He is quoted as saying to Edna, "You take over, you're the best man I've got." Edna did, of course, an incident which captured the imagination of the public right around Australia and the world. One leader in the *Weekend Australian*, many years later, stated, "Edna rides small in the saddle, large in legend."

R. M. Williams comments about the Zigenbine family in his autobiography, *Beneath Whose Hand*,

> The whole family including Edna, perhaps especially Edna, were accomplished drovers, and their feats were yarned about over a hundred campfires in every season.

The following year Edna took a mob of Banka Banka bullocks from the Territory, down to Lilyvale, near Winton, and then took another mob from a station near Boulia into Winton. At about this time she met John Jessop, and after spending some time with her mother in Tennant Creek, flew back to Winton where she and John were married.

They continued droving together for about six years. Their son Jack was born in 1954 and Edna left John in 1960, settling in Mount Isa, Queensland. She was determined that Jack would receive a proper education, something she was never given.

Edna helped found the Mount Isa Pony Club and for twenty six years was in charge of the local pound, a familiar sight riding through town early in the morning with stray stock. More recently she has been recognised

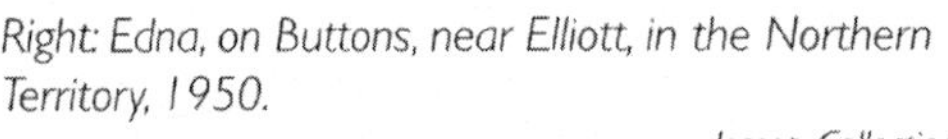

Right: Edna, on Buttons, near Elliott, in the Northern Territory, 1950.

—Jessop Collection

for her long term involvement with the Mount Isa Rodeo.

As Edna said recently in 'Cattle Pads', the newsletter of The Drovers' Camp Association Inc., Camooweal,

> I have had a fairly hard life and things were tough sometimes. But the freedom of the bush and the countless nights under the stars, miles from cities, walking with the mobs, seeing all the wonderful places and antics of animals and the peace and quiet have made it all worthwhile and I wouldn't change it for quids. Gone is that life forever and I wish some of the kids of today could have the chance to experience the life I knew as a youngster.

Sadly, only Edna, Joe and Mavis remain of that generation of this legendary family.

In the early 1980s, Australian legend, singer Slim Dusty, released a song by Stan Coster called *Give My Regards to Edna* as a tribute to her ability. It is still available on a compact disc titled *The Man Who Steadies The Lead.*

Edna's spurs were given to her by station owner Jack McConochy when she was about sixteen years old and are visible in many of the early photographs of her. I remember them clearly as they were longer in the neck than the average spur at that time.

The spurs above left were also Edna's, quite light and compact, and were 'her last working spurs' which she used while running the Mount Isa pound. I was very moved when Edna presented them to me a few years ago when I visited her in Mount Isa.

Clockwise from top: Two pairs of spurs. Edna's, left, and her father Harry's. A closer view of one of Edna's spurs. Edna at Newcastle Waters, Northern Territory, about 1946. Edna on Buttons, with Banka Banka bullocks, between Banka Banka station and Rankine Store, Northern Territory, 1951.
—Photos: Don Corcoran, Carmel Williams, Jessop Collection, Jessop Collection, Kim Corcoran.

Top: Camfield Creek, Northern Territory, in 1942. From left, Mavis Zigenbine, Edna Zigenbine, Sid Bird, Kathleen Zigenbine, David Bird and Harry Zigenbine. This was when the Zigenbine family left Butru and travelled over to Wave Hill to start droving for Vestey's. Harry had a fall from their wagonette in severely wet conditions on the Georgina River, which accounts for the sling on his arm.

—Jessop Collection

Above left: Harry Zigenbine, Springvale, Western Australia, about 1950.

—R. M. Williams photo, in Jessop Collection.

Above right: Harry Zigenbine, Winton, Queensland, 1951.

—Jessop Collection

Former drover, Jack Sammon,of Rydal, New South Wales, has written the following poem about Edna's trip from Bedford Downs to Dajarra in 1950.

Edna Zigenbine

When Edna got the message she was working in the town
She'd grown up in the bush and hoped to settle down,
But her father had an accident, droving on the track
And needed her to take his place until he could get back.
Now stock routes were a man's domain in nineteen fifty two
And having women in charge of stock; a thing they didn't do.
But Edna knew the droving game and didn't have a doubt,
She took those fifteen hundred steers and started on the route.

With a team of native stockmen and pack horse plant behind,
She headed off to Queensland, when permits were all signed.
Over dry and barren plains and ranges rough and red
A thousand long and lonely miles extended out ahead.
With eyes bloodshot and weary, she watched the mob go by
In choking dust that billowed up into a cloudless sky,
Her thoughts were of the trip ahead and challenges she'd face
And hoped she would be good enough to take her father's place.

As they crossed the Jump Up she scanned the brooding sky
And prayed to God it wouldn't rain while in the Murranji,
For drovers dread the Murranji when storms come rolling in
When cattle rush off camp at night to thunder's deafening din.
There's many who have met their match in scrublands dense and black
So Edna didn't take a chance when on that dreaded track.
And she hurried past lonely graves where several men have died
In those sombre lancewood scrubs that clung to the track beside.

When they got out on the Barkly where miles drag slowly past
The plains spread out before her and steers were quiet at last
But she couldn't take things easy, they still had miles to go
And the plains still hold dangers as all the drovers know,
She worried if there's water at the windmills up ahead,
Or maybe she should have taken another track instead.
As she nursed the lame and lagged that struggled on behind,
She did her best to feed them with what grass she could find.

She saw the white horns glisten in the pale moon's eerie light,
As she took her turn on night watch when all was still and quiet,
While singing to the cattle as she slowly rode around,
To the sound of creaking leather and hoof beats on the ground.
Lonely curlews joined in chorus with their haunting cry,
While the cross turned slowly over in the southern sky,
When all was bathed in darkness save the fire's ruddy glow,
She allowed her thoughts to wander while riding to and fro.

It took her almost half a year to bring those cattle down;
Along the dusty stock route to that little railway town
When the trip was over she put the cattle on the train,
Then she turned around and headed straight back out again.
There were other mobs of cattle to bring in from the west,
And Edna is now a drover, as good as all the rest,
Before the day's of women's lib and that sort of thing began
She proved that she could do a job as well as any man.

When Edna took her father's place, he was filled with pride,
He taught her well in ways of stock and taught her how to ride
But Edna didn't want his praise she just had a job to do,
To help him out when he was ill and get the cattle through.
'Though she's proud of her achievement, no one would ever know,
She doesn't talk about herself or let her feelings show.
So I'll dedicate these lines of verse to a friend of mine,
A woman of the outback, Edna Zigenbine.

Jack Sammon ©2000.

Jack Sammon, left, Edna Jessop and George Booth photographed at the Drovers' Camp Festival in Camooweal, Queensland, July 2002.
—Courtesy The North West Star/Carpentaria Newspapers, Mount Isa, Queensland

In September, 2007, in her eightieth year, Edna Zigenbine Jessop finally succumbed to cancer in the Mount Isa Hospital. She was buried at the Sunset Lawn Cemetery after an emotional outdoor service attended by over 150 people. Many former drovers and ringers were there and the following two poems indicate the respect felt for this unassuming and legendary woman.

Poems for Edna

For the sake of the meet and the muster
The rides over sand ridge and plain
For the sake of the old days whose lustre
Will never shine round us again
In mind of the head rope and halter
The mounts in the dawn and the dew
We have laid these few words at the altar
Of mateship in memory of you.

Eugene Kostin

If there's a cattle camp up in the blue
Where the stock horses whinny and stamp
And if there are mobs to be mustered and moved
We know who'll be running the camp
And taking the last watch – a Camooweal girl
Will be holding her own with the men

So fill up your quart pots and drink to our mate
'Til we all meet with Edna again
She has packed her last pack and buckled her spurs
For her ride to that big boundary gate
So let the clods fall ever gently and slow
It's goodbye to a fair dinkum mate.

Kelly Dixon

Many writers and commentators have stated that Edna could not read or write. This is not correct. It is true, that having been born and raised on the road, she never received a proper education, but over the years she was able to teach herself to read and write. I have many cards and notes that Edna has written to me during the last thirty years.

She was very skilled in working leather, and I am proud to have some examples of her craftsmanship in my collection of bush memorabilia.

Some typical ringer's gear from the 1950s – Edna made the belt.
Photo: Don Corcoran.

Edna Zigenbine Jessop and Don Corcoran, Mount Isa, 2004.
Photo: The North West Star, published by Carpentaria Newspapers Pty Ltd.

Mick Bower

Katherine, Northern Territory

MICK BOWER and I first met in Sydney in our early teens through a mutual interest in studying and collecting live reptiles. We both left the city about the same time to work in the bush. Mick went to Rowena and I went to Burren Junction, both places in North Western New South Wales.

Working on sheep stations gave us the opportunity to learn to ride and to start understanding stock. Of course, in those days the sheep was king in much of rural Australia and no one dreamt that cotton would ever be grown in this country.

The Northern Territory and cattle beckoned, with books such as Ion Idriess' *Man Tracks* and Vic Hall's *Outback Policeman* and *Dreamtime Justice* fuelling our interest. In those days *Hoofs and Horns* was a magazine which gave excellent coverage of rodeos, the movement of stock and the drovers involved, and outback characters and events in general, particularly in the North.

We eventually left our jobs on sheep stations and headed back to Sydney where we caught the train to Mount Isa, Queensland, a trip which commenced on a Sunday, and delivered us to Mount Isa on Wednesday, after changing trains in Brisbane and Townsville.

We hitched a ride to Camooweal and camped there on the Georgina for a couple of days, eventually getting a lift across to Tennant Creek, in the Territory, where we were hired by Edna and John Jessop.

As mentioned earlier, we were droving for Edna and John, with a mob of cows from Helen Springs into Dajarra, about three months on the road.

Mick Bower, about 1970.

—Corcoran Collection

After being paid off there we took the train across to Rockhampton to ride in the 'Rocky Roundup', which was about the biggest rodeo in Queensland at that time. I recall that four of us left Dajarra on a crowded passenger carriage, hooked behind the guard's van on a cattle train.

At Duchess we got off to wait for the train from Mount Isa to take us to Townsville on the coast. This was the relatively new diesel train *The Inlander*, and we surely had to talk hard to convince the guard, in his resplendent blue uniform, that one of the ringers, Jimmy Lace, was indeed sober.

Jimmy caused much amusement among the passengers while trying to decipher the meaning of a sign indicating that the rubbish bin was under the cold water tap. The sign was worded 'Refuse Container Under Cool Water Alcove.' Jimmy's argument to the world in general was along the lines of, "How can I refuse a container when no one has offered me one, and who the hell is this Al cove, anyway?" A while later I stopped him walking out through the carriage door, looking for the toilet, while the train was at full speed. Everyone was relieved when we decided to leave the train at Charters Towers for a look around the town.

After riding in the Rocky Roundup Mick and I went back to New South Wales, working as station hands in the Central West for about six months. Mick eventually headed back to the Territory and I got a position with Simba Film Productions, a documentary film unit working in the Territory and the Gulf country. Some knowledge of the bush and my ability to catch snakes and crocodiles helped me to get the job.

Mick stayed on in the Territory and the Kimberley, including droving for Mick Cussens with a mob from Birrindudu to Helen Springs, and again for Edna and John Jessop with a mob from Helen Springs to Dajarra. Mick was also ringing on Gordon Downs and Birrindudu and was later head stockman on Nicholson, Manbulloo, Nutwood and Limbunya.

He eventually settled in Katherine, working for many years at the meatworks, and still lives there with his wife Nida.

Mick and Nida, Katherine, 1967
—Bower Collection

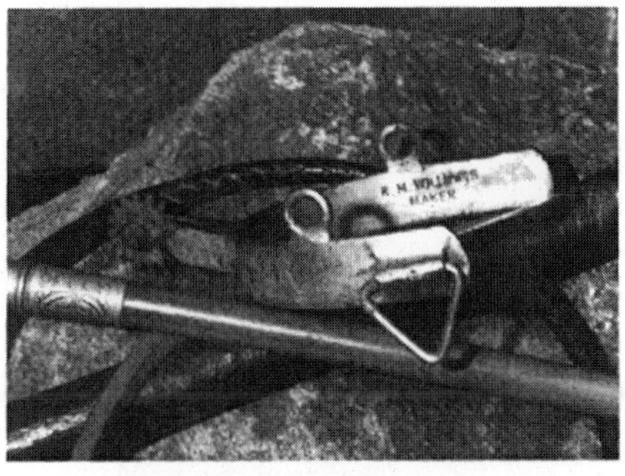

Mick has used many styles of spur over the years, and at the moment has a pair of Willoughby spurs, which he used upside-down, swapping the left and right spurs. Tied under the boot they are easy to run with and good for hanging on when riding rough horses and bullocks. Mick featured prominently at the Katherine rodeos for many years.

I continued working in the bush until 1957, including droving in the Territory for Larry Darcy and Keithy O'Keeffe, ringing on Willeroo for Tom Humphrey, surface work at the Rum Jungle uranium mine, ringing on Oban, near Dajarra, Queensland and as a station hand in North Western and Central Western New South Wales

Mick and I haven't seen too much of each other over the last forty years, but I was pleased when he was in Sydney in the early 1960s and officiated as godfather to our son Allen. (Mick's real name is Allen).

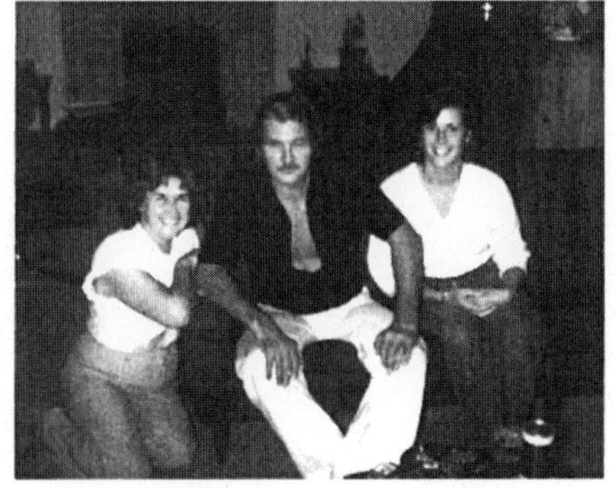

I took the adjacent photo of Mick with my wife Margaret and daughter Lesley Anne during one of his rare visits to Sydney, about twenty years ago, when many horses were re-ridden and many snakes recaptured.

Top: A Willoughby spur shown upside-down.
—Photo John Swinfield

Geoff Allen

Sydney, New South Wales

I MET GEOFF ALLEN in recent years in Sydney after reading a poem he had written about Merle 'Terry' Humphrey, the wife of Tom Humphrey, who was manager when I was at Willeroo.

Geoff had worked for Tom on Gordon Downs in the West and, like anyone else who met Terry, admired her greatly. Since those days Geoff has published *Ballads of the Kimberley and Other Wild Places* and two novels, *The Gun Ringer* and *Outlaws of the Kimberley Underworld*, the last two published by Outback Books and based on real people and events.

I have included here the poem about Terry Humphrey, Geoff's story, 'Memories of the Wave Hill Spur' and a second poem 'Just a Dag'.

HER WAY

"Do you think it's wise," the
Big Boss asked,
"To have them here with you?"
He smiled and said it kindly,
For they were only new,
And coloureds in the dining room,
Went against the grain
Of the fine old English Company,
On its far flung domain.

The woman eyed him coolly,
And a vision floated past,
Of her father at the table,
With folk of every caste.

Top: Geoff Allen. —*Photo Martin Brannan*

Right: Tom and Terry Humphrey with their children, Mark and Dale, Gordon Downs, about 1955.
—*Photo courtesy Terry Humphrey*

No matter who the
mail truck brought,
They always came inside,
Shearers, drovers, station hands,
Children shy, wide eyed.

Old Captain sitting proudly,
The last of his wild band,
Accepted by the people,
Who commandeered his land,
Abu Sal, the Afghan,
The old Chinese who cooked,
Judged by how they grafted,
Not the way they looked.

"I come from far west Queensland",
A soft smile swept her face,
"Where everyone was welcome,
To eat and take their place,
I never knew the colour bar,
Until I came out here,
And I assure you it won't flourish
While Tom's your overseer."

The Big Boss never answered,
Good men were hard to find,
She could sit them in the bedroom,
Were she so inclined.
He bid good-day, and drove away,
To view a neighbouring block,
And forgot about the woman
And her western stock.

I was filling up the woodbox,
A Sunday morning chore,
And heard it all quite plainly,
From my spot outside the door,
They're getting into trouble,
For treating us so well,
Then she came out smiling,
And banged the smoko bell.

"I heard him, inside, Missus,
What he says is true,
We may be on full wages,
But never be as you,
It's only causing problems,
We'll eat back with the cook"—
But she stopped me in an instant,
With the fiercest kind of look.

"I never heard such nonsense,
I'll do as I think right,
You're on the station ledger,
As stockmen, classed as white,
You'll eat here in the dining room,
With Tom, the kids and me,
That's the way we do it,
Any place we be."

When supper times were finished,
And things all cleared away,
We'd talk a bit of horses,
And what we'd done that day,
Tom might plait a hobble strap,
Or thumb a magazine,
And sometimes tell a tale or two
Of places they had been.

And later in the starlight,
Trudging back to camp,
Swags stuck in the saddle shed,
Beneath a carbide lamp,
We wondered at those people,
Who cast no jibes or slurs,
And every man amongst us,
Would give his life for hers.

Memories of the Wave Hill Spur

It has been said that when I first turned up in the Kimberley my possessions were a swag and favourite bridle and when I left eleven years later I had only the swag. That's not quite right as when I arrived I also had a greenhide whip I'd made and a pair of spurs. When I arrived at Ord River station I was smartly told to throw the whip away, "as cattle in this country run ten mile when they hear a whip cracked" and the spurs created a knowing grin. So I left the whip behind when we went out mustering – though it came in handy later when I went on the road with cattle to Wyndham – but I was stuck with the spurs. And they weren't much use as the knowing looks suggested. They were a light pair with short necks and rode all over my boots during the day's hard galloping. We each rode three horses a day in the stock camp so you can see the kind of country we were in. The horsetailer met us at the dinner camp with our afternoon muster mounts, took our jaded morning muster horses back to camp with him and when we got to the bronco yard about sundown we caught our yarding up horses.

There was a part Aboriginal chap in the camp, George Hamilton, a smart little stockman, twice my age, who always beat me and everyone else to the lead. One day he lent me his spurs, he called them Wave Hill spurs, a term new to me at the time, but as soon as I slipped them on I was struck with the way they fitted neatly to the shape of my R.M. boot heels. George had also fashioned a piece of light harness leather to the shape of his instep and that, together with the way they sat low on the heel and their weight, kept them in place all day. We also got involved in throwing bulls and whilst no spur is designed for running with over rough terrain, they never caused us a problem. The rowels too were blunt enough not to rip our blankets of a night when we slept in our boots, spurs to the boot front, as we often did when we had a mob of toey freshly mustered bullocks on the camp a few yards off the fire.

George said he had swapped the spurs for a new hat from Smokey Saville, one of the Queensland drovers' men who had come out the previous year to lift a mob of fifteen hundred bullocks and take them inside to Dajarra. Swapping was quite common as you never got much chance to go to town – except at races time once a year when you were probably too drunk to buy anything – so when a stranger you liked the look of or an old acquaintance turned up it wasn't unusual to swap shirts or leggings or anything else that took each other's fancy. You'd probably say something like, "Geez, I wouldn't mind a pup out of that shirt." And next instant it would be stripped off and the swap made. Those Queensland drovers, as we called them, were our best chance of learning what was going on around the country and no doubt the benefits of the Wave Hill spur were spread by that source. The Kimberley was a pretty isolated place, generally only one white bloke in the camp and there wasn't a great deal of moving around between stations let alone anyone heading into the Territory for a job ringing. Towards the end of the fifties though, they began to turn the tracks into graded built up roads and that caused a lot more traffic to flow to the West.

Eventually a hawker by the name of 'Happy Jack' turned up at the station I was ringing on and I was able to buy a pair of Wave Hill spurs for myself. I suppose I paid dearly for them as a man didn't hawk goods over those roads and distances for nothing, but cash was something we didn't think about much and anytime we needed anything, if we couldn't book it down at the station store, we got a sub from the bookkeeper. That's how I would have paid Happy Jack.

One time I had gun ringer and fighting man Jack Vitnell in the camp with me and he was amazed none of the boys had spurs. Flamboyant and free with his money, Jack sent to Fred Gutte, the blacksmith at Wave Hill station, for six pairs of Fred's spurs for the youngest and smartest of the stockboys. "Never let me see them off your feet." Jack growled. I don't know whether it was Jack's threat or the spurs but they certainly got up with the lead after that!

Part Aboriginal-Chinese stockman Johnny Ah Won turned up early one year to take a mob of 500 fat Mistake Creek bullocks down to Wyndham and the first day he met us at the yard where we were shoeing up a new plant of horses he clanked along with a pair of Wave Hill spurs on his boots two feet long in the shank. He'd had Fred Gutte make them specially for him as a bit of a joke but the stockboys didn't know that and eyed them off with amazement. He came out mustering with us for a few weeks until we had the last of his mob made up but he changed the stunt spurs for a normal pair of Wave Hills when he rode.

Johnny was about fifty at the time, quite a big solid fellow and very easy going. He'd been reared on Rosewood station with Johnny Kilfoyle and was still a smart man. We always jumped off to throw bulls or old pikers but Johnny would gallop alongside and grab the beast by the tail and send it rolling as he swept past Then he'd jump off to where it was lying stunned and if any of us were watching, straddle it and give it a rake or two along the ribs with his Wave Hills. It took split second timing to make this play because if you were a fraction too wide of the animal or missed the tail the beast could twist its head and sink a horn into your horse's guts. I know because after doing it a few times and thinking I was a second Johnny Ah Won I made a poor attempt and got my horse killed and was a whisker off getting horned in the thigh as well.

But any type of spur was better that none. You'd spend a pretty frustrating day kicking your horse along if you left your hooks by the fire. Those horses were no fools, the minute they felt your boot heel they'd lay on you all day, whereas you only had to touch them a few times with the spur early on in the day to make them stride out and walk properly. We never had to spur our good mustering horses hard after cattle. They enjoyed the chase as much as we did and the moment we sighted cattle we'd hold our mounts in, lash them a couple of times with the reins, touch them with the spurs and they'd be off after them as soon as we loosed the reins.

But getting your horse moving was only one aspect of using spurs. They were also helpful when riding a rough horse although a lot of riders wouldn't try it. They'd be reluctant to mount a tight horse with a pair of hooks thinking they would only make the horse buck worse, which they probably did, but they were also a great help in hanging up. The idea was to swing on quick and get a good grip by jamming your spurs in behind the horse's shoulders. "Grab 'em by the spur" as the saying went and the Wave Hill spur was just the right size for that. Of course, top balance men wouldn't ride that way, the soles of their boots wouldn't shift from the irons with spurs on or not.

I've always maintained there were only two types of rough riders, balance riders and grip men, and here I'm talking about station ringers, not rodeo riders, who were something again. I suppose the two supreme examples I came across in the North in the fifties were Cammy Cleary and Jack Vitnell. Cammy was all balance, to perfection, Jack on the other hand was a very powerful man and used his strong thighs to maintain a grip. Of course he had a certain amount of balance as he rode in local rodeos where he had to spur fore and aft. He was a born showman and would twist around while a horse was bucking – if he had any sort of an audience – and grab it by the flank to "give it a bit of a lift" as he would say. Naturally he wasn't balanced in a position like that.

The quiet retiring Clammy Cleary also wasn't above a bit of showmanship if he was in the mood. He'd stand pensively alongside a known buckjumper in front of a bunch of ringers as though he'd rather be anywhere but where he was, then suddenly turn towards the animal and swing on. But as he swung on he'd deliberately give the horse a whack in the guts with his knee and of course it was bucking before he could get set in the saddle. But that didn't worry Cammy, "Give 'em a bounding start" he'd say with a shy grin later after he'd ridden the horse out.

I'll close off with a short poem I wrote about a mate of ours who wouldn't think of mounting a roughie without his hooks on. I mention 'attending', for those who don't know the term, 'attending' was when the adjoining station gave notice that it would be mustering along the joint boundary and it would be in your interest to send a couple of men over to attend the muster and cut out your cattle. Otherwise their calves would be branded with the other station's brand and be eventually turned off as cattle belonging to that station. Of course, you always took a good cutting-out horse along with you.

Just A Dag

I'm thinkin' back to Pigeon Hole an' Sammy Lew, the dag,
He dinkum wouldn't know sometimes the night watch greatcoat
from his swag,
Nearly every day he'd be with his bridle inside-out,
Up before the dawn an' still asleep no doubt,
Catch his horse, saddle up an' wake up later on,
And ride across and ask you where the camp had gone.

Wasn't what you called a dill, a dag, that's what he was,
Never cared what people thought, smart rider, as good in Oz.
Me and him attended once, his cutting horse went lame,
They lent him one, the other camp, 'Killer' was its name,
Anyway, we catch the thing, I know how Sammy feels,
When suddenly he gives this wail, 'Have to hang up by me heels!'

Lost his spurs! Dinkum, mate, how could a ringer lose his hooks?
He rode that way, understand, not like they teach you in the books,
But jammed them with his spurs and hung in hard and tight,
Look out any rogue horse then getting' smart and squealin' fight,
Rode 'em, but never thought he could, had no idea at all
We reckoned he was best, scarcely ever took a fall.

Anyway, everybody's lookin', thinkin' that he's in a funk,
"Damn the hooks," I says, "Get on! They'll call you for a yella skunk"
But he won't, not in his boots, pulls them off! The dag!
Jumps on an' lets his callused heels serve him as a jag,
Yeah, rode him easy, like I said, ever see a Lewis couldn't ride?
Never knew him different no matter what we tried.

Gerry Ash

In 2003 I received a letter about the gold-plated trophy spurs mentioned in the story I had written about Lloyd F. Fogarty of Timber Creek, N. T., from Gerry Ash, of Derby, W. A.

Gerry wrote:

'My reason for writing is in regards to the Wave Hill spurs owned by Lloyd Fogarty. George Bates had nothing to do with getting the spurs done, they were my idea. I wrote a letter to Angus & Coote in Sydney telling them what I wanted done to the pair of Wave Hills I sent with my letter.

'That was – polished and engraved, sterling silver rollers and gold-plate the spurs. A letter came back from Angus & Coote saying that they thought they were a wonderful trophy for a bush race meeting. I can't recall what they cost.

'Jerry Woods was in the Gordon Creek camp with me - the cream of the joke is that I never got to the races. Jerry took the spurs into the meeting. I had a bad buster and was laid up back at Gordon Creek.

'I am including a photo of a pair of spurs I have had and used since 1954. They are made by Fred Gutte and they are just conventional pattern and not angle heeled – the only pair of conventional pattern I have seen made by him, though he probably did make more of the same.

'You will notice in the photo he uses the same studs as his angle heel type. A thing that always got me about Gutte spurs was the fact that the studs were driven into the heel band cold, they will never shift. I've seen this happen, when a bloke tried to alter the spurs with heat, the studs fell out.'

Although we spoke on the phone several times, I never did meet Gerry, who died of cancer in 2005.

Gerry Ash at Gordon Creek.
Photo Gerry Ash.

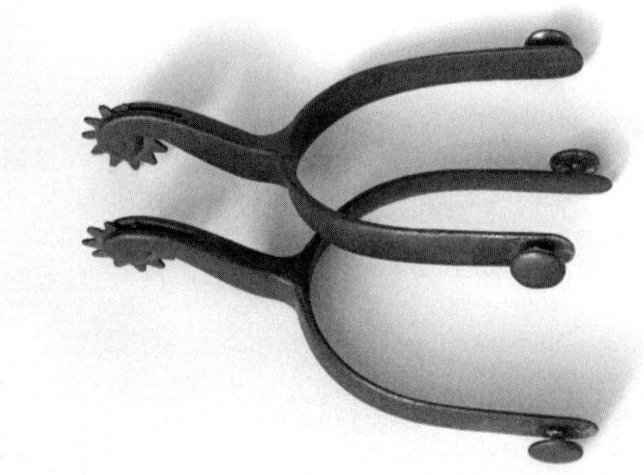

Gerry Ash's Wave Hill spurs.
Photo Kevin Shaw, Derby, W.A.

George Booth

Cardwell, Queensland

GEORGE AND I had been corresponding for about five years and met for the first time at the Drovers' Camp Festival at Camooweal in 2000 where he was inducted into the Drovers' Camp Association Hall of Fame.

George's parents, Johnie and Mary Booth were the last of the teamsters working out of Burketown, hauling ten ton loads through the Gulf and into the Territory. George had his first droving plant in 1947, taking a mob from Hughenden to Woodhouse near Ayr. This was a packhorse plant and in later years he used a wagonette and then a truck.

When I contacted George after the Festival to arrange to call in and see him he said, "Come whenever you like, I'll get mother to put more water in the soup." His wife Julia, a softly spoken Scot, is well qualified to put more water in the soup, she was George's camp cook for about five years, mainly in the Gulf and around Richmond and Cloncurry.

George commented that in those days the term 'Boss Drover' was not used, the boss was simply called 'the drover.' If someone came into the camp looking for the boss they would ask for the drover, the others in the camp were ringers, horsetailer and cook.

On Wave Hill spurs George said, "In the early '50s I was heading through Wave Hill on my way to Gordon Downs to pick up a mob and rode up to the smithy to get some spurs. Fred had spurs there already made up, but because I wear a small sized boot, he made mine while I waited, using an old car spring. Each spur was forged from one piece of steel and fitted to my boot heel and I asked him to make the necks a bit shorter than usual so I could run with them."

"The 9 point rollers were punched out with a cold chisel, after first cutting the round shape from the same metal as used for the spurs. He fitted the short steel roller pin by punching the hole for the pin while the shank was white hot, then tapped in the hot pin and married it to the steel of the shank. He didn't

George, photographed at Longreach about 1998.
—All photos courtesy George Booth

even have to use a file to dress the end of the pin on each side of the shank. It was eleven years before the pin wore through on one of my spurs and I lost the roller."

"Fred made them within the hour and I think I paid £1 or £2 for them. He always made spurs as mates, and was careful to match them. He was a big solid man with a chest like a barrel."

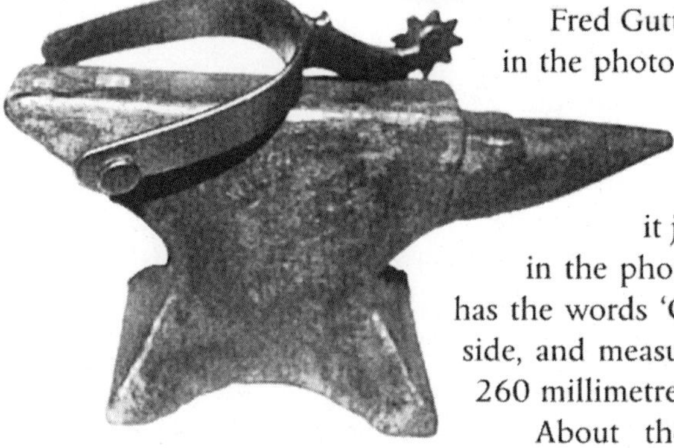

Fred Gutte's 'trade mark' can be clearly seen in the photo at left – the 'point,' or projection, at the base of the neck was created when Fred, filed a groove on each side of the neck, where it joins the heel band. The small anvil in the photo is a No. 5, made by Wilkinson, has the words 'Queens' and 'Ley' stamped on one side, and measures 120 millimetres in height and 260 millimetres in length.

About the use of spurs, "Spurs are for emergency use only, don't sit there going dig, dig, dig all day or the horse will get doughy and won't take any notice when you do need to use them. When working in the yards I turn my spurs around to the front, because of their shape the Wave Hill spurs sit perfectly on the instep. A lot of riders automatically hook the spurs underneath when a horse stumbles, to lift him up, so after a while when the horse stumbles he takes off immediately, expecting the spurs, and leaves the rider behind the saddle."

George recalled that while on the road in the early '40s his uncle, Malcolm Douglas, saddled his horse one morning and walked over to the fire to have a cup of coffee. He had the reins over his arm and something startled the horse and made it buck. Its front hoofs went straight onto Malcolm's heels and smashed them and as a result he afterwards had to have square heeled boots and special spurs made by R.M. Williams.

When I showed George a sketch of drover Harry Zigenbine he said, "He used to do the sword dance to his own accompaniment on a concertina and was one of the fastest men on his feet I've ever seen, even at 23 stone. I once saw him sitting cross-legged around a fire with other blokes and in a second he was on his feet and donged a bloke on the other side of the fire who'd apparently upset him."

The photo on the following page shows Julia Booth with a batch of bread she has just baked in a Bedourie oven. This was on the road about 1962 with a mob of Dunbar cattle to be put on the rail at Mungana, near Chillagoe, in Queensland.

George used to breed mules for stock work. "We had every colour of mule, bar grey, they were great for droving and as good as a stock horse if you handled them right."

While we were yarning I mentioned how much I had missed hearing the curlews and dingoes, who were ever-present but distant companions during the nights while on the road. George produced a photograph he had taken years ago, showing a curlew lying motionless, relying on its camouflage for protection.

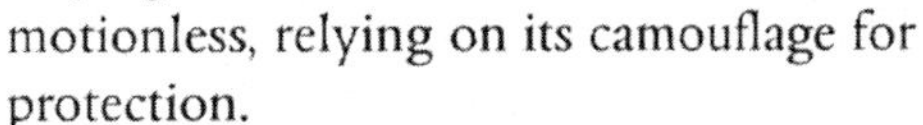

When I left the bush and settled in the city, I always had a poem by Bruce Simpson, titled 'Curlews' displayed on the office wall to remind me of those droving days and nights.

Accordingly, both Bruce's poem and George's photo are shown here:

Curlews

Do the curlews still mourn
On moonlight nights,
Through the tea tree flats
On the Queensland coast?
Like lost souls doomed
To a futile search forever.

Their burden of grief seemed
To wax with the moon,
To a tortured climax
Of exquisite sadness

Above: George with mule at the junction of the Lynd and Mitchell rivers in 1962.

When the full moon turned
The forest into a fairy-land
Of black and silver.

Poor desolate shy curlews
Their cries come to me yet
From across the years,
Like the keening notes
Of some old violin
With a sob in it's throat
That plays but the one tune
Over and over.

Ron Bostock

Rathdowney, Queensland

I first heard of Ron Bostock from his brother Bluey who I met at the Drovers' Camp Reunion at Camooweal in 2000. Since then I have had many phone conversations with Ron who, in his seventies, is still actively involved in breaking and training horses. His daughter Susan provided the following profile.

Ron was born in the thirties and with a father in the Armed Forces moved around a lot, attending fourteen different schools before leaving at the age of fourteen. Reared on the land he started riding horses for local horse breeders around the Ipswich area and it was here that he found his true calling and began a lifelong career in the breaking and training of horses. Ron also enjoyed the sport of boxing in his spare time, fighting numerous title fights and barely missed out on a Queensland title when he was sixteen. He was runner up for the title of 'Golden Gloves' and went on to fight some of the best in the country as a professional.

During these same years he began a 'love affair' with riding rough stock, first in the back paddocks and yards where he broke and trained station horses and soon in rodeo arenas all over the country. Ron spent over six years following the rodeo circuit, competing wherever the prize money was good, riding bulls, bareback horses and saddle broncs. A good all-rounder, Ron had his share of wins and placings out of the three rough stock events. In the late '50s and '60s, in the days of the Australian Rough Riders Association on the Queensland run, most rodeos were two rounds and a final and you needed to be a consistent and tough stock rider to be in the money.

Ron and his wife Joan bought a cattle property, Dundee, at Taroom on the Dawson River in Central Queensland and his rodeo days came to an end. Using his property as a base he broke and trained horses all over the country for many top breeders and property owners. His natural affinity with animals was well renowned and his 'methods of handling' adopted the friendly approach and his horses were much sought after. Ron's talents were very diverse and he produced some of the best campdraft, show-ring, stock, station and pleasure horses around. As his experience and expertise grew, so did his reputation and Ron also found himself teaching people how to handle their horses and how to get the most out of them. He always maintained that if you didn't teach the owner to continue the good work, his newly trained horses would soon develop bad habits. It is this commitment to his work that has endeared him to many well known horse people over his entire working life to this day.

During their time on the property, Ron and Joan's five children were being taught the 'tricks of the trade' with eldest daughter Carol enjoying huge success in the show and campdraft ring. All were very adept with horses and were breaking in alongside Ron as soon as they could climb the stockyard fence. Ron also began training trick horses and taught his children Susan and Ian the art of trick riding at a very young age. The talented youngsters toured all over the country with their father, astonishing the crowds and appearing at numerous national finals and large country shows and rodeos from the age of eight. Ron's repertoire also included 'Liberty Horses,' a team of seven horses working totally free in a big arena carrying out complex manoeuvres, as well as exhibitions of riding on highly educated horses working without saddle or bridle, amazing audiences wherever they performed.

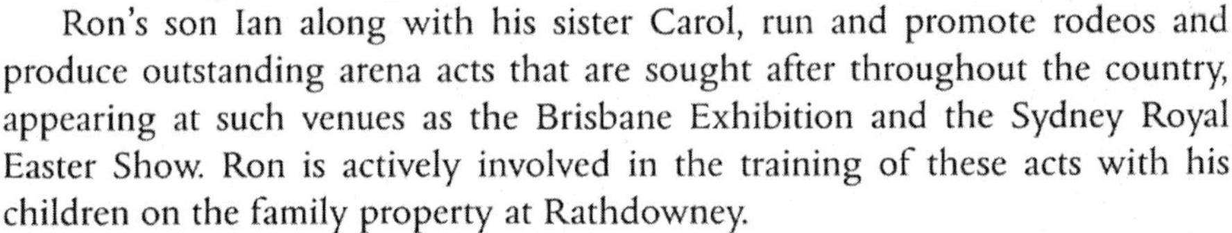

The family also produced Australia's first bullfight in the seventies, with a two round challenge to a Spanish matador to come and fight bulls Aussie style, with 'the kill' being a hand placed on the charging bull's head! When Ron's brother Bluey Bostock, a well known rodeo clown, was injured during the second round , Ron took his place in the arena to fight bull for bull against the Spanish matador.

Ron's son Ian along with his sister Carol, run and promote rodeos and produce outstanding arena acts that are sought after throughout the country, appearing at such venues as the Brisbane Exhibition and the Sydney Royal Easter Show. Ron is actively involved in the training of these acts with his children on the family property at Rathdowney.

Over the years Ron has dabbled in art, working with charcoal and later oils to produce a style of work that is hard to find in the present day art world. His outback canvases depict man and animal in typical everyday scenes and his attention to detail and ability to paint a 'picture that tells a story' has

Ron Bostock riding in the Rocky Roundup, 1959.
—All photos courtesy Ron Bostock

ensured wide exposure of his work. Ron's late father was a talented artist, as is his sister and his daughters Susan and Rhonda enjoy continuing success in the art world. Susan's paintings also reflect her upbringing on the land and her love for Australiana, and she attributes her artistic achievements to the continuing guidance and motivation she receives from her father. The pair often paint side by side with a father/daughter exhibition planned for the near future.

Ron has had no formal training , yet his art is that of a true Australian horseman and artist, a man of the land whose love of nature and all things Australian shines through in the richness of his work. Now in his seventies and enjoying great health, he is still breaking and training horses and animals and continues to capture our beautiful bush and its characters on canvas.

Ron wrote to me about spurs he has made over the years.

> In 1958 I was breaking in horses at Jindabyne down in the Snowy Mountains. I did four rodeos while I was there and I decided to build myself a pair of bull-riding spurs, different in length and angle to the ones I was using. In those days availability of these types of things was more difficult and without the variety we have today. The surest way to get what I wanted was to build them myself.
>
> On the way to the first rodeo I called in to a blacksmith's shop and built the heel of the spur using the blacksmith's forge and anvil. On the way to the next rodeo I stopped at a welding works and used steel bolts to fashion the shank. Some cutting and welding later, I arrived at the third rodeo with my new spurs ready to go. These spurs were great, I liked the extra weight and they were the only spurs I used when riding bulls after that

Top: Carol Bostock doing the first catch on a six year old in the breaking yards on Glenaughton station, Carnarvon Range country in the Taroom area, one of the stations that Ron broke in for every year. Carol is using a bush to relax the horse, while puttting a halter on at the same time.

Above: Ron giving a newly broken colt its first ride out of the yards, breaking in for Clem Davey, Roundstone station, Moura, central Queensland, in the 1960s.

In about 1972 I decided my daughter Carol, still a juvenile, who had done very well at local campdrafts, needed a better pair of spurs. The idea I had was a spur that sat high on the boot to make contact easier but sloping down some so that the contact was not too direct and would still have some give as a result. Some years later when Carol went to New Zealand to work with blood horses, I started using these spurs myself. I am still using them today; they have been in use some thirty years. They have done a few miles and trained a lot of horses.

Over the years I have made a number of pairs of spurs for my children and myself – spurs for poddy riding and for general horse work.

I also asked Ron for his views on using spurs and he sent the following article:

Spurs and Young Horses

As a horsebreaker, my use of spurs on a young horse is only a very small part of their training. By the definition 'young', I am referring to the horse that is in the early stages of training and is therefore green or inexperienced. Also referred to as 'colts', this is a bush term used to describe a horse in the process of being 'broken in', or if you like – started under saddle.

Firstly I get my young horses going with a dressage whip, legs and bare heels in and around the yards and then progressing out into the open paddock. As he develops and reaches the stage in his training when he is ready to learn more about body control, I will introduce the spur quietly to give more emphasis to my leg. This would be backed up with the use of a dressage whip applied in conjunction with the leg and spur and used behind the leg. This combination of leg, spur and riding whip is a three way feel and easier for the colt to understand.

These early sessions are about the colt learning how the rider's legs can control the colt's hindquarters. It is about shifting his hindquarters or holding them in place and shifting his front end or setting the colt up to take a particular lead. This is the start of many things to do with controlling the colt's body. You are teaching the colt a language – be it silent – and you will therefore have the means to be able to ask of him what you want at any time.

The way to teach this language is to start very small and build gradually with the early lessons taking place in the yards. This early introduction to the

The spurs Ron made for his daughter, Carol.

spur is not intended to be a 'go faster lesson' but more about 'listen to what my legs are telling you'. I start by teaching all the moves separately and he will respond to the different combination of aids later. I begin by applying pressure, small enough so as not to panic him but persistent and annoying enough to cause him to want a way out.

Immediately reward the first move he makes in the right direction no matter how small this response may be – 'this is the key'. Immediately take all pressure of and leave it off long enough for him to feel the release of pressure and to get comfort from that release. It's this 'release of pressure' that he will remember and this is where the light begins to switch on. He will look for it again and his response will come more quickly next time with less pressure needing to be applied.

These lessons need to be short and you want him calm enough to think. The colt learns that the spur is a backup to the rider's leg – and you need him to be able to feel that he can move away from the spur and leave the spur behind. My spurs are blunt and loose on my boots with no tie strap underneath the boot ensuring their contact remains soft. The spur on a young horse is just another training aid that you are teaching him how to respond to. This knowledge will make life easier for him later with someone else on his back.

I do not use spurs to put 'go' on a young horse (to teach him to move fast), I find a dressage whip used well back on the rump is much easier for him to understand. I would say the spur is useful to help put a finer touch on a horse that is already going, that is he has advanced enough in his training to have a basic understanding of aids and response.

Horse training is about doing only that which gets a good result and never persist with anything that is not getting a clear understanding. Go back to the drawing board and come at it from another angle, what works for one may not always be right for the next horse.

Whether I am mustering cattle on a young horse or just riding from A to B, I ride always as a teacher, I ask many things of him along the way and I help him to get it right. And I ride to save him, I ride to save his mouth, to save his wind, and to save his 'light feel'. There are many ways to save him and still show him how to get the job done. I prefer to train at a slow pace as it is here that you can teach him his lessons, while he is calm, fresh and ready to 'listen'. If your horse has not got it right, come back to a slower pace and do more work. A rider's job is to show him and help him – **Do not blame your horse for what you have not yet taught him!**

A sharper spur to achieve more pace, a bigger, flasher bit to get more stop or to pull harder for a faster turn – **this is not the way and it does not work!** He will give all of these things freely when you train him and show him how and then ask him in the correct manner. You do not achieve a softer mouth by making it sore – you get a softer mouth by working on his brain. Apply a spur to the belly of an untrained horse and he will wonder why you are being nasty. The untrained horse will push back at you in defence, he will not know that you mean to go forward or shift over, unless you have first taught him.

If you are a thinking horseman who can ride all day with spurs on your boots and not use them or use them little and wisely – that is okay. However if you are a young fellow who likes the pace and wants to be getting up there on the blade every chance you get, I would suggest you leave the spurs off your young horse. You would be better off to break off a sucker, leave some fine branches on, strip off the leaves and this will help you show him 'go' and will give you more chance of getting out of the way if a bull comes back a bit mean.

One cannot write a definite 'how to' to do anything; it depends on the horse and his stage in the training at the time. What was right for him yesterday, I could change tomorrow. It differs from horse to horse and it changes from day to day, it would be better to say – be flexible and find what works for that particular horse at the time.

Ron also wrote the following poem for inclusion in this book.

The Horseman

His hair is grey but he is not old
He walks with purpose in his stride
He values friends and knowledge shared
And a better horse to ride.

A horseman speaks a language clear
To any breed or age
He trains with neither force nor fear
He lets understanding be the gauge

The horse will answer and respond
With honesty and deed
To place his trust and follow
The man that takes the lead

Gifted is the man
That can a message give
A horse, that he may read
New rules with which to live

A good man looks to read him
Treats him not a fool
There's learning worth a dozen books
With the horses in their school

Horsemen down on through the ages
With timing and feel, positioning and pace
Help the horse on through the stages
Respect and understanding are the base

So give me a horse that has a good rein
That carries his saddle well
Give me a horse that will never gall
A horse that has never fell

May he pick a track that's straight and true
When the pace is on
Game enough to crash the suckers through
And never a foot put wrong

A horse to ride through rocks and rough
Up on the mountain side
Where a horse needs be more than tough
To be drafted off to ride

So little time left the long shadows say
The horseman limpy with rain and cold
He watches all with a sharp eyed gaze
His hair is grey but he is not old.

Buck Buchester

Kalkarindji, Northern Territory

THE SINGLE SPUR shown here was recently given to Mick Bower by Neville John 'Buck' Buchester and has an interesting history.

When Buck was running the camp on Camfield in 1963, this spur was one of a pair of Wave Hill spurs given to him at Lignum Hole by part aboriginal ringer Sabu Sing.

Sabu Sing was born on Delamere in 1940 and from the age of about four years old was raised by Manbulloo manager Tom Fisher. In March, 1952 Tom went down to manage Wave Hill and Fred Gutte made the spurs for Sabu the following year, when Sabu was 13 years old.

When Buck obtained the spurs they were apparently without rollers as subsequently another ringer, George Man Fong, from Delamere, who was working at Camfield at the time, made the rollers for Buck from an old shovel blade.

This spur is not as heavy or as angled to the heel as are all other examples of Fred's spurs, perhaps reflecting the fact that it was made for a young boy.

Sabu had two other pairs for Fred's spurs made, one pair when he was about fourteen years old, and another pair a couple of years later.

From Humpy to Homestead, the Biography of Sabu, by Pearl Ogden, is the story of this young man, born

Top: Sabu Sing's spur. —Photo Kim Corcoran
Right: Buck Buchester, photographed in 1953 when he was head stockman on Moolooloo.—F.H. Johnston Collection, National Library of Australia

in an Aboriginal camp and who, with limited formal education, eventually reached managerial level in the pastoral industry. Sabu, who had been left at Manbulloo by his mother in 1945, returned there in 1978 employed by Vestey's as manager, a remarkable achievement for a man of his background. Sabu was killed in a motor vehicle accident in the Territory in 1993.

The photograph on the the right shows Sabu yarding cattle at Nutwood Downs, Northern Territory, in 1981. He is wearing his Wave Hill spurs and riding one of his quarter horses, Doc's Leo. This photograph, featured on the front cover of *From Humpy to Homestead*, has been included with the permission of Pearl Ogden.

Buck Buchester and George Man Fong, like Sabu, spent much of their working life in and around the Victoria River District.

On the 4th April, 2003 a one-and-a-half-times lifesize bronze sculpture of a horse and rider, called 'The Pioneer', was unveiled in Katherine, paying tribute to the stockmen and pioneers of the Top End.

Former stockman and helicopter pilot Archie StClair sculpted the statue for the 'Katherine Icon Project'. This project had been initiated by Terry Underwood of Riveren Station on behalf of the Northern Territory Cattlemen's Association for the Year of the Outback.

Top: Sabu at Wave Hill when he was about 17 years old.
—Sampson Collection

Left: George Man Fong, Hidden Valley homestead, Northern Territory, about 1962
—Scobie Collection

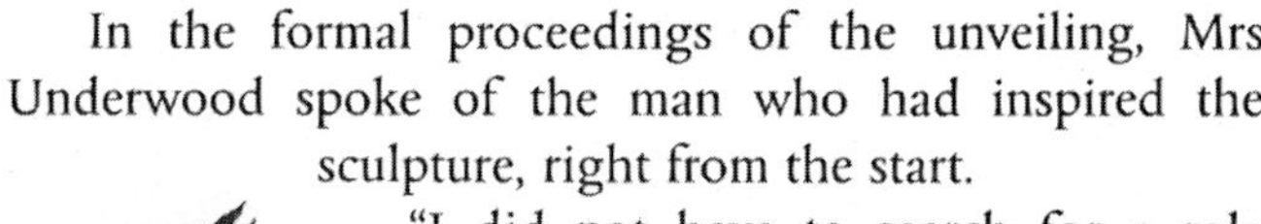

In the formal proceedings of the unveiling, Mrs Underwood spoke of the man who had inspired the sculpture, right from the start.

"I did not have to search for a role model – there was one obvious person, one who was beyond dispute, qualified in a number of ways," she said.

"With the blessing of Dorothy and the family, I announced that Sabu Peter Sing was the role model for the Katherine Icon.

"A gentle, humble man, he was our mate. He rode beside my husband John and many of you gathered here today. Sabu's outstanding skills as bushman, horseman, stockman and cattleman were widely recognised and acclaimed.

"Sabu epitomised different races and cultures. At Wave Hill station he met his match and in 1970, Dorothy became his wife and soul mate. Tragically killed in 1993, Sabu's spirit lives on through his children – Samantha, Gregory, Lionel and Damien.

"And now, through Sabu, the chosen representative of all people – blackfella, whitefella, yellafella – our history and heritage will be immortalised.

"We are all inextricably linked."

Buck Buchester and other workmates of Sabu gathered on horseback to form a Guard of Honour when the sculpture was unveiled.

The statue of The Pioneer..
—Photo courtesy Katherine Times

Frank Bunyan

Frank Bunyan was born in Walgett, N. S. W., in 1950 and at thirteen years of age, worked for his father, Bluey, and his uncles, who were drovers, while the family was living at the 23 Mile Tank, or Tull's Bore, on the Hungerford Road, out of Bourke. He helped take mobs of cattle to Tancred's Meat Works, which employed about 300 workers in Bourke at that time.

He also did a trip with his father's pack horse plant, taking a mob of about ninety horses from Noondoo, near Dirranbandi, just over the Queensland border, to Bourke, about four weeks on the road. He was getting paid £1 a day and reckoned he was a millionaire.

Frank related that he bought his first pair of R. M. Williams boots in Bourke, and was so proud that while walking along the main street to show his mates, and looking down at his boots, he collided with a post in front of the barber's shop and broke his nose in three places.

In the seventies and eighties he worked as a ringer in stock camps around the Georgina River, Winton, Boulia, and Bedourie including Cluny, Marion Downs and Thylungra stations, mustering cattle to go on the road trains. For a couple of seasons between jobs he also worked on maintaining the Dingo Barrier Fence on the Thargomindah – Bulla Downs section.

Later he worked for about fourteen years for Queensland Railways on the building and maintenance of railway bridges.

Reading through Frank's story I note that the word 'work' appears often. He was typical of so many young men in the bush, who took whatever job was available - there was plenty of work around and no one expected a handout.

Frank has accumulated a collection of spurs, horse bells, and other bush gear, including a Monty Scobie stockwhip – the Scobie family were regarded as amongst the finest whip makers in Australia, from the 1930s.

Shown is a very old pair of Wave Hill spurs, which Frank bought from George Thompson, who used to run the hotel at Daly Waters in the Territory, which have since been refurbished. Also shown is a pair of unused Willoughby spurs, which belonged to his father.

Frank has a pair of spurs stamped 'Sorensen' on the inside of the heel band, believed to have been made in Injune, Queensland. I have written about Niel Sorenson in 'The Blacksmiths' section of this book but have not seen any of his spurs. The spelling on Frank's spurs differs to other references I have found to the blacksmith Sorenson at Injune.

At the time of writing, Frank, who lives in Mitchell on the Maranoa River, is involved, with all other residents, cleaning up the town after the recent disastrous flooding in that region of Queensland.

Frank Bunyan on Dusty.

Frank Bunyan's relic Wave Hill spurs.

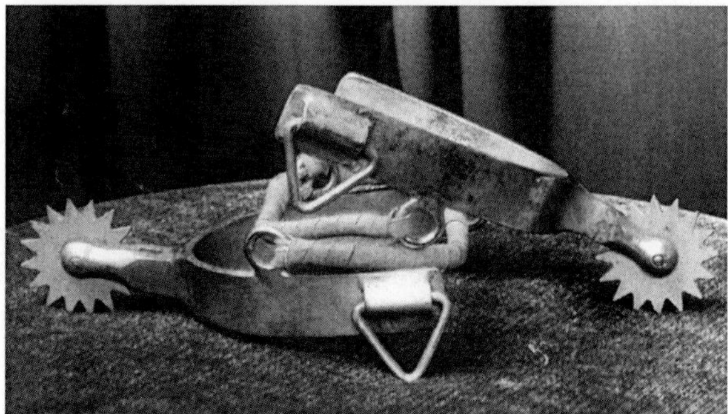

Frank Bunyan's Willoughby spurs.

Photos: Frank Bunyan.

Stewart Campbell

Mitchell, Queensland

I FIRST HEARD of Stewart Campbell's long necked spurs while in Birdsville, Queensland, many years ago and eventually contacted him at his property, Clara Vale, near Mitchell.

When I spoke to him he said, 'I think I've got the longest spurs in Queensland.' At that time, because of the condition of the roads, I was not able to visit him, and the photographs were recently sent to me by Mrs. Campbell.

His spurs, as can be seen at left are about 115 millimetres long in the neck, the rollers, are 65 millimetres in diameter, with eleven teeth, each 25 millimetres in length. They were made by Stewart prior to 1947 and it is unusual for spurs of that time to have separate studs for the strap under the boot.

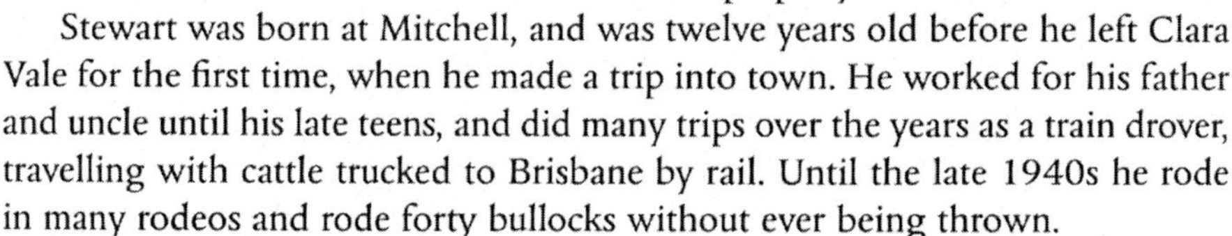

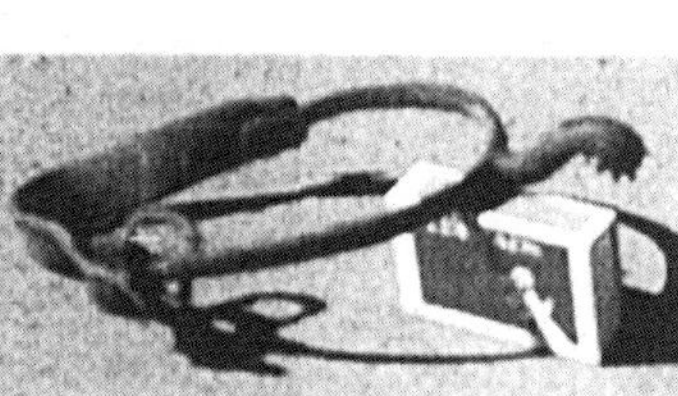

The single spur on the right belonged to Stewart's father, James Peter Stayte Campbell, also known as Gill, who was a part time jockey and rode his own horses in the local races and over hunt hurdles at shows. Clara Vale has been owned by the Campbell family since the 1890s and there used to be a race track on the property in the 1920s and '30s.

Stewart was born at Mitchell, and was twelve years old before he left Clara Vale for the first time, when he made a trip into town. He worked for his father and uncle until his late teens, and did many trips over the years as a train drover, travelling with cattle trucked to Brisbane by rail. Until the late 1940s he rode in many rodeos and rode forty bullocks without ever being thrown.

Stewart Campbell passed away in late 2002 aged ninety years.

Top: Stewart at Clara Vale in the 1940s

—Photo courtesy Mrs Campbell

Tony Clark

Ellerston, New South Wales

Tony Clark was born in Bathurst, New South Wales in 1939 and as his father was a police officer, the family was usually transferred to a new town every four years. He grew up in Bathurst and Rockley and attended primary school in Bourke, Merriwa and Taree – secondary schooling was at Newington College in Sydney.

In 1957 he commenced work as a jackeroo on Glensloy station, Young. The owner, Allan Gordon with J. D. MacLeod, Bill Kelly and Neville and Clive Milson had visited Wave Hill station in the Northern Territory a few years earlier when Tom Fisher was the manager. Fred Gutte was the blacksmith at that time and Allan bought a pair of his spurs which are still at Glensloy with Allan's son, Jimmy.

Allan's many stories about Wave Hill, Tom Fisher and ringer Sabu Sing influenced Tony who subsequently went to Wave Hill as a jackeroo in 1959. He started in No. 2 stockcamp with head stockman Rod Russell, attending mustering at Inverway station, when Pat Underwood was the owner and George Hamilton was head stockman.

Tony said of George Hamilton, – "George was the smartest man I've ever worked with in unfenced country with wild cattle. Another man of his calibre was aboriginal stockman Johnson Hatwood who worked with me when I was managing Nutwood Downs."

Overseer Barry LeRoy left Wave Hill in 1960 and was replaced by Ralph Hayes whose brother Lynn became No. 3 camp head stockman. Sabu Sing ran No. 1 camp, Jim Tough became improvements overseer and Tony took over No. 4 camp. A highlight of the season was attending mustering at Mount Sanford station, when Elmore Lewis was head stockman there.

Tony at Wave Hill, No.2 Camp, 1961.
—Photo courtesy Tony Clark

In 1961 Len Brodie took over No 4 camp and Tony ran No. 2 camp, attending musters that year on Hooker Creek station, where Bob Savage was head stockman, and at Inverway, where John Underwood was head stockman.

Tony left the Territory in 1962 to work as an overseer for Clive Milson on Cardross station, Goulburn, New South Wales and married Sue McGilvray in 1964. Two years later he moved to Funny Hill station at Binda as manager for Sir James Carr. He went back to Wave Hill in 1969 as overseer when Ralph Hayes was manager and was next transferred to Nutwood Downs as manager. When he left Nutwood in 1978 Sabu Sing was appointed as the next manager.

Since 1979 Tony has worked as general manager of Ellerston station at Scone for Kerry Packer.

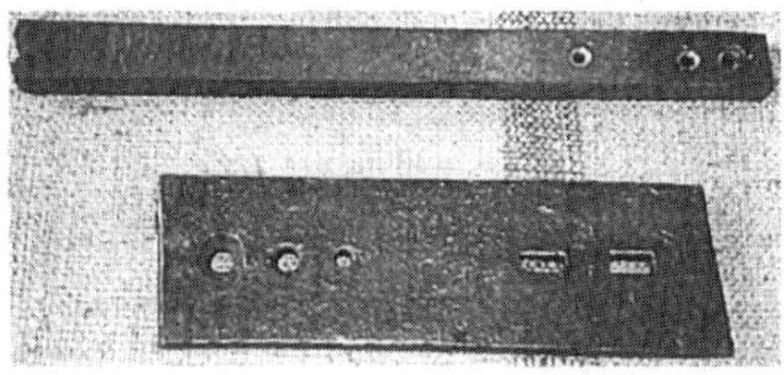

In April, 2003 Tony attended the unveiling of a bronze statue of a horse and rider, titled 'The Pioneer', in Katherine, a tribute to the stockmen and pioneers of the Territory. This statue is of Sabu Sing and as a former work mate, Tony took part in the ceremony as one of the horsemen in the official Guard of Honour.

In 1959 during the wet season, at Wave Hill, Tony, Colin Wardell and No. 4 Camp head stockman Jim Tough made four sets of spurs using the bar and swedge plate shown above. The bar is 460 ml long, 40 ml wide and 22 ml thick while the plate is 320 ml long, 100ml wide and 15 ml thick.

Colin Wardell had worked on Wave Hill from the late 1940s to the early '50s as head stockman of No. 1 Camp. He had become quite an experienced blacksmith, sometimes working with Fred Gutte during the wet seasons. When Fred left Wave Hill, about 1956, he gave the swedge plate and bar to Colin.

At the time of making the spurs Colin was contract fencing and yard building at Wave Hill, and died only a few years later while droving with Charlie Swan. After Colin died the swedge plate and bar were purchased by Pat Underwood of Inverway and are now in the possession of his son-in-law John Westaway.

Colin, Jim and Tony each made a pair of spurs, in the style of Fred's design, and then together made a pair for ringer Lynn Hayes.

Step 1. First a piece of ¾ inch round mild steel, about 5 inches long was split with a hacksaw, about a 2½ inch cut.

Step 2. The uncut half of the round steel was heated to red, and drawn out on the anvil face, using a flattener, to create the neck or shank.

Step 3. The swedge plate was placed on the anvil face, with the rectangular hole over the anvil hardie hole. The cut end of the round steel was heated to red and the shank end was dropped through swedge plate and hardie hole. The cut end was opened with a hammer handled chisel to separate the heel bands, which were then hammered down flat onto the swedge plate, leaving the spur as a 'T' shape, with flat 'wings'.

Step 4. The 'wings' of the spur were re-heated, the shank held with the tongs and the spur placed on the anvil horn so the 'wings' or heel band could be shaped to the boot heel by hammering them down onto the horn. The inside of the heel band was slightly angled to fit the boot heel.

Step 5. The shank was re-heated, the heel band and about ¾ inch of the shank was clamped in the vice, and the hammer used to achieve the upward curve of the shank.

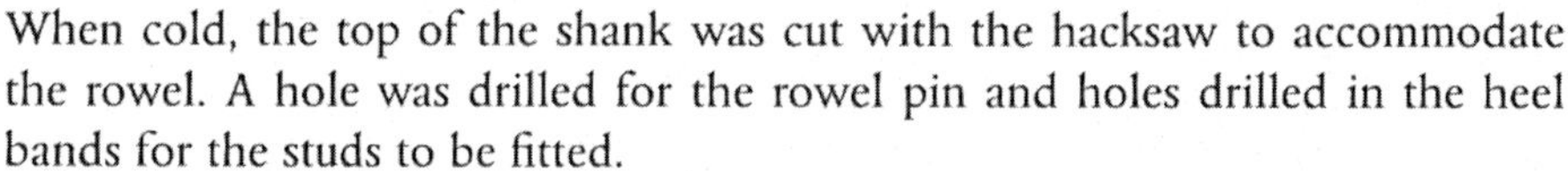

Step 6. The top of the shank was heated, and hammered on the edge of the anvil face to create the rowel housing.

Step 7. The shank was re-heated and the final curve of the shank shaped on the anvil horn. When cold, the top of the shank was cut with the hacksaw to accommodate the rowel. A hole was drilled for the rowel pin and holes drilled in the heel bands for the studs to be fitted.

Step 8. The swedge bar, which had a countersunk hole drilled through it to form a 'mould' for the stud, was used next. A ¾ inch section of ¼ inch rod was cut almost through, heated, then drawn out to fit through the hole. The hot section was twisted off and hammered into the 'mould' to make each stud. The stud was then tapped hot into the hole in the heel band and riveted in from the inside using a ball peen hammer.

To finish off the spurs a 12 inch flat file was used to remove any rough spots and a groove was filed on each side of the shank, at the bottom where it joins the heel band, with a round file. Two grooves were filed across the top of the shank near the heel band with a three cornered file which was also used to tidy up the rowel housing. R. M. Williams ready made rowels were then fitted.

Tony commented that spurs were a bit like the spare wheel on a motor car—'If you didn't have them, that's when you would need them.

Tony recalled that while they were making the spurs the Wave Hill manager Tom Fisher would come to the smithy to see how they were doing. Tom told them that Fred Gutte used to get two new files from the station store each

The spurs made by Tony Clark in 1959 at Wave Hill.
—Photo Don Corcoran. Photo previous page John Westaway

Friday night, made his spurs over the weekend and by Monday the files were too worn out for station work.

Tony's father, Frank Clark, was born at Uralla, New South Wales, on 10th July, 1902 and joined the New South Wales Mounted Police at Redfern, Sydney, on 19th September, 1924. The horse was still his means of transport when he was stationed at Rockley in 1944. From there he went to Bourke, Merriwa, Taree and Gosford and retired at Broken Hill as Inspector 1st Class on 10th July, 1962.

He now resides in Parkes and on his 100th birthday representatives of the New South Wales Police, including a contingent of Mounted Police, escorted him to a civic reception at the Parkes Council Chambers.

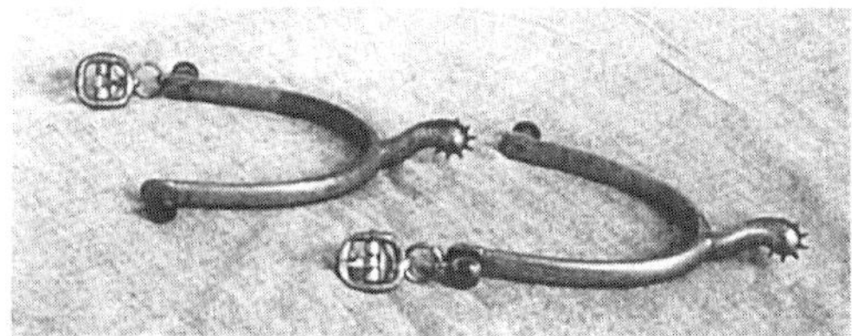

Top left: Buck Buchester, Greg Scott and Tony Clark at the unveiling of 'The Pioneer'.

—Photo Jane Jackson

Top right: Tony's spurs, made to sit low on Cuban heels.

—Photo Dean Stibbs

Right: Constable Frank Clark at Redfern Police Training Centre in 1924.

—Photo courtesy Tony Clark

Above: Frank Clark's spurs. These spurs were not Police issue, but of an approved style which recruits were recommended to buy from a saddler's shop opposite the Police Barracks,

—Photo Don Corcoran

Mick Daffy

Colac, Victoria

MICK DAFFY LIVED and farmed at Eurack about thirty kilometres north of Colac, Victoria where he bred horses, including Shetlands, and was a stock agent in Colac for Dalgetys and J. G. Johnstone & Co.

Mick's daughter Christine Sommerville, of Colac, said, "He picked up stock from farms prior to sale day, worked in the saleyards and then took sold stock back to the properties of their new owners. He was a drover with two great dogs and mainly worked around the mid 1920s to the late '40s in this district. He said his spurs were unique because of the placement of the rowel which meant that he could control his horse with minimal leg and heel movement.'

Mick's spurs are made of steel, have straight 25 millimetre necks and the rollers are placed horizontally. Although not unique, this type of spur was far less common than those with the rollers placed conventionally. Spur retailers generally referred to this style as having horizontal, cross or side rowels.

Top: Mick at the Colac Show in 1938.
Above: Mick's spurs.
—Photos courtesy Christine Sommerville

George Day

Avon Downs, Northern Territory

WHEN I WAS DROVING for Larry Darcy in about 1952 we were fairly short handed. There was myself, another ringer and George Day as cook and horsetailer. Later on Larry's brother Sonny joined us as cook. This was a pack horse plant and I learned a lot from Larry.

I used to yarn a lot with George and found he was formerly head stockman at Avon Downs, which I understand in those days was owned by the Peel River Pastoral Company which was part of the Australian Agricultural Company, the oldest pastoral company in Australia.

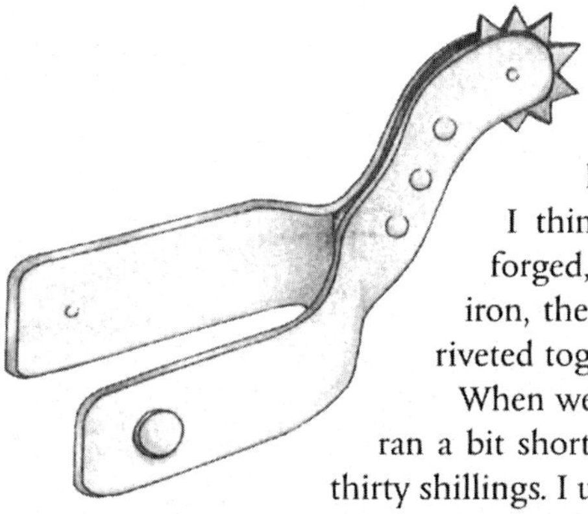

George had a pair of iron spurs which he had made himself while on Avon Downs, I think from old water troughing. They were not forged, but each spur was made from two pieces of flat iron, the heel bands shaped to the boot, and the necks riveted together.

When we were paid off in Dajarra, Queensland, George ran a bit short of cash and I bought the spurs from him for thirty shillings. I used them for many years but passed them on to a mate when I left the bush.

These spurs were fairly well known as a couple of years after buying them, when I was ringing on Oban, near Dajarra, someone asked me if George had died when they saw me wearing them. They believed that was the only way George would have parted with them.

As the spurs are long since gone, I have included a sketch.

—Courtesy Longina Phillips Designs

Rob Dempster

Rob Dempster, currently living in South Australia, comes from a family who spent their life on cattle and sheep stations. His father Mick (James Ivan) Dempster was a Kidman drover and head stockman, as well as a contract tank sinker and earth mover, working much of the time throughout the channel country of south western Queensland.

In 1940, the War Office, desperate for beef to be shipped out of Wyndham, W. A., engaged Kidman's to seek out competent cattlemen to be sent to Victoria River Downs. Mick went there as a ringer, later to be a drover of cattle to Wyndham, then head stockman at Wave Hill in 1944.

In 1945 Mick managed Limbunya station for Vestey's. His wife, one of the few white women in the district, worked in the pack horse mustering camp as cook, with all aboriginal ringers. As Mick later said, 'The Limbunya boys were the best men I have ever worked with, black or white – none better –very smart men.'

As well as Limbunya, Mick also managed other stations in South Australia, New South Wales and Queensland, including Granite Downs, Idracowra, Alcoota, Elkedra and the family property Joulnie, later inherited by Mick when his mother died.

Rob was born at Alice Springs, when Mick was managing Alcoota station. The family returned to Joulnie in 1956 and it was there, at ten years of age, that Rob first worked in a packhorse stock camp. Bert Olds was in charge and when mustered, the cattle were walked to the rail head at Cockburn.

While at Joulnie in the 1950s, Rob was able to further pursue his education at Broken Hill, working as an apprentice fitter and machinist at the Zinc Corporation Mine qualifying as a Diesel Mechanic, Welder, Fitter and Machinist, amongst other skills, but never stopped his hands-on involvement with horses and livestock.

Rob worked with his father for nearly thirty years, in stock camps and driving heavy machines until 1979 when Mick died on Sanpah station, ten miles from the Tindara ruins, his childhood home.

In 1983, Rob travelled alone with a pack horse plant, from Broken Hill to Adelaide, a distance of about 580 kilometres, carrying a letter from the Mayor of Broken Hill, to be handed to the Mayor of Adelaide, inviting him to attend Centenary Celebrations in Broken Hill.

During his years of living and working on stations in remote regions Rob has been continuously mentored by aboriginal and white ringers and drovers.

As a consequence, he is a recognised and respected horse breeder, breaker and trainer, and presently has commitments breaking and training horses in Japan, where he generally spends two three-month periods each year.

Over the years Rob has collected spurs which are of specific interest to him and I have included photographs of these spurs and their stories.

Mick Dempster's spurs were purchased from Fred Gutte at Wave Hill for £2 in the late 1940s. Rob, of course, used them after his father died. They were stolen at one stage, but after ten years he was able to recover them.

Rob's own spurs are also from Wave Hill – as a ringer on Nockatunga station, in south west Queensland Rob worked with horsetailer, Keith Oats, who was a former drover and ringer, originally from Jundah.

In 1984 they were moving a mob of about 1400 bullocks from Conbar to Nockatunga, and over the campfire at Rocky Tank, the first night out, the talk eventually got around to spurs. Keith mentioned he had a pair of Wave Hill spurs in his swag which he had bought from Fred Gutte for £2 years before, while droving in the Territory. A deal was done, Rob got the spurs for $60 and has had them ever since.

Another pair of spurs in Rob's collection were once owned by Frank Judd, former stockman and saddler. Frank, now in his eighties, was born in Adelaide. At fifteen years of age he got a job working for saddlers, collar makers and leather merchants, Julius Conn & Co, in Leigh St, Adelaide. He learnt the trade, at a time when the firm was committed to supplying World War 2 military orders.

Eventually, he headed north and got a job on a Kidman station near Bancannia This was a property on the Broken Hill line called 'The Selection', run by Jack Otto Watt. He was soon taking mobs of Kidman cattle to the rail head at Cockburn.

Frank's last job on the road was a trip of some months with boss drover Leo Whitely, taking a mob of channel country bullocks from Durham Downs to Deniliquin, near the N. S. W. Victorian border.

Until his retirement Frank worked as a saddler He had a business at Meadows in S. A. for many years and later worked from home.

Frank's spurs are unusual, as can be seen in the photographs, as one spur has four studs on the heel band, and the other has just two.

Rose Rawlins Coppock of Alice Springs, has written the following story about a pair of Wave Hill spurs:-

'In 1955 Tom Rawlins (my Dad) was running Bohemia Downs, between Louisa Downs and Christmas Creek in the Kimberley. Bohemia Downs was a small place bought by H. V. Leonard, a businessman of Sydney, then Perth, and brother-in-law of R. M. Williams. Leonard bought Bohemia because the stock route was too dry to move cattle that R. M. had contracted for him to buy for Kurundi, Leonard's place in the Territory. With 'walkabout disease' rife and few horses on Bohemia, it was arranged for stockman/drover Ron Ogilvie to walk about 100 Territory horses, mostly unbroken, from the Alice Springs area. Alone for the most part, swapping youngsters for reliable mounts whenever he could en route, Ogilvie eventually arrived. Waiting at Bohemia for Connellan's mail plane to visit Hall's Creek, he showed us the spurs he had bought from a blacksmith at Wave Hill when he worked in the stock camp there, some years earlier. The story was that the blacksmith made spurs in his spare time for sale to station ringers.

'After Ogilvie left for Hall's Creek to catch the plane back to Alice Springs his Wave Hill spurs were found, left behind at the quarters. We had no forwarding address. Needing spurs to keep awake an old pensioner horse I rode there, I took charge of them. They returned to the Territory with us in 1956. I needed them more than ever when Tom bought sheep – and three horses to shepherd them with – on a Grazing Licence on the Hanson River that we called Numagalong. We ran sheep for about eighteen months; the country was dry and sandy, eagles and dingoes plentiful.

'Tom saw Ron Ogilvie in Alice Springs, mentioned that his daughter had the spurs, and would he like them back?

'The response was, 'No, let her keep them. I've got others now.'

'Fifty plus years have flown by. Unused since the sheep venture at Numagalong, I am happy to pass on the Wave Hill spurs to my friend Rob Dempster, knowing that he will treasure them as I have done for the outback history they represent.

'I found my Wave Hill spurs and photographed them, along with my R. M. boots and a dish my father made from roofing iron. It was our laundry tub and bath at different times.'

Rose also wrote about her father's spurs:-

'My father, Tom Rawlins was born at Cockburn S. A. on 29 December, 1897; a stockman and drover from the age of fourteen; head stockman at Tallawanta, an outstation of Lorraine in Queensland at seventeen, he did a host of bush jobs that included well-sinking; fencing; yard building; erecting tanks, troughs, windmills; whip and rope making and managing stations. Tom gave away all his bush gear in 1942 when he understated his age to join the Army. The war in New Guinea was at its height. Tom was discharged from the Army two years later to look after Willowra station, N. T., whose owners faced manslaughter charges that were later dismissed. Tom probably bought the spurs from R. M.

Williams in 1944, when he began to replace the bush gear he had earlier given away.

'Still riding horses until he retired, he sank his last well and built his last dwelling at TiTree Well on the Stuart Highway north of Alice Springs in 1966, where he passed away on the 22 November, 1978.'

'Bush Tracks and Desert Horizons', written by Rose Rawlins Coppock of Alice Springs, and published in 1999, is a detailed history of her family living in Central Australia from 1938 to 1960.

All photographs by Rob Dempster.

Rob Dempster in Adelaide, 1983.

Rob Dempster with friends in Japan.

Mick Dempster's Wave Hill spurs.

Rob Dempster'sWave Hill spurs.

Frank Judd's spurs.

One of Rose Rawlins Coppock's Wave Hill spurs.

Rose Rawlins Coppock's Wave Hill spurs and other gear.

Tom Rawlins' spurs.

Kelly Dixon

Camooweal, Queensland

WHEN WE VISITED Kelly at his home in Camooweal he showed me two pairs of spurs. The first were Bronc spurs, purchased from saddlers Syd Hill in Brisbane, and the second pair were made in 1987 by a spurmaker in Beaudesert who sold his spurs through Greg Grant Saddlery in Brisbane. *(These spurs are stamped inside the heel band with Leo Benjac's trade mark. Don C.)*

Kelly, at left, photographed by the author during his visit, was a ringer on Tanbar, Babiloora, Victoria River Downs, Galway Downs and Bulloo Downs and in 1948, '49 and '50 he did droving trips with Johnny Darcy from Victoria River Downs to Walgra, Queensland.

He was manager of Buckingham Downs in Queensland from 1956 to '59, then in the Territory managed Helen Springs from '59 to '61 and Numery from '81 to '85. For twenty years he was involved in the transport industry interstate.

Kelly has owned two pairs of Wave Hill spurs, "The first pair I bought when I was on Victoria River Downs in 1949, Fred sent them over on the MacRobertson-Miller mail plane from Wave Hill for a cost of two pounds ten shillings. They were the best spurs I've owned, they sat right down on the heel and didn't need to be tied down. When working in the yards I turned them around and they didn't flop about. Fred's spurs had the right length and rise in the neck for the average rider to spur without needing to put the leg back. He made the rollers from shovel blades and old crosscut saws. I bought a second pair in 1952 but later gave both pairs away."

Kelly is a poet, and founding President of The Drovers' Camp Association, based in Camooweal. Formed by Aidan Day, John Gill and the late Peter Clausen, this association has objectives which include the preservation and safe storage of authentic artefacts, documents, photographs and records relating to the droving industry in Australia.

The symbol of the Drovers' Camp Association is the Wave Hill spur, and as stated in their newsletter 'Cattle Pads':

> The unique Wave Hill spur was designed and made by Fred Gutte, who was employed as a blacksmith by the Vestey Company on Wave Hill station in

> the Northern Territory. Being purpose built at the request of several drovers, it soon became a necessary item for all who worked in droving plants. The Drovers Camp Association has adopted the spur as a symbol of the droving industry in Northern Australia.

We had met Kelly a number of times before our visit and were very impressed when he greeted us with the fact that he had written a poem for me entitled 'Where Are My Spurs', and here it is:

Where Are My Spurs?

Where are the spurs which used to grace my boots when the world was wide?
And where are the mates who rode with me, and the horses we used to ride?
Where are the men of the camps of then, where have those bushmen gone,
The fellows who used to wear spurs like mine, how many have since moved on

To some other life in a different world, where saddles are things of the past,
And friendships form in a hasty way, where friendships often don't last
As they did back then when my world was wide, and only the rich were poor
When it came to friends, and the stockman's home, was under the hat he wore!

And where is the quart I used to boil, with my mates in a drovers camp?
By some sleeping mob on a windy night--- I still hear the restless stamp
Of the horses tied to a night-horse tree, and a watching rider's song
Comes yet to me in the midnight hours, in this world where I don't belong.

Oh, where is the whip I used to swing, in the face of a wayward stag,
Which broke from the wings of a yard somewhere, and where is the saddlebag
That hung from the dees of the Schneider stool, tied down with a greenhide lace,
To keep it free from the clawing scrub, when the cleanskins used to race!

The swagwrap too, where is it today, the old Birkmyre "eight by ten"?
And the collar-check rug that was favoured too, by most of the droving men?
Well, it's lost somewhere in the mists of time, today they are using furs
And their swag-wrap now is a poly tarp, and a motor bike don't need spurs.

But our world must change, as the years pass by, that's part of a price we pay
If we want the things for a better life that we didn't have yesterday
And I must accept all the change I've seen, though it's hard to put aside
All the memories of the 'other life'-and the times I used to ride;

Or yarn with the mates I knew before, in the gold of a campfire bright,
Or race with that whip I sometime swung, at a galloping mob at night.
And those spurs of mine, and that saddlebag, and the quart I can't locate
Were the trappings of Life, when my world was wide – but I willed them away to a mate

Who has long since given them on again to another in need, I trust,
Another who hopefully wears them well, but forever I feel that I must,
Every now and then, when the house is quiet, allow my mind to roam,
To the land beyond, to those spurs of mine, and a world that was my home!!

Those spurs of mine were seldom red, with blood lest an urgent need
Was born when a charging beast bailed up, and I called for a turn of speed
From my horse to save both he and I, and that's when the worth would shine,
Of a pair of trusty bushman's spurs – like those Wave Hill spurs of mine!!

* * *

While we were in Camooweal Kelly had just written a poem for the family of his friend "Hippy" Phillip Wilson who had died in hospital shortly beforehand. With his permission I have included it, as to me, these verses describe the best attributes of the typical outback stockman.

One Of The Vanishing Breed

He was born to the sound of the hoofbeats, and a world of the cattlecamp's dust,
Like his father, a horseman before him, he was one of a breed we could trust–
He lived by the spur and the stockwhip, with hobble and halter and girth
His breed are the breed which some boast of,
boasted the salt of the earth.

Accepted by all who knew 'Hippy', he was
welcomed wherever he rode
With none ever able to turn him, away from
the pathway he strode –
He always rode tall in his saddle, you could
bet he'd be first to the lead,
If a mob were to break for the timber, he
was one of a vanishing breed!
I am thankful I knew Phillip Wilson, I am proud that
he claimed me a mate,
I know he'll take charge of the musters, when he
rides through that boundary gate,
Where the silver-shod horses are waiting, and buckles
and bits are of gold,
And the herds of the heavens are wheeling, and
cattlemen never grow old!

Phillip 'Hippy' Wilson.

—Photo courtesy Kelly Dixon

Lord, you've taken from us a real favourite, for reasons which only you know–
And I hope I will meet up with 'Hippy', again, when my time comes to go;
Guard his young family now, Lord please, and give them the comfort they need
And you've won your big stockcamp a good man – one of a vanishing breed.

The sound of the hoofbeats will echo, and the song of the stockwhip will ring,
While ever we've cattle to muster, the saddleman still shall be King –
But each time we lose men like 'Hippy', we lose men with skills that we need
And we don't breed 'em now like we used to – they are men of a vanishing breed.

Let the clods of this country that birthed him, fall gently today on his grave,
Let him ride through the herds of the heavens, where belly-high grasses will wave.
Keep a place in his camp for my swag, Lord, tell 'Hippy' I hope he'll find need
For another old bushman who knew him, as one of the vanishing breed!

For Kathy and family, from Kelly and Marian Dixon, Camooweal. 'Hippy' was a bloke who typified the real Australian stockman, a nice man, and we shall miss him always.

Here is another of Kelly's poems:

Yesterday's Ghosts and Me

Sometimes at night I go down to the place
Where the Georgina waters are quiet,
When the birds are all camped on the coolibah limbs,
And the moon casts a ghostly light
When the night breeze whispers through the silken grass,
And stars paint a silvered roof,
While a lone swan trumpets his sad refrain—
To the beat of a distant hoof.

It is then, only then, I hear the bells
And the chime of the hobble-chains.
When I close my eyes, I can see the sweep
Of those rolling Barkly plains.
The pungent scent of the horses' sweat!—
And the redhide reins I still feel—
And I hear the jingle of Wave Hill spurs,
On some long-dead drover's heel!

There comes to me, too, the lilting sound
Of a watching drovers song
As I swear I can see a travelling mob,
Fifteen hundred strong—

Where the Buchanan wanders—
Flinders and Mitchell are waving stifle high,
Like they used to be for my ghosts and me,
When we'd beaten the Murranji!

The lancewood crackles like lightning bolts,
And a bellowing cook I hear
Thundering hooves, a red dust cloud,
And the smell of nighthorses' fear—
The roaring rush of a maddened mob,
From a camp where the bullwaddie grew,
And the sound of bells on the plant at night,
Those awe-filled nights we once knew.

I picture the spread of a Kimberley mob,
With the wings a mile apart—
On the sundrenched plains of the Tableland,
And it gladdens a drover's heart.
Ah! a camping mob on a moonlit night,
With the Southern Cross on high,
And the sights and sounds of the rosy dawns,
Of those wonderful days gone by!

Yesterday's ghosts are always there,
They wait, 'cause they know I will be
Where the lone swan trumpets his wild refrain,
And old campsites I can see—
It is there the music of hobble chains,
And the Condamines sweet and free,
Comes, borne on a breeze from the droving days—
To yesterday's ghosts and me!

John Joseph Donnelly

aka Jerry Randall, Northern Territory

When Margaret and I were travelling in Ireland in 2000 we met an Australian couple in Dublin, Norman and Geraldine Mead, from Caloundra, Queensland. Quite naturally, the conversation turned to spurs! Geraldine told me that she had a pair of spurs won by her father, at the Esk Show, in Queensland in the 1920s.

When I eventually contacted Geraldine back in Australia she told me the following interesting story about a very interesting character.

Geraldine's father John Joseph Donnelly, was born at Augathella, Queensland in 1913. The brass spurs shown here were won by him for calf roping at the Esk Show when he was thirteen years old. His father was acting Sergeant of Police in Esk at that time.

"Dad finished his senior schooling at Nudgee College and spent two years at the Brisbane Polytechnic. He became a Sound Motion Picture Projection Engineer and worked as a projectionist at Brisbane's Regent Theatre.

"He joined the Air Force in 1942, was slightly wounded in the bombing of Darwin and was discharged in 1945. Dad won the leases for some land in the Northern Territory in a poker game and by 1948 he leased three lots, all in the name of Jerry Randall, the original lessee.

"On the smallest lot he built a tourist camp, 'Randall's Ranch', and on the other lots he had licences to shoot and destroy 700 buffalo, 3 years and over, as well as a licence to graze stock on Crown lands.

"Bill Hambly-Clark of Adelaide, proclaimed as 'Australia's Most Progressive

Clockwise from top: Randall's Ranch letterhead; John in the 1940s; the 1926 trophy spurs; and 'Jerry Randall' in the 1960s.
—Photos courtesy Geraldine Mead

Gunsmith and Sporting Hunter' and 'Australia's Ace Marksman' used to take tours to 'Randall's Ranch'. People would fly into Darwin and Dad would pick them up and drive them out to the camp in his old blitz truck.

"Dad also wrote articles for *Outdoors & Fishing* magazine and managed theatres in Queensland after he left the Territory. He then went to England to study at the London School of Film Technique, later working for the British Army in 'The Army Kinema Corps' in Aden. He also worked with tourist guide and hunter, Jan Voss, in Addis Ababa and spent time in Kenya on an elephant cull.

"After returning home he spent a few years in New Guinea before retiring to Russell Island in Moreton Bay, Queensland and died in 1979."

The Drovers Camp Association – Camooweal, Queensland

CAMOOWEAL, on the Georgina River in western Queensland, was the jumping off point for drovers heading into the Territory. In the 1940s and 1950s, at least thirty drovers paddocked their horses on the Town Common, with about 1500 horses spelling there, and many of the drovers living in the town. In those days Camooweal was regarded as 'The Drovers' Town'. At the start of the droving season they would muster their plants, stock up for the trip, and head west - after only thirteen kilometres they were through the Territory border gate.

In 1996 a local group decided to hold a Festival each year to commemorate and preserve the history of the droving era, and so formed the Drover's Camp Association with the following objectives:

1. To erect a building to be known as the Drover's Camp which will provide safe storage and preservation for authentic artefacts, documentation, art and photographic treasures from Australia's droving industry. The buildings shall also contain audio-visual presentations, interactive and interpretive displays.
2. To ensure the building becomes a focal point where living drovers and their descendants can meet with other people to share their experiences with peoples of all ages, to stimulate and sustain community interest in the significance of the droving industry.
3. To construct and maintain a National Shrine to acknowledge the contribution to Australia's cattle industry development by stockmen and stockwomen of all races. Such acknowledgement of their contribution will assist in the reconciliation process.
4. To stage an annual Festival to celebrate the contribution of the drovers and their families and to provide a venue for a reunion of old mates of the droving era.
5. To be a part of a successful and integrated tourism strategy with emphasis on the unique outback heritage of Australia.
6. To introduce commercial and income generating opportunities and to become fully self supporting.
7. To create jobs for unemployed people in the area.

It is fitting that Kelly Dixon, Camooweal resident and former drover, was elected the Founding President. The first Festival was held in 1997 on the banks of the Georgina River and after a few years the site was moved to the Camooweal

Race Club

In 2002 the committee secured a block of land on the Barkly Highway, one kilometre east of the town. This is now the venue for the Drover's Festival, held in August each year over a three day period and now attracting over 3000 visitors from within Australia and overseas. The Festival events include country music, bush poetry, a talent quest, a street parade, yarn spinning, an old time dance, an art and photography competition, a whip cracking competition, the Aussie Post mail race and bronco branding. (If you don't understand what bronco branding is, come and have a look)! The Camooweal Race Day is held on Saturday, the second day of the Festival.

In line with its aims and objectives, the Drover's Camp now has a Memorabilia Shed, with historic displays and an art gallery, a stage, a bar, catering, toilet and shower facilities and stockyards All of this has been achieved in fifteen years by the generous efforts of countless volunteers and the support of Events Queensland Regional Development Program, Mount Isa City Council, Myuma Pty Ltd, Southern Cross Media and Xstrata Mount Isa Mines along with other local business entities.

Liz Flood has been the Drover's Camp Association President since 2004 and with her husband Col, has overseen much of this development.

The present Committee are:

- Liz Flood, President,
- Russell Young, Vice President,
- Carmel Williams, Secretary,
- Ellen Finlay, Treasurer,
- and Col Flood, Paul Finlay, Tony Anderson, Minnie Kenna, Kathy Green and Dave Green.

The Patron of the Drover's Camp Association is former boss drover, Pic Willetts, of Camooweal.

Drover's Camp Association Patron Pic Willetts 1988.
Photo: Pic Willetts.

Sign on the Barkly Highway. Photo: Liz Flood.

Drovers in the Memorabilia Shed at the 2011 Festival.
Photo: Liz Flood.

Charlie Edgar

Pentland, Queensland

CHARLIE EDGAR AND I had been corresponding for about two years while we were living overseas and it was a real pleasure to finally meet him, with his wife Laura at Pentland, Queensland.

Margaret and I had been camping at Porcupine Gorge north of Hughenden, and were delayed there for a few days by heavy rain which made the roads impassable, even for the Toyota Troopy. Consequently when we visited Charlie and Laura we were covered in mud and a bit on the scruffy side. We needn't have worried, we were made most welcome and over many cups of tea and later a meal we swapped yarns and Snuffler Oldfield jokes and reminisced about 'the days when the world was wide.'

Charlie's family has been in Pentland since 1885, when his grandmother's family, the Taylors, owned stores and the hotel. His father, Albert Edgar, was a drover and Charlie was a ringer for four years on Blackbraes, north of Hughenden. His spurs, R.M.Williams' Angle Heels, were given to him when he was sixteen years old.

He had his own droving plant for a while and was head stockman on Carpentaria Downs and Longton. He then went to the Territory on Willeroo, Helen Springs and Innesvale, then back to Pentland in 1970. He was contract mustering with his own plant until '84, head stockman on Wanda Vale for a time, then went to the west side of Cape York to de-stock Arakun.

Top: Charlie at Pentland, 2000. —*Photo Don Corcoran*

Above right: Charlie, on right, with ringer Herbie Bosel on Gregory Downs, north of Hughenden. Charlie was 18 years old and boss drover for the first time.

—*Photo courtesy Charlie Edgar*

Charlie went to Katherine in '86 as head stockman at the meatworks but later 'retired' after being badly horned there. For the last four years he has been the organiser and president of the Pentland Campdraft Society. He has a great sense of humour, a flair for poetry and a never-ending supply of jokes and stories.

Here are two of Charlie's poems.

Last Muster

I've been a top-notch ringer, in the stock camps way out back,
I've done my share of droving, down along the Birdsville track,
I've mustered on the Gilbert, the Mitchell too as well,
I've camped beside the Staaten, where the mossies bite like hell.

I've lain awake and listened to the clink of hobble chains,
Away from noisy cities, and the smell of diesel trains,
I've duffed my share of poddies, beyond the Great Divide,
I've broke horses on the Basalt where you really have to ride.

I've saw the drought and hardship, watched the pouring rains,
Saw the fogs come drifting in, across the blacksoil plains,
I've been out on the Roper, saw the Daly in full flood,
Ran scrub bulls on the Flora, with hornsaws dripping blood.

I've ran the wildest cattle, with the wattle scrubs in bloom,
Jammed them in the coachers, then yarded with the moon,
I've swam the mighty Burdekin, when she's been bank to bank,
I've rode my share of horses, the quiet one and the rank.

I've watched the years pass swiftly, with that I must abide,
I've turned myself to pasture, in the Towers Eventide,
I often sit and wonder about the old brigade,
Snow, Big Jack and Lancey, with a good horse on the blade.

I've nearly reached the turning, it is time to say hoo-ray,
My legs are getting feeble, and my hair is silver grey,
I've been summoned to one last muster, on the big run up above,
I've saddled up old Bullwaddy, to do the work we love.

Rusty Spurs

I see you admiring my trophies, ribbons and cups galore,
Slide that door back laddie, and feast your eyes on more.
There is the whip I used on Gilgai to win a local cup,
The bracelet I won with Zulu Chief, and Splinter the jockey up.

You question this rusty trophy, the straps all perished and worn,
Look on them with dismay, show your derision and scorn,
Given to me as a young lad, by the boss of a big Kimberley run,
Fitting they hold pride of place, now their life's work is done.

They have helped run many a scrubber, shoulder many a cow,
With me in many a tight spot, those spurs are all rusty now.
They were once new and quite shiny and jingled a merry tune,
With Ivanhoe stags on nightwatch, singing my songs to the moon.

Made on a Territory station, shared in many a rodeo thrill,
Brainchild of Fred Gutte, blacksmith, on Vestey's station Wave Hill.
Wore them to draft, and to party, many the tale they could tell,
Wore them that day in the limestone, the day old Acrobat fell.

They were my mates, and one thing I silently vow,
I will never be parted from those spurs that are all rusty now,
When it is time to meet my Maker, and I take the final bow,
I trust they bury with me, those Wave Hill spurs somehow.

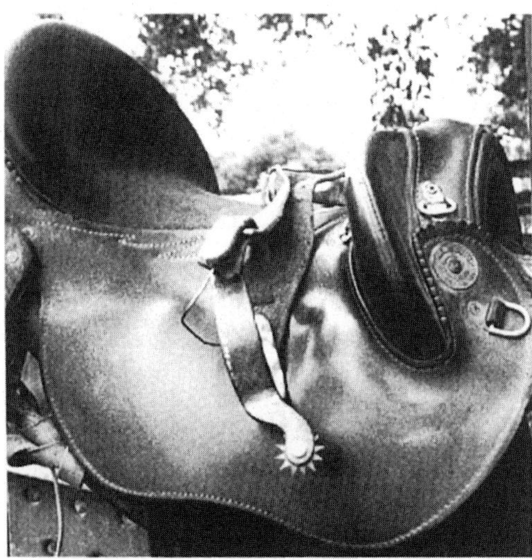

Charlie's Angle Heel spurs.
—Photo Don Corcoran

George 'Blue' Ellis

Sydney, New South Wales

GEORGE "BLUE" ELLIS, at 12 or 13 years of age, while living near Midland Junction east of Perth, Western Australia, bought a pony and used to work around the abattoirs and saleyards, moving stock from the saleyards into the paddocks and then back to the abattoirs.

Later on while living in Perth near a dairy, he used one of the dairy horses to take the cows out to graze after the morning milking. He learned to move them along nice and easy so they would be relaxed and feed better, which would be reflected at the afternoon milking. All good training for later life in the bush.

When Blue was about 15 years old he got a job as a rouseabout in a shearing team, (his father had been a shearer, then a wool classer in the 1920s). This led to work on sheep and cattle stations in the Gascoyne district of Western Australia, before going to the Territory and working at the Rum Jungle uranium mine. After the wet season that year he went south, heading for Alice Springs, but stopped at Dunmarra station and worked as a ringer.

He next went with drover Jeff Nixon taking a mob of cattle from Willeroo down the Dry River Road to the Murranji Track, and across the Barkly to Morstone station in Queensland. After that trip he returned to Dunmarra and ran the stock camp until the end of the dry season. The next year he went over to the Kimberley as a ringer on Argyle Downs and at the end of the season he returned to the Gascoyne district.

In 1956 Blue was back in Queensland at Winton, and at the end of the year was ringing in the Nebo district, near Mackay, before going out to Helen Springs station in the Territory. After a short stay there he went to Iffley station in the Gulf country. The next two years were spent working around the Winton area as a ringer, fencer and yard builder.

Blue on Nugorra, at Wallah station, near Narrabri, New South Wales, in 1962.

—Photo courtesy Blue Ellis

He next took a trip down into New South Wales and turned his hand to timber felling and oyster farming. Then he went back to station work on Wallah station, near Narrabri, as a stud groom with Angus cattle. From there he moved on to farm management and earth moving plant operator. He later went into road transport, first as a driver and later as an owner-driver. This work took him to Sydney and kept him and his family in that city until he retired in 1995.

Blue bought his Wave Hill spurs from Max Schober's store in Elliott, Northern Territory in early 1953, paying £5 for them had the following comments to say about the use of spurs,

"First off, long necked spurs for a long legged rider - the reason, the spur makes contact with the horse sooner and therefore hasn't got the impact that a short necked spur would have, used by the same rider.

"Next, the rowel should be made with widely spaced points, because they will roll with ease and not clog up with sweaty hair and make the rowel point like a spear point.

"The Wave Hill spur design has both of these features, as well as being tempered so they won't crush down onto your heel in a fall, or bend if they are kicked. I've had my spurs kicked off my boot heels in one kick, both spurs at once.

"Some people will tell you that spurs shouldn't be used.

"I tell those people I have respect for the horses I ride and will always wear spurs on my boots. You never have time to put them on when you do need them.

"A station horse has no reason to get out of the way of a beast when it charges, not until after it has been horned, then it's too late. The spurs get the message through quick and easy. Some people argue that a stick will do the job just as well, but a stick and/or riding crop, whatever you may use, is carried in the hand and can get in the way. Spurs on your boots are right there on the job.

"Fred Gutte's Wave Hill spur has the correct angle, inside the heel band, to fit the heel of the riding boot, and all the spurs he made had that angle. He must have checked the angle of each heel band on the under side of the anvil horn.

"Because of that angle, the Wave Hill spur would, and did, fit well when it was turned over the instep, when working on foot in the yards, you didn't get tripped up, nor did you lose them.

"I've never had to buy or borrow any spurs since I've had my Wave Hill spurs.

"By the way, a horse always knows when you have spurs on your boots without even using them. I've seen riders that use the small rowelled type spur and because they can jam up with loose hair, get very little response from their horse. These riders have their spurs in a vice, trying to sharpen the points, the first chance they get, and that is not the answer, bigger rowels are what is needed, so they will roll.

"Swan necked spurs were without the shape to fit the boot and had to be strapped on tight otherwise they would fall off very easily.

"I've seen spurs as strong as Wave Hill spurs, but they were much heavier and did not fit the boot very well.

"I believe spurs are a must, even on colts after they are going, that is to say, as soon as they know how to go. The spur can keep them going straight, without needing to pull them about by the mouth and making it very sore, because the mouth is so sensitive. It takes time for the mouth to toughen up without losing its sensitivity, otherwise the colt will end up with an iron mouth, which nobody wants to happen."

These photos show how well the spurs fit the boot heel and how they sit securely on the instep while working on foot.

—Photos Don Corcoran

Blue Ellis (front right) and mates after branding on Iffley station. Photo Ian Kelly.

Lloyd L Fogarty

Timber Creek, Northern Territory

THANKS TO A LEAD from Darrell Lewis I was able to locate a pair of Wave Hill trophy spurs, owned by Lloyd Fogarty, of Timber Creek.

Lloyd's trophy spurs.
—Photo Terri Fogarty

In 1953 Lloyd won the Gordon Creek Trophy at the Victoria River Downs races, Northern Territory. The trophy was a gold-plated pair of Wave Hill spurs, engraved on the heel band of each spur, 'Gordon Creek Trophy, V. R. D. 1953.

George Bates, who was a head stockman on V. R. D. at that time, organised the gold plating of the spurs.

Lloyd was ringing at Auvergne and won the race on Curlew, an Auvergne horse. Curlew was a grey gelding by Dalwind, a Durack stallion by Windbag, who had won the Melbourne Cup in 1925.

Lloyd wrote to me of his background,

"I was born in Mitchell Queensland on 5th July, 1928, my mother was Ethel Doris Park and my father was George Nudley Fogarty. My first five years were spent at Murra Downs, west of Bollon and the next seven years at Bellevue near Jericho. My father managed the two small sheep properties for the same owner R. McClymont.

"These were very hard years and I learnt to ride and do all manner of bush work. School was by correspondence in the early years and I finished up at Longreach State School with a high scholarship pass and 96% in maths.

"We moved from there back to Mitchell and I did droving and station work then kangaroo and brumby shooting with horses before acquiring a Ford truck. I then did contract yard building and fencing in Queensland and at Goonoo Goonoo south of Tamworth in New South Wales.

"My father, who was always known as Mick, was then manager of Caldervale station for Australian Agricultural Company. The boss of the company, Dolph Schmidt, asked us to go to the Northern Territory and Western Australia to take

over their newly acquired Durack stations, Auvergne, Newry, Argyle and Ivanhoe which they got in 1950. My parents, two brothers and myself left Caldervale in March 1951 with two trucks and a Willys Jeep and arrived at Auvergne, which was Dad's headquarters, on 7th April, 1951. I did some contract work but was soon talked into the head stockman's job, £10 a week, wild cattle, scrub bulls and rough holey ground!

"I was married in January, 1954 and took over the management of Auvergne in 1955 when Dad moved to Argyle for three years before retiring. I was promoted to Pastoral Inspector and later Regional Superintendent of the four stations. Much improvements were made and the company was doing well till the big beef slump in the mid '70s and then the Ord River Dam put half of Argyle, the best station, under water and Ivanhoe under farming. The A. A. directors decided to sell out and bought Brunette Downs.

"I was sold with the place and Gunn Rural Management, financed with overseas capital, took over. They did no good, other companies got involved and eventually Kerry Packer's company took over and is now doing well.

"I didn't get on well with the new owners and by 1980 started looking for new ground. Luckily the Wayside Inn at Timber Creek was for sale so we didn't have far to go, it was only 50 miles away. I didn't get much thanks for the thirty years I put in but was pleased to be able to visit

Top: Lloyd on Rogilla in 1955.
Right: Lloyd outside his Timber Creek store *(see next page).*

—Photos courtesy Lloyd L. Fogarty

my father's grave at Auvergne where he had passed away peacefully after my mother was killed in a road accident.

"We did very well at Timber Creek and built up a very profitable business which we sold in '92. My wife Camille and I have three sons, two daughters, and fifteen grandchildren. They are all doing well with good jobs and their own homes, two families here and three in Darwin. We have leased land here at Timber Creek and run 900 head of Brahmans and 50 goats."

Lloyd has been actively involved with the Timber Creek Race Club Inc. since the first races were run there in 1968. He has acted as secretary and president and at the final race meeting, held on Saturday 8th September, 2001, Lloyd, finished his 'President's Message' in the front of the race book with,

"I trust you enjoy your weekend at Timber Creek and if you can't back a winner maybe you can catch a barramundi."

This seems to be a good idea as indicated in the photo on the previous page, which shows Lloyd outside his store in the 1980s.

George Foot

From near Woodhouse station, Ayr, Queensland

THE PHOTOGRAPH at left, of George P. Foot of the 5th Light Horse, shows the uniform and one Light Horse spur clearly. George was a friend of Charles Frederick Schultz, the father of Charlie Schultz, and sent two photo/post cards to Charles senior from Persia in 1914.

The notation on the back of one of the post cards reads as follows:

Machine Gun Section
5th Light Horse
Second Expeditionary Force

Dear Charlie
Just a P.C. to show you what I look like with part of our rig out. The gun I am on can fire up to 600 shots a minute, not bad. The barrel is inside another tube which is kept filled with water. A merry Xmas to all at Woodhouse.

It is understood that George Foot came from the Dubbo area in New South Wales and had a station on the eastern side of Woodhouse station, near Ayr, Queensland. He never returned from the war and is believed to have been killed at Gallipoli.

Charles Schultz senior, was the manager of Woodhouse station near Ayr, in Queensland, and his son Charlie, was born in Charters Towers in 1908. When young Charlie was nineteen years old he became the manager of the badly run-down Humbert River station in the Victoria River district of the Northern Territory.

Over the next forty-four years Charlie built this station into one of the showpiece properties of the North and became one of the Territory's best

—*Photo courtesy Darrell Lewis, from the Charlie Schultz Collection with the permission of Charlie's daughter Mrs Betty Atkinson*

known identities. He died in Proserpine, Queensland in 1997, aged 89 years, and a memorial plaque detailing his life and achievements has been set up near the Humbert River homestead. The biography, *Beyond the Big Run*, co-authored by Darrell Lewis, is the story of Charlie's life and a history of Humbert River station.

The origin of the Light Horse spurs shown below is not known, but they have five-pfennig pieces, dated 1913 and 1917, as rollers.

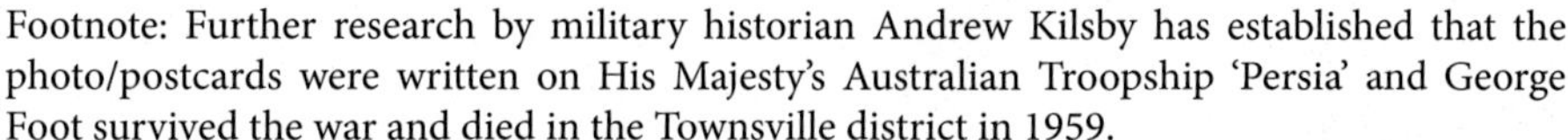

Footnote: Further research by military historian Andrew Kilsby has established that the photo/postcards were written on His Majesty's Australian Troopship 'Persia' and George Foot survived the war and died in the Townsville district in 1959.

Charlie Fuller

Victoria River Downs, Northern Territory

It is unusual to find photographs of ringers where spurs are visible, but this one is certainly worth including.

Taken on Victoria River Downs, it shows, from the left, Frank Spencer, drover Charlie Fuller, with his spurs turned forward, and Ted Martin, son of the manager, Alf Martin, who ran VRD for about 25 years. Next is Doris Roden, the daughter of book keeper Jack Roden, who was on the station from about 1925 to 1953, then Jack Knox and Frank Reynolds, both head stockmen, and an unknown man.

Reynolds was on the station from about 1925 to 1953 and Knox was there between about 1934 and 1938, so this photo would have been taken during that four year period.

Doris was a beautiful and vivacious young woman, and understandably very popular with the men.

—Photographs by Darrell Lewis from the collection of Chris Woodland (top) and, above, from the Roden Collection.

Bill Hamill

Yelarbon, Queensland

Bill Hamill, former ringer, drover and Vestey's station manager, is the author of *From the Top Rail* and *Don't Trot the Bullocks* and lives on his property Curriba at Yelarbon in South Eastern Queensland.

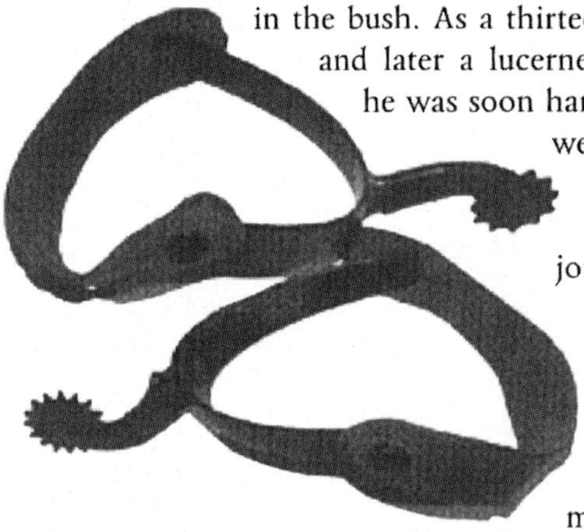

From The Top Rail is an account, mostly humourous, of Bill's life in the bush. As a thirteen year old he worked on a dairy farm, and later a lucerne farm which used draught horses, and he was soon handling four and six in hand. In 1939 he went to Manbulloo, near Katherine in the Northern Territory, as a stockman and in late 1940 went down to Sydney and joined the Army.

In April 1944 after discharge from the Army he went back to Manbulloo and was appointed head stockman. He later worked on Mistake Creek, as manager at Inverway, and in 1955 was manager on Ord River where he remained for five years.

Bill's Wave Hill spurs are on display in The Australian Stockman's Hall of Fame at Longreach in Queensland. He has owned three pairs of Wave Hills while in the Territory, buying a new pair each time he lost one. The surviving pair were purchased in 1952 for £3 when Bill was manager of Inverway, and donated to the Hall of Fame "as my Yamaha does not really require them during a day's muster".

Fred Gutte, the blacksmith at Manbulloo, arrived there in April, 1944, the same month that Bill returned. Bill's recollections of Fred are set out in the section dealing with the blacksmith spurmakers.

Bill told me, "Fred made his spurs from any steel that was available, and forged each spur from one piece, using only hacksaw and hammer."

Bill's Wave Hill spurs.
—Photo Jenny Wilson, Australian Stockman's Hall of Fam

Len Hill

Charters Towers, Queensland

After about three years of corresponding, Len Hill and I finally met at the Drovers' Camp Festival at Camooweal in 2000 and again later in the year, with his wife Robin, over tea and fresh scones at their home in Charters Towers.

While at Camooweal Len was inducted into the Drovers' Camp Association Hall of Fame, being the only man there who had been droving down the Canning Stock Route, which runs for a thousand miles from Wiluna to Halls Creek in Western Australia.

Len, a quietly spoken man with an excellent memory, first worked in the bush at Tootra sheep station in the Moora district of Western Australia in 1944, then as a ringer on Carnegie station near Wiluna, and on Wongawol and Windidda. In 1945 he took a mob of bullocks from No. 9 Well on the Canning Stock Route to Carnegie with Jim Clarke. In 1946 with boss drover Ben Taylor, the last of the Canning drovers, he took a mob of 58 unbroken horses up the Canning with a small plant and two boys, taking 10 weeks. They then returned with a mob of 600 Bililuna bullocks, an 18 week trip. Len recalls that it was necessary to wear a pistol at all times to show that you were armed to deter attacks by blacks, "as they knew what revolvers could do." On one occasion, when threatened by a black, Ben shot the koondie (lethal throwing stick) out of his hand.

Around that time Len, with Jim Clarke, took a mob of bullocks from

Len, in 2000, with his Wave Hill spurs (top) and with Ben Taylor in 1985.

—Photo at top, Don Corcoran and, right, courtesy Len Hill.

Wongawol to Leonara, near Kalgoorlie. He also did three trips from Wongawol to Wiluna with station cattle, one with George Lannigan, one with Ernie Hanlon and one with Henry Ward.

Len kept a day by day diary of those times, the only such record according to the Battye Library of Western Australia.

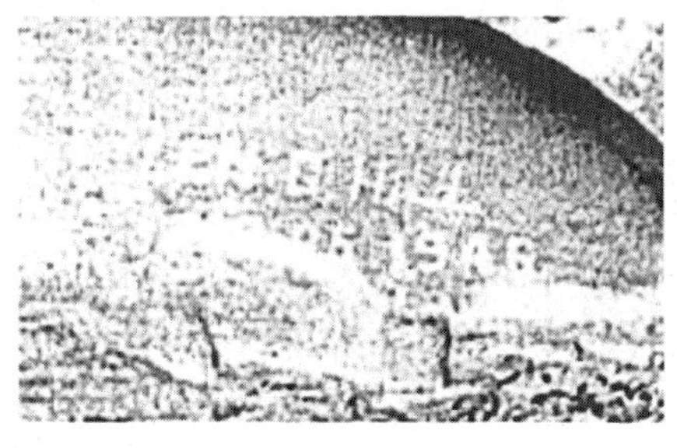

Len was head stockman on Flora Valley for five years, one year at Nicholson and two years with Vestey's droving boss Paddy Conway, checking the mobs on the road from the West to Top Springs and Wave Hill. He spent one season on Coolullah, north of Cloncurry, then back over to the West, marrying Robin in 1958 and managing Nicholson, Ord River, Turner, Mistake Creek and Spring Creek until 1980. After a year in Perth they returned to Christmas Creek on the Fitzroy River for three months, then managed Go Go station for seven years, retiring to Toowoomba and finally settling in Charters Towers.

He first met Fred Gutte while breaking in at Flora Valley in '49. Fred used to do a circuit repairing gear on Ord River, Gordon Downs and Territory stations, spending maybe a couple of months at each station.

"I gave Fred a hand to set up the blacksmith's shop and had collected some charcoal from the open fires at the stockcamp for him, but he only shook his head in disgust when he saw it, saying he would show me what timber he needed and would burn his own. He inspected the station woodheap and pointed out the size and age of timber he wanted, solid Snappy Gum and Bloodwood, semi-green or dead, with hollows free of rubbish, no decaying sections, no bark and no dirt. Dirt eventually produces clinker in the base of the fire which burns and distorts material. For welding in the forge he suggested I keep my eyes out for Supple Jack and Black Heart Coolibah, which he intended to burn separately.

"Arriving at the shop next day with lengths about 3 feet 6 inches, I saw he had 44 gallon drums ready with the tops cut out, and I inch holes spaced around the bottom of the drums, to activate an upward draft once the fire was burning. Fred keenly watched the burning, often stoking and rearranging the fire with a long rod like a professional baker. Before the timber was burnt out

A rock face at Durba Springs, on the Canning Stock Route, where Len chiselled his name in 1946
—Photo courtesy Len Hi

he would close the top with the original lid that had been cut out, using ant bed made into a stiff pug with water. The bottom air holes were sealed with earth shovelled into a pile around the base and the fire allowed to cool.

"Once re-opened the freshly burnt charcoal could be shovelled out in pieces the size of a cake of soap, which produced excellent heat and broke up again during use in the forge. His ultimate aim, he said, was to do away with ash as much as possible. A drum of charcoal would generally last a little over a week. Once it became too fine it was thrown out.

"Fred made his spurs from three quarter inch round mild steel, first splitting the required length by cutting it with a thick hacksaw to within three inches of the end, finishing the cut on an angle. With three or four pieces cut he would shape them hot into a "T" shape then throw them onto the dirt floor to cool.

"Then, using the flat part of the anvil, near the horn, he would heat and draw out the neck, holding the steel with the tongs in his left hand, hitting it with the hammer, and squeezing with the tongs to form the rough shape of the neck. Next, holding the neck with the tongs, he would heat and shape the two sides of the heel band on the top of the anvil horn, the angle of the initial saw cut making it easier to fashion the distinctive shape which allowed the spur to sit low on the heel of a riding boot. The neck was then finished and the slot for the roller cut with the hacksaw. Fred never left hammer marks on the spurs and was very careful to match each pair. I never saw him use a swedge to shape the heel band or shank.

"Fred made the pegs or buttons for the straps in a 'mould', a piece of steel plate about a half-inch thick with a hole drilled and countersunk to the required size of the peg. A short piece of rod was hammered hot into the hole to shape it and then fitted to the heel band. In the case of my spurs, however, he used tank bolts.

"The distinctive slots on each side of the neck at the base were cut with a round file to dress up the spur, as was the slight indentation at the base of the neck. He made the rollers from old heavy duty cattle troughing, cutting out a square, then taking off the corners and filing the teeth with a triangular file.

Len's Wave Hill spurs.
—Photo Don Corcoran

"Fred cleaned up the spurs and took off the rough spots with a coarse file as there was no grinder or electricity in the station blacksmith's shop, and with my pair, painted them with silver paint. He did not use spring steel as has been claimed, it would have been too difficult to cut, but he did temper each spur to spring steel consistency before fitting the pegs and rollers.

"He was a master blacksmith, coachbuilder and wheelwright, no job seemed to be beyond his ability. He made brands, chains and hooks, and refaced and tempered all types of blades, with all welding being done in the forge, which had a winding handle rather than bellows to blow the air.

"The Wave Hill spurs sat low on Cuban heeled boots and were light. I used a strap under the boot to stop them moving up when running. He certainly made spurs with different widths of heel bands to fit small and large boots and made the shanks of different lengths.

"Fred left Wave Hill about the mid 1950s when Peter Morris came (he had taken over as General Pastoral Manager from A.S. Bingle at Vestey's). Maybe Mr. Morris reckoned Fred was using too much company time and material to make spurs. I was on Wave Hill for a time in 1958 and Fred had left by then.

"I think I paid 30 shillings for my spurs, but believe the price varied considerably depending on who you were. The figure of £3 as a general station price seems to ring a bell, but the hawker's price would have been about £7. Maurie Metyard and Ben Humphreys, hawkers around the East Kimberley stations, used to sell Fred's spurs.

"Fred was a great man to improvise and very, very careful with his money. I doubt if he ever bought anything to make his spurs, but scrounged it from the stations and their rubbish tips, which naturally had lots of pieces he could use for any of his repair work for that matter. He was probably in his early sixties when I met him and apparently without ailments common to blacksmithing, such as a bad back.

"He was a solid man with a friendly disposition and quiet ways. He always presented himself neat and clean at the table, heaped his plate to the top and never complained about the food.

"Being bald almost to the ears, he encouraged the hair on both sides to grow sufficiently to enable it to be combed over his head and plastered down. Sometimes it came unstuck while hammering over the forge on a hot day, sticking to his face. Choosing the right time he would stop, comb back the hair and characteristically pat it down firmly before recommencing the job. I guess he felt the little he had was worth looking after."

Peter Hogg

Willeroo, Northern Territory

PETER HOGG was a ringer on Willeroo in the late 1940s and early '50s, and was given his Wave Hill spurs by Harry Huddlestone, who was running the camp there at that time.

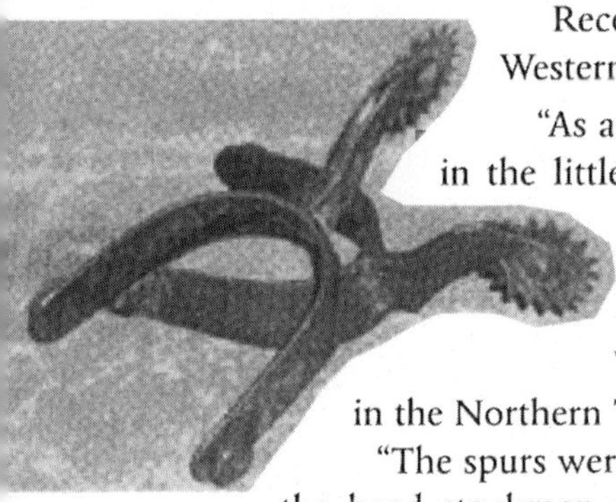

Recently, Peter's son, Neil Hogg, of Kinclaven station, Western Australia, wrote to me:

"As a small child I remember a pair of rusty old spurs in the little shed in the back yard of our home in Victor Harbor, South Australia. My father, Peter Hogg, had owned them since 1949. My parents, Peter and Margaret, were employed and living on Willeroo station, eighty miles west of Katherine in the Northern Territory following the Second World War.

"The spurs were given to Dad by Harry Huddlestone, who was the head stockman at Willeroo. Harry and Dad were good mates, so Harry had the spurs made by Fred Gutte, the blacksmith at Wave Hill station.

"When I was eighteen years old, in the '70s, I was able to fulfil my dreams and go up north to work on cattle stations as my father had done. I worked on Nicholson, Limbunya and Flora Valley stations. When I first went there I often heard people mention the famous Wave Hill spurs and thought back to the shed in the back yard at home and the pair of rusty old spurs, so I had Mum send them to me.

"When they arrived they were without rowels or straps so I fashioned some new rowels from an old fan blade from a motor car and the straps out of good quality Vestey's leather.

"I used the spurs on a daily basis from then on. Once, when we had spent all day drafting cattle on the flat, (I was using my gun cutting horse, Little Bit), I realised one spur was missing. I spent hours after everyone else had knocked off for the day, searching the area until I found the lost spur.

"To this day both spurs have pride of place displayed in the hallway. They

Peter Hogg's Wave Hill spurs.
—Photo Elise Hogg

stand as a legacy to the time this family has spent in the Territory and as an heirloom for future generations."

The adjacent photos were taken on Seemore station, near Kalgoorlie, Western Australia. Seemore Downs is now owned by the Hogg family and has been renamed Kinclaven.

As Neil has pointed out, they are photos of father and son riding father and son.

Top: Peter Hogg on Topaz, in the yard at Seemore Downs, in the 1960s.
Above: Neil Hogg on Shamrock, son of Topaz, Seemore Downs, mid 1970s.
—Photos courtesy Barbara Hogg

Roy Hulbert

The following is an extract from a letter received from Roy Hulbert of Bangalow, N. S. W. in 2004:

Dear Don,

A friend of mine gave me some old copies of the Hall of Fame newspapers and in a 2002 issue I saw your letter telling us you were writing a book on spurs and spurmakers of Australia.....

I am an old Territory drover going back to the fifties. My brother Bob and I lived in Camooweal and worked for boss drover Stan Fowler. We took 200 head of unbroken horses from Avon Downs near Camooweal out to the Kimberley and dropped them on three different stations viz Newry, Auvergne and Ivanhoe which was just across the border in W. A. We then picked up 1250 head of stores from those places and brought them back to Queensland.

We took the plant back to Victoria River Downs the following year and picked up 1000 head of fats from there and took them down to Wyndham Meatworks. I've been through the Murranji a few times so I reckon we earnt our money.

However, to get back to the spurs which I bought off an old drover in Camooweal in 1953. I used these old spurs the whole time I was droving in the Territory, I was only 18 years old at the time. They are not Wave Hill spurs but are very similar. They were a pretty flash pair because as you can see they were once chromed. I don't know if they had a particular name.

I am retired now of course and just have a property here at St. Helena running a few head of cows & calves etc. Don't use the old spurs much but have kept them all these years along with my old quart pot & a few other pieces of memorabilia from my droving days. Hope you appreciate the pictures and it would be nice to hear from you, (I saw Tom Willoughby win the open bronc ride at Rockhampton in 1951),

Regards,
Roy Hulbert.

I telephoned Roy soon after and had a number of conversations in the following months but was saddened to hear recently that he passed away in 2008. Almost 600 people attended his funeral service at the All Souls Anglican Church at Bangalow, where he and his childhood sweetheart, Jan Jarrett, were married in 1957.

Roy, well known in the bowling fraternity, was one of the district's leading greenkeepers for over thirty years, working at both Byron Bay and Bangalow Clubs. He was the secretary of the Northern Rivers Greenkeepers Association for twenty five years as well as being made a Life Member. After retiring, he worked voluntarily on the Bangalow greens he so loved.

He will also be remembered for his singing and guitar playing at every chance – the guitar always went into the car before anything or anybody else. He actually bought his first guitar in Camooweal when he was about eighteen years old and along with his camera, took it everywhere he went.

Roy and Jan had four children, Alan, Wendy, Noel and Owen, between 1957 and 1972 and at the time of Roy's death had ten grandchildren.

Roy Hulbert's boot, spurs and quart pot'

Roy left his name on an Auvergne boab tree.

Roy Hulbert in the 1950s.

Ian Kelly

IAN KELLY was born in Winton, western Queensland in 1937. He grew up on a sheep and cattle station, Happy Valley, a property of 150,000 acres about 100 kilometres southwest of Winton, where his father was manager.

After attending boarding school at Charters Towers and then the Abergowrie Agricultural College near Ingham, Ian worked for his father for about a year. Then he got a job as a stockman, or ringer, on Lorraine station, on the Leichhardt River between Cloncurry and Burketown. This was a property of 1,800 square miles, running about 60,000 head of cattle, with two stock camps.

Ian worked in Don Schultz's camp and looking back at those days, when everyone slept on the ground in their swags, worked unlimited hours six days a week and rarely saw the homestead, as a nineteen year old he was very happy. Like most young blokes of the day he was proud to put in a good day's work for his pay and keep.

Later he got a job as a ringer on Helen Springs, a Vestey's station just north of Tennant Creek in the Territory, at that time managed by Andrew Geddes, with Peter Appleton as head stockman. It was here that Ian noticed that some of the ringers were wearing a style of spur that he had not seen before. He found that they were the Wave Hill spurs, made by blacksmith Fred Gutte on Wave Hill station, another Vestey's property. Ian arranged through a visiting stock inspector to get a pair from the Elliot store and used those spurs until he retired from stock work.

Ian met Blue Ellis on Helen Springs and later they both headed into Queensland, working for a time on Iffley station, between Julia Creek and Normanton.

Over the next few years he moved around Queensland, amongst other jobs working as a wool presser in the shearing season, sleeper cutting, contract ringbarking and cane cutting.

Next Ian bought a carrying business at Marmor, south of Rockhampton and eventually moved to Rockhampton, working for the local gas company driving LP gas tankers all over central Queensland.

Now retired, with three adult children and five grandchildren all living in Brisbane, Ian and his wife Margaret have settled at Sandstone Point, near Bribie Island.

Ian Kelly on colt, Lorraine station.
Photo Ian Kelly.

Ian Kelly's Wave Hill spurs.
Photo Fred Bienvenu.

Kerry Kendall

Middlemount, Queensland

KERRY KENDALL was born in 1948 in Townsville, Queensland and grew up in the suburbs. At the weekends he often went to a dairy farm at Upper Ross, owned then by Huey and Ma Collins and their daughter Gloria Gollogly. It was there he learnt to ride and met a lot of drovers bringing mobs from the Gulf and the Charters Towers area to the meatworks at Townsville.

Kerry wrote to me about his ringing days.

"My first job, at the age of sixteen, was on Dotswood station, Charters Towers when Bob Morrison was the manager. Dotswood was a bullock depot for the store cattle that walked down from Strathmore and Van Rook stations in the Gulf. They also had a large breeder herd and a lot of good men worked there at the time.

"I have always regarded Ray Davidson as one of the best and the Mossman brothers, Jim, Tony and Bernie were also very handy in

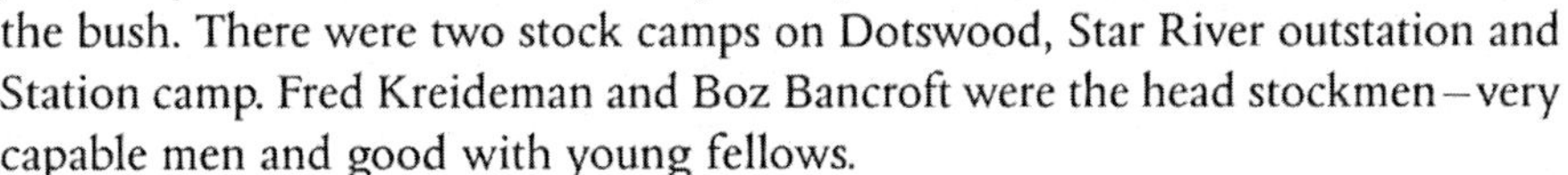

the bush. There were two stock camps on Dotswood, Star River outstation and Station camp. Fred Kreideman and Boz Bancroft were the head stockmen – very capable men and good with young fellows.

"At the end of '68 I left Dotswood and started work on Rutland Plains, north of Normanton in '69. After a couple of years there I went to Moray Downs near Clermont in the brigalow country for some time.

"Next I went across to the Territory, ringing on Cresswell Downs, buffalo catching with Norm Bright around the Adelaide and Finnis Rivers and fencing with Dave Keir on Delamere. Later I came back into Queensland, working around Julia Creek on Caiwarra and Canobie stations.

Kerry on Dotswood station, giving Snowman his second ride after handover from horsebreaker Tony Mossman.

—Photos courtesy Kerry Kendall

"When the beef slump came in the seventies I worked around Mackay for the cane growers who had horses and cattle, breaking in and also fencing and yardbuilding. I gave the ringing away in the eighties owing to back problems.

"I've kept in touch with the game and still visit mates on properties in Central Queensland and the Gulf. I've always been interested in collecting bush memorabilia from the stations and mustering camps. I also collect Australian art, by such artists as Hugh Sawrey, Eddie Hackman, Sir Daryl Lindsay, Albert Namatjira and Cliffy Robinson. Books on Australiana are another field of interest.

"As far as Australian poetry goes, apart from the old favourites I rate Bruce Simpson, Lex McLennan, Kelly Dixon and Geoff Allen up there with the best. I am a Life Member of the Australian Stockman's Hall of Fame and am proud to have contributed to the restoration of the grave of Nat Buchanan at Walcha in New South Wales, one of our greatest explorers and overlanders.

"In June and July, 1998 I was a member of Bruce Simpson's second expedition around Glenormiston, Herbert Downs and Marion Downs in Western Queensland searching for traces of the 1848 Ludwig Leichhardt expedition."

Here are some spurs from Kerry's collection.

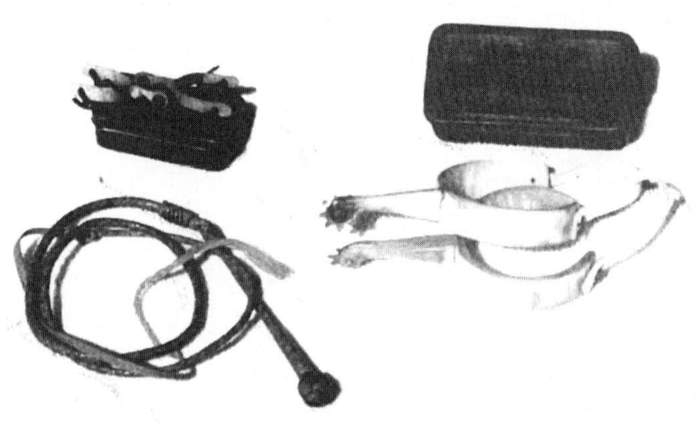

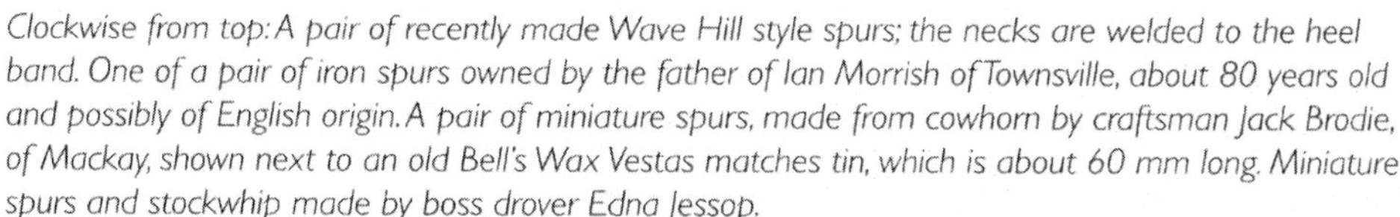

Clockwise from top: A pair of recently made Wave Hill style spurs; the necks are welded to the heel band. One of a pair of iron spurs owned by the father of Ian Morrish of Townsville, about 80 years old and possibly of English origin. A pair of miniature spurs, made from cowhorn by craftsman Jack Brodie, of Mackay, shown next to an old Bell's Wax Vestas matches tin, which is about 60 mm long. Miniature spurs and stockwhip made by boss drover Edna Jessop.

Eugene Kostin

Brunette Downs, Northern Territory

EUGENE KOSTIN, former ringer and drover and currently working at Brunette Downs in the Northern Territory, brought some old spurs with him to the Camooweal Drovers' Camp Festival.

Eugene found the spurs shown here when he cleaned out the back room of J. J. Cronin's old store at Camooweal in 1951 or 1952. They were in an old suitcase with letterheads dated 1929, otherwise nothing is known of their previous history. Each pair have necks about 44 millimetres long, brazed onto the heel band.

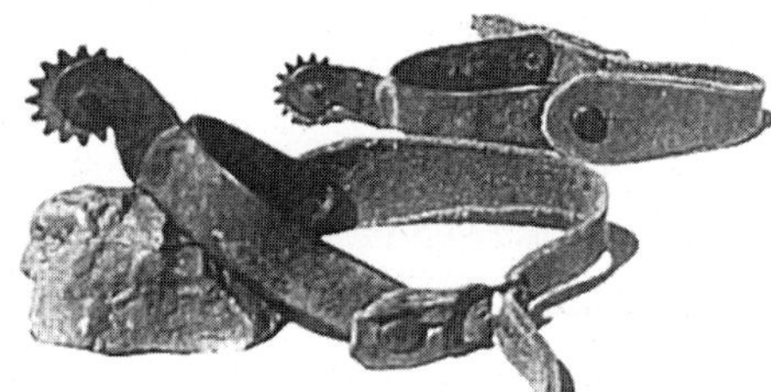

Top: Eugene Kostin, (left), and Keith Luscombe, Camooweal, 2000.
—Photos Don Corcoran

Peter LeDuff

Adelaide, South Australia

When I contacted Peter LeDuff about his spurs which had been pictured in the Australian Stockman's Hall of Fame newspaper, he wrote back with the following background:

"The Fred Gutte spurs that I have are two and a half inch goosenecks. Fred made each from one piece of steel, using only the forge and a file. The rowels and pins were hardened also by tempering in the forge. He filed grooves at the base of the neck, one on each side. Even after four or five trips on the road there was little sign of wear.

"They were made to fit R. M. Williams riding boots. From memory I think they cost about two pounds, this was in '46 or '47 at Wave Hill. Wages then were one pound a day droving, and three pounds ten shillings a week station wages. Fred was a nuggety man about fifty years old.

"I went to work for Noel and Ma Healy at Dunmarra when I was sixteen and finished up in the stock camp. Later on I worked there for Jack Williams contract mustering and branding.

"My road trips were with Keith Henderson, Jeff Nixon and Clarrie Pankhurst and on one trip with Clarrie we had Edna Zigenbine as a ringer, I knew her father fairly well.

"After managing Arkaringa Station out from Oodnadatta I wrote to Max Schober at Elliott to find the whereabouts of Clarrie, I wanted another job. Max asked me to come up to Elliott to run a plant for him of which he was the executor, after Norm Stacey died at Newcastle Waters. I took the plant to Wave Hill and shifted 1250 head to Morstone. That was the last trip that I did in the Territory."

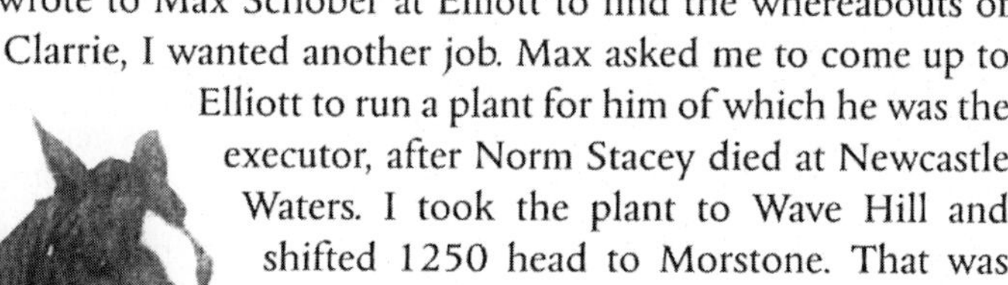

Top: Peter's Wave Hill spurs. Centre: Emily and Clarrie Pankhurst with Peter, right, Lucinda Queensland, 1995. Left: Peter at Burta station, near Broken Hill, New South Wales, about 1945, on a thoroughbred called Sack of Gold, from a neighbouring station.

—Photos courtesy Peter LeDuff

Keith Luscombe

Pittsworth, Queensland

WHEN I MET Keith at Camooweal in 2000 he showed me a pair of spurs made in the early 1960s by Barry Blain, who used to run the Caltex Garage there. Keith had them made in the style of the Wave Hill spur, angled to fit the boot heel, and Barry forged them from car springs.

Keith, a former ringer and drover, with his wife Roberta, set up a transport company at Pittsworth in 1979, running local and interstate bulk carriers and road trains.

Later on Keith told me about his ringing days in Queensland and the Territory,

"I left Pittsworth when I was 15 years old to work on Eastern Creek station at Mitchell. I broke my arm riding a calf so I came home after 9 months. My father, Jim, had his mate Stan Fowler visiting from Camooweal. Dad and Stan had both left Pittsworth in about 1918 and were droving and ringing together in the Territory and Western Queensland for 18 years. Dad met Mum at Windorah and they got married and settled back in Pittsworth.

"I had always wanted to go droving like my father so when Stan went back to Camooweal, I went with him. That was in 1955 when I was 16 years old. I did four trips with store cattle from Auvergne station to either Brighton Downs or South Galway. Drove fats from either Brighton Downs or Cluny station into Winton and fats from South Galway to Quilpie. Then with Stan Fowler drove a mob of cows and calves from Headingly station to Alroy Downs.

"With Dave Allworth as boss drover, I went with another mob of cows and calves from Headingly to Rockhampton Downs, and then was contract mustering with Ian McBean on Dalmore station when it was sold to Alroy Downs. I went with Ian to Coolibah station and mustered horses, then went to Auvergne station. Took delivery of a mob of store cattle that we delivered to either Avon Downs or Headingly. A few years later Ian McBean drew Innesvale station and I went to work for him there for ten months.

Keith, 17 years old, on the road between Cluny station and Winton.
—Photos courtesy Keith Luscombe

"In between droving cattle I worked on Austral Downs and on separate occasions attended musters on Lake Nash, Barkly Downs, Woorona, Avon Downs and Rocklands. I later did a part trip from Victoria River Downs to Walgra with Bill Walters who had Cammy Cleary's plant. A couple of his men left and he was short handed. Drove a mob of cows and calves from Austral to Norfolk on agistment then a few months later went back and mustered them and took them to Mount Isa and trucked them. Took another mob of cattle from Austral Downs to Dajarra and trucked them.

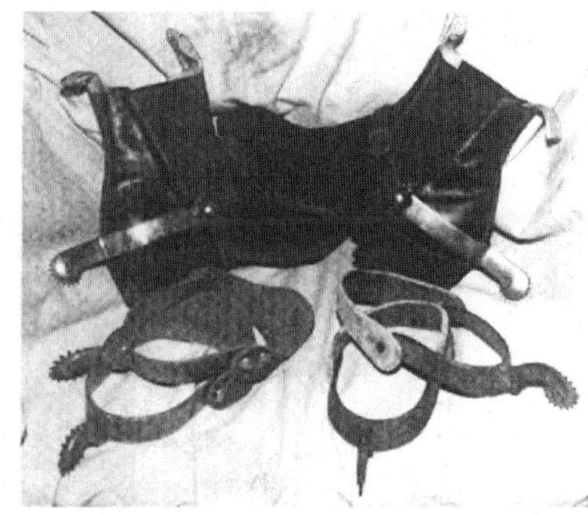

"In 1968 I got word my Dad was ill so I came home to be with him. I didn't return to Camooweal until I heard about the Drovers' Reunion and now go back each year."

"When I was on the road droving I generally didn't wear spurs, but certainly would use them whenever we were campdrafting, and a bit of pace was needed."

The photo above shows Keith's spurs, the pair on the boots belonged to the late Bernie Belford, who was droving out of Goondiwindi with Tom Fry and Keith Strohfield when he was 14 years old. Keith met Bernie through the transport industry and they became firm friends. The spurs in the foreground are R. M. Williams' Swan Necks and the Barry Blain spurs.

Ray Macnamara

Born in Quilpie, south west Queensland, in 1929, Ray Macnamara grew up during and after the depression on his father's property, Prairie station, on the eastern side of the Bulloo River. It was there he was given a good grounding in horses, cattle and sheep.

He was educated by correspondence schooling, then boarded at Downlands College in Toowoomba, and later at Marist Brothers College in Ashgrove, passing his Scholarship examination before leaving. However, he returned home to help his father on the property and took other work in the area as well, as his father sometimes could not pay him a wage.

At seventeen years of age Ray was offered a job on Lissadell station in the Kimberley, which was being managed by his uncle, 'Galloping Paddy' Macnamara. He had only been six weeks in the camp for the bullock muster when the head stockman was sacked and Ray was given the job of running the camp. This entailed being in charge of about twelve aboriginal stockmen and 25,000 head of cattle on a million acres of country which he didn't know. For the first eight months on Lissadell Ray never slept in a bed.

When the mustering camp was shut down for the wet season, Ray broke in horses. For each horse he broke in there was a bonus of £2 a head on top of wages. After about eighteen months on Lissadell, Eric Durack, manager of Argyle Downs, offered Ray the job of droving Argyle Downs, Auvergne and Newry cattle to the meatworks at Wyndham. Ray gladly accepted, and in the one season delivered seven mobs, totalling 6000 head, to the meatworks.

This part of Ray's life is well documented in his book *The Way it Was* published in 2002.

In 1950 he returned to Queensland as his parents had sold Prairie and he wanted to visit them before they moved from Quilpie. While there he was offered a job by Colin Watts on Giberoo. He had also been corresponding with Betty Hearle of Caboolture for some years, so he took the job at Giberoo and married Betty that same year.

Speaking of his days as a young man, Ray said, 'I loved the land and stock and it was my life's ambition to get a bit of dirt of my own at some stage in the future. While they were working for the Watts family, over a period of five years, Ray and Betty applied for no less than 176 ballot blocks, before winning the ballot for the subdivision of Wyaga, northwest of Goondiwindi, in 1956. This block of 3,400 acres, in belah and brigalow country, was literally a wall of scrub.

Ray said of this property, which they named Alice Dale, 'If I'd had two goannas, I would have had to put one of them on agistment, that's how thick the scrub was when we got there!' Ray and Betty had six girls and two boys who grew up on Alice Dale, and the scrub block, which couldn't sustain a goanna in 1956, won the Queensland Trade Cattle Championship in 1983 for a pen of three Simmental-cross steers.

Over the years Ray was very much involved in producer politics. He was elected secretary of the Yelarbon branch of the Queensland Grain Growers' Association and in 1975 was the foundation chairman of the Goondiwindi branch of the Cattlemen's Union.

He continued to serve in many positions in the Cattlemen's Union, including Regional Chairman and Councillor, for two three-year terms, Queensland Chairman and National Vice President in 1984-5. He was voted onto the Cattle Council of Australia for the years 1988, 1989 and 1990 and has also served on the local Fire Brigade Board and as a member of the Waggamba Shire Council for twelve years.

After breaking in hundreds of horses in the Kimberley, then at Giberoo and Tobermorey, working for the Watts family, and later on his own property, Alice Dale, Ray estimates the tally would exceed 500 head. But today, finally retired and living a quieter life in south east Queensland, he has even stopped breaking in horses.

Ray Macnamara, Argyle Downs.

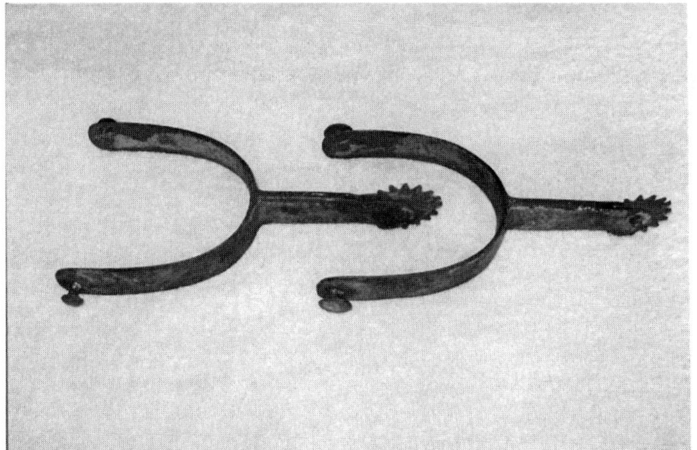

'Galloping Paddy' Macnamara's spurs,
made on Wave Hill in the late 1930s.
Photos Ray Macnamara.

Thorpe McConville and 'Wild Australia'

When I started working in the bush during the early 1950s, firstly in north west N. S. W., then western Queensland and the Territory, I heard many stories about Thorpe McConville and his 'Wild Australia' show. There were songs and poems about the star buckjumper Rocky Ned, and although 'Wild Australia' closed down about 1951 there were still ringers and station hands around who had been employed as roughriders, or had competed in the show when it passed through their town for cash prizes to stay the distance on one of the buckjumpers.

Eventually when I settled near Myrtleford in north east Victoria in 2003, I met Thorpe's son, Ray, who has a nearby property, named 'Thorpeville', in memory of his father. Ray has compiled an excellent work titled *Thorpe McConville's WILD AUSTRALIA – History of a Famous Showman and the Riders Who Rode with Him.*

From Ray's book I have written a brief account of this legendary horseman whose name is so familiar to many of the older riders in the outback.

Thorpe McConville was born at Tarago N. S. W. in 1890, and as a young man became a breaker and dealer of horses in the Yass district. There he soon made a name for himself as a horseman and roughrider of note.

In 1910 arrangements were being made in Australia to take a team of roughriders and buckjumpers to England for the ceremonies at the coronation of King George V and Thorpe was included in the Australian team. The name 'Wild Australia' was adopted and the show, described as 'An exposition of genuine bushmanship,' was first staged at the Crystal Palace, London during the Pageant of the Empire celebrations.

After many performances were given in England Thorpe left the 'Wild Australia Show' in 1911 and sailed to America, joining up with the '101 Ranch Wild West Show' in Oklahoma.

Thorpe caused much astonishment when he first appeared in the show in his Australian riding outfit - a slim youth of twenty years, fresh complexioned and wearing skin-tight white riding breeches, white shirt and concertina leggings. It was no wonder he earned the name 'Tenderfoot'. He led out his first horse, with a flat saddle and no stirrups, and refused to mount while it was being held. Thorpe then vaulted lightly into the saddle and showed the crowd how to ride!

The fun loving cowboys in the show took great delight telling the hard bitten westerners that their wild horses could be ridden by a tenderfoot on a flat saddle who rode in his long white underwear! Their delight knew no bounds when the 'tenderfoot' did all that was asked of him, and more – Thorpe was the draw card of the show.

Thorpe achieved the honour of being the first Australian roughrider to appear in England and America.

After returning to Australia after a year in America, Thorpe ran the Gillenbah Hotel in Narrandera, N.S.W. during the First World War. He had been ruled as unfit for military service because of blindness in one eye.

In 1920 Thorpe assembled a team of young roughriders and horses and held his first 'Wild Australia' show in Hyde Park, Sydney, where it ran for eight weeks. The well cared for animals, riders dressed in spotless whites, absence of crude jokes and with Thorpe himself as ringmaster, was a combination that gripped the imagination of the public and enhanced his reputation as a professional showman.

Over the next three decades the show developed into Thorpe McConville's 'Wild Australia Rodeo and Circus', performing in hundreds of venues in Victoria, South Australia, New South Wales and Queensland, their last season being 1949-1950. Thorpe McConville died in Narrandera in 1953.

In compiling and publishing his father's story, from scrap books, press cuttings and by talking with people who still had memories of the shows, Ray McConville has ensured that the history of this great Australian show, and the people who made it all possible, will not be lost.

Thorpe McConville aged 21 years.

Billy Jonas, Jack Morrissey, Thorpe McConville and Ned Lloyd, part of the roughriding team which went to England, 1911. Photos Ray McConville.

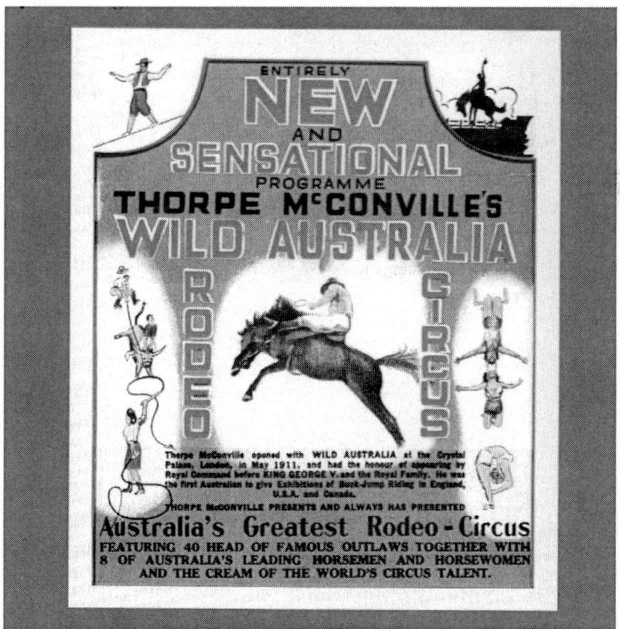

'Wild Australia' poster, 1920s.

Photographs Ray McConville.

Jim Marshall

Burrumbuttock, New South Wales

Jim Marshall has written regarding the spurs, shown at right, which were used by his mother-in-law, Geraldine Pennefather, in the 1930s during Ladies' Polo and Point to Point events.

One pair of these spurs was used in the Peninsula Polo Club Interstate Ladies' Challenge Match, South Australia versus Victoria, won by Victoria in November, 1934. Point to Point racing was a type of steeple chasing, very common in Victoria at that time. The R. M. Williams Willoughby spurs are my own, I bought them in 1965 for £3.

The Willoughby spurs, at left, clearly show the angling of the necks and the removable screw for easy changing of the rowels.

At right is a pair of spurs made by Jim's son, Sam Marshall, in 2001 at the Longreach Pastoral College, Queensland, when Sam was a first year student there.

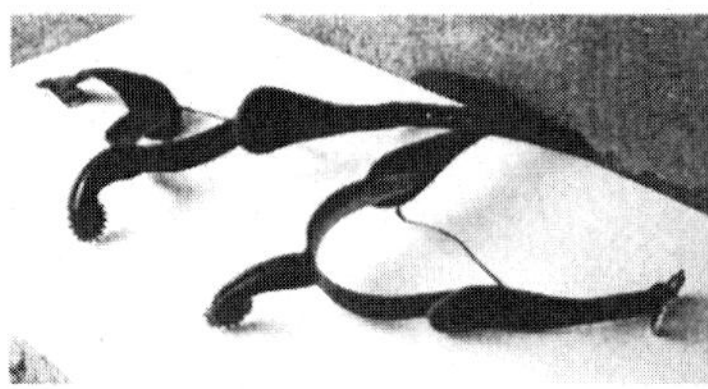

—Photos courtesy Jim Marshall

Gerry Mullins

Mingela, Queensland

THE SPURS at right were donated to the Australian Stockman's Hall of Fame by Gerry Mullins in the 1990s. Apparently he had made them from an old shovel when he was a young ringer.

When I tried to locate Gerry, I found that he had died in 2002 in his early nineties. He had worked as a ringer in his younger days and served in the Army, seeing service in New Guinea, during World War II.

After the war he worked for the Queensland Railways as a ganger in the fettling gang based at Mingela, until retirement.

Gerry was interested in photography from his youth and I understand the University of Townsville has a collection of his outback photographs.

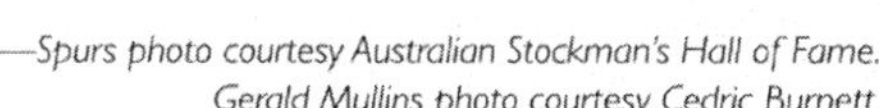

—Spurs photo courtesy Australian Stockman's Hall of Fame.
Gerald Mullins photo courtesy Cedric Burnett.

John Nicolson

Halls Creek, Western Australia

THIS PHOTOGRAPH of John Nicolson was taken on Buffalo Springs, Northern Territory, in 1962, and shows his Wave Hill spurs hanging on the saddle. John bought two pairs of Wave Hill spurs from Syd Hawks' store at Top Springs for "about £2 a pair, in 1954 while I was working on Victoria River Downs".

John was born in Victoria, attending school at Wangaratta, and in 1950 went to Brunette Downs in the Northern Territory, and then to Victoria River Downs for two years. He worked there for Buck Buchester who was running the Moolooloo stock camp.

In the 1950s he worked in the Clermont district of Queensland and later went across to manage Fitzroy Station back in the Victoria River district. In 1959 he worked for Peter Murray on Coolibah, who then acquired Buffalo Springs.

In 1963 he went to Bullo River, working for Charlie and Sara Henderson, and became a partner there in 1966. He was bought out in 1974 and was then contract mustering in North Queensland for about ten years, later becoming involved in gold prospecting in Hall's Creek, Western Australia, where he still lives.

—Photo from Nicolson Collection courtesy Darrell Lewis

Clarrie Pankhurst

Lucinda, Queensland

In July, 1993, Clarrie Pankhurst was celebrating his 72nd birthday with his wife and droving partner, Emily, and many friends, in the local pub at Lucinda, in North Queensland. Clarrie commented during the night, "There's not too many of us left, love, we're a dying breed."

Author and friend Anne Marie Ingham was present and the idea of a book recording the Pankhurst legend was born, resulting three years later in the publication of *The Boss Drover and his Mates.*

This book tells the story of Clarrie, born in Renmark, South Australia in 1921, and his childhood on the Murray River. Clarrie's mother had been widowed with four children and subsequently married a widower, Jack Carpenter, who also had four children. Another four children were born in the years following and by then Australia was in the grip of the Depression.

Life wasn't easy but it was a happy family, with nothing wasted and everyone pulling their weight to keep fourteen mouths fed. At the age of twelve years Clarrie left home with his older brother Frank, working their way north to Queensland. The pair split up in Queensland, with Clarrie, a boy, working at many jobs and experiencing the worst side of adult human nature.

Clarrie became a highly respected ringer in the Northern Territory and by 1943 had put his own droving plant together, accepted by the Vestey company as competent to be included amongst the drovers who lifted mobs from their Kimberley and Territory stations each year.

There were many heartbreaks, but Clarrie always seemed to come out on top, building on his experiences and being prepared to work at anything. He was a highly successful drover, eventually being joined on the road by Emily as cook, with many of these trips detailed in the book.

It was on the Murranji that Emily had a frightening experience, which in hindsight is amusing but could have been tragic. A gigantic bull buffalo had joined the mob of cattle and was not intending to leave. The ringers tried unsuccessfully to drive him off so Clarrie had no option but to shoot him. He dropped the beast in its tracks and suggested that Emily sit on the huge bull's back so he could take a photograph.

Emily climbed onto the buffalo's neck and spread her arms along the horns. Clarrie, who was peering through the viewfinder of the little camera, suddenly became aware that there were two baleful black eyes staring back at him. In an instant the beast was on its feet and Clarrie was running for the truck with the charging animal snorting down his neck, and Emily still on board. At that

moment Emily's cattle dog jumped at the beast's lowered head, causing it to wheel and gallop into the scrub. Fortunately, with a deft movement or two, the buffalo offloaded his unwanted rider very quickly, and crashed off through the tangled scrub.

This story was told many times around the campfires of the stock routes and later, stockman, drover and bush poet George Crowley wrote a poem, 'Emily's Ride to Fame', which is featured in the book, along with many other great stories.

Clarrie owned a pair of Wave Hill spurs and about 1988 donated them, along with his Levinson's drover's watch, to the Newcastle Waters Drovers' Museum which was set up in the old store there.

He died in March, 2000 and I met his wife, Emily, later that year at the Drovers' Festival at Camooweal.

Emily later gave me the photo of her and Clarrie, taken at Townsville in February, 2000 and the following tribute to Clarrie, written by Kelly Dixon of Camooweal.

His Last Nightcamp

He has guided the leads of a hundred mobs, from the runs of the Great Outback–
He shouldered the spirit of true mateship, 'midst the trials of the Murranji track–
He has laughed by the fires the drovers lit and wept for a good horse lost–
His handshake carried the seal of trust and his friendship came without cost.

Born of a breed which our land once knew, out where the scrubs were dense–
Where freedom for all was undeterred, by the sight of a boundary fence!
We say farewell to a bushman proud, who has hung up his bridle today;
And we beg you to somehow soften the fall of the clods of the red, red clay.

When you shovel the soil of this land he loved, to shelter his camping place,
We know that his judge upstairs will approve, of how Pankie ran his Life's race.
He sometimes faltered, like most of us do, but he always regained his stride,
Then raced again for the winning post and he suffered his losses with pride.

We hope there's room in the big stockcamp, where the grasses will always be sweet,
For a drover to ride with his mates again and we hope once again we will meet
With Pankie, a mate from yesteryear, where the nighthorses restlessly stamp
'Neath a supplejack tree, near a camping mob, when we go to *our* last nightcamp

Ralph G. Proctor

Lilydale, Victoria

RALPH PROCTOR, born in 1915 in Hay, New South Wales, left school at the age of 15 years and spent the next nine years in Queensland, working on the following stations,-- Ambo, Ingela near Windorah, Weewondilla, Russleigh, Ardglen near Cunnamulla, and was 4½ years on Isis Downs, near Isisford.

Isis Downs was a stud sheep property of 420,000 acres in those days, breeding horses and running Shorthorn cattle. The manager at the time was Bruce Johnson and the overseer was Doug Harris of Hay, New South Wales.

While on Isis Downs Ralph had a pair of spurs made by the station blacksmith, whose name he cannot recall, each spur being forged from one piece of steel. In 1988 Ralph presented these spurs, along with a quart pot and pouch purchased in Longreach in 1930, and a photo of a white Brahman bull, (one of the first to be imported to Wealwondangie, Springsure, in 1934), to the Australian Stockman's Hall of Fame in Longreach, Queensland.

In 1939 he left Isis Downs and drove down to Melbourne where he joined the Royal Australian Air Force for the duration of World War II, spending 2½ years in England.

The photo at top left on the following page shows Ralph at Hay, New South Wales, with his 1932 Austin Heavy 12 utility, on his way to Melbourne, Victoria, to enlist in the Royal Australian Air Force.

In the photo at top right, Ralph, centre, in battle dress, poses with his English crew at Harwell, near Oxford, England, in 1944. Ralph was one of seven Australians in 295 Squadron, Royal Air Force. The aircraft is a Stirling, later to be withdrawn by Bomber Command in favour of the Halifax and Lancaster.

Also on the following page is a portrait of Ralph, photographed at Lilydale, Victoria, on Anzac Day, 2001. The medals on his left breast are: 1939–1945 Star; Air Crew, Europe, France and Germany; Australian War Medal; Australian

One of Ralph's spurs.
—Photo Jenny Wilson, Australian Stockman's Hall of Fame

Defence Medal; Australian Service Medal with Oak Leaf, denoting 'Mentioned in Despatches for Distinguished Service'.

The badge below the medals is the Glider Pilot Regiment, 38 Group, of the Royal Air Force, responsible for the airborne movement of troops.

On his right breast are Commemorative Medals for Arnhem, Holland and Caen, Normandy, France.

Ralph was recently awarded a Diploma of Honour from the French Government in recognition of his involvement in the D-Day Landing in Normandy, on June 6th, 1944.

Ralph's collection of war memorabilia is now on display at historic Mont de Lancey, Wandin, Victoria.

Above right: Ralph on stock horse Robroy on Penjobe station, part of the original Wealwondangie station, near Springsure, Queensland, about 1980.

—Photos courtesy Ralph G. Proctor

In December 2005, Ralph G. Proctor's autobiography, *Aim High – Proc's Journey*, was launched at the Mont De Lancey Historical Museum at Wandin in Victoria, two months before his 91st birthday. As Ralph states in his book – 'I very much want to share some of my experiences of the 1900s and the war years – especially with the younger generation. This is my story of living in a time that changed the world'.

During the previous ten years, around Anzac Day, Ralph had been invited to address local primary and secondary schoolchildren. Ralph found that the students were very interested to hear about events and activities during the war years. They asked many questions and were eager to know more. With this in mind Ralph decided to part with his personal collection of wartime memorabilia and share it with the community. It is now on display at the Mont De Lancey Historical Museum.

In September, 2004, Ralph and other veterans were honoured guests of the British and Netherlands Governments in Holland, commemorating the 61st Remembrance Day of World War 2.

Ralph G. Proctor (left), and John Yull, R.A. F. 295 Squadron, outside Eusebius Church, Arnhem, Holland, 2004. Photo, Ralph G. Proctor.

Ernie Rayner

Darwin, Northern Territory

ERNIE RAYNER was born in Cairns, Queensland, in 1941 and soon after his family moved to Maryborough. He attended school at the Convent and Christian Brothers in Maryborough, and then Caloundra State School.

Ernie recently told me about his younger days:

"After a couple of years at Caloundra I was sent to the Christian Brothers in Gympie, but after a punch up with one of the Brothers I was duly expelled and so ended my formal schooling years. I was just thirteen years old, had not even finished Year 7, nor sat for the Scholarship Exam.

"My first job was working in a furniture factory in Maryborough for about eight months. In 1955 my mother was offered a job cooking on Maylands station near Muttaburra and I was also given a job as a jackeroo, and spent three years there. After that I did some droving, fencing, cordwood cutting and odd jobs for eighteen months.

"In late 1958 I rode a buckjumper in Sam Fuller's Buckjump Show at Muttaburra which resulted in a job offer in the Northern Territory by Peter Murray, a man who was to be my future father-in-law.

"In 1959, with Neville (Sandy) Little, I drove my 1935 Chevrolet utility to Coolibah station in the Victoria River District of the Territory, arriving there in June. The idea was that if I didn't like working with wild cattle I would go back to the sheep country. Forty four years later I am still in the Territory!

"When I arrived at Coolibah I met Pauline, Peter Murray's eldest daughter, and when our eyes met, that was it for both of us! We were married four years later in 1963, with two additions to the family, a daughter Pamela in 1964, and a son, Dan, born in 1971.

"I worked at Coolibah under head stockman Les Little, a good horseman and cattleman. I finished up at the end of 1960, then put in the next season at Victoria River Downs, (VRD), working in the Gordon Creek camp under Gerry Woods, and then went to Willeroo as head stockman, with Jack Pender as manager. I pulled out after six months as he reckoned I was too hard on the blacks.

"I then went back to Coolibah and ended up going to Bullo River with a contract mustering team from Coolibah, led by Les Little, with John Nicolson, Oliver Roberts and eight or ten blacks. Ray Locke from Aramac in Queensland had drawn Bullo River in a ballot. I put in the rest of the year between the two stations.

"All Land Ballots held in those days were open to the public. To be eligible, applicants had to show they had plant, equipment and experience, plus financial backing or money in the bank. The Land Board would weed out the unsuitable ones – those who showed promise were drawn from names put in a hat, so to speak.

"In 1963 I joined up as a Stock Inspector with the Animal Industry Branch (AIB), spending a year in the Darwin and Katherine districts. During the next four years we lived at Top Springs where I was responsible for that district for two years, and then spent two years in the Wave Hill region.

"The duties of a Stock Inspector included supervision, inoculation and dipping of all travelling road cattle, except stock going to slaughter at an abattoir, where we were responsible for issuing 'Permits To Travel Stock'. The inoculation program was part of the Pleuro Pneumonia Campaign, requiring the inoculation of all calves at branding time and the blood testing of all road cattle and herds for Pleuro. All reactors were shot and a post mortem carried out, with samples taken sent to the laboratory for testing.

"Other responsibilities in those days were many and varied, such as being ex officio wildlife rangers and some-time veterinarians, as we had to castrate and spey stock and put down cats and dogs on occasions. I imagine that stock inspectors today have different duties.

"In 1964 I was digging around in the rubble of the burnt out Top Springs store and found a pair of Wave Hill spurs, which I cherish to this day as they are a relic of a past era.

"While on the subject of spurs, I was never a great lover of wearing them as I found them too dangerous while jumping off to throw a beast by the tail, as you could get your feet tangled and then be in serious trouble!

"Apart from this they are very handy while on the face of the camp cutting out, as a horse will respond with just a touch at the right time. Also while shouldering a beast, you can get a horse to come onto the animal with a bit of spur from the other side. I will say though, spurs on the heels of the wrong man's boots can make or break a potentially good horse, and a lot of horses will tend to cower with too much use of spurs.

"I left the AIB in 1968 and started on my own, doing contract fencing, yard building and equipping bores, primarily in the Daly Waters area, at Kalala station, working for the manager, Ray Easey.

Ernie Rayner's Wave Hill spurs. Having been born in the forge, they are certainly none the worse for wear after the fire at the Top Springs store.
—Photo Todd Sinclair

"In 1971 I struck up a Contract Bull Catching partnership with Maitland James (Len) Hayes, and in 1972 we drew a mini pastoral lease, Ballongilly, forty kilometres west of Katherine, where for the next twenty three years we eked out a living. After five years Len signed his share over to me and I was the proud owner of my own piece of dirt!!

"During this time Len and I started up a small abattoir and a butcher shop, located on the Collins and Hayes family property, Uralla Park, just south of Katherine. Later we also bought the town butcher shop from Northern Meat Exporters. Len and I dissolved the partnership in 1986, resulting in my purchase of Len's share in the town butcher shop. I then gave Vince Jones, who had been with us for years as mainstay and manager of the shops, a share in the town shop to stay on, which he did. We sold the shop a few years later when the town started to boom with the development of the RAAF Tindal Airbase.

"We stayed on at Ballongilly till 1994, when my wife and I moved to Darwin. I do odd jobs now, just to keep my hand in and to keep me off the streets.

"Sadly, two of my old mates and partners, Len and Vince, have 'shook the hobbles', so to speak, along with Gerry Woods, the head stockman from Gordon Creek."

Top: Ernie at Coolibah station, top, 1960, with 'flat top' Wondoan in the background, and, above, having a break from branding, Willeroo station, 1962.

—Photos courtesy Ernie Rayner

Cliff Robinson

Townsville, Queensland

Cliff Robinson's family are counted among the founding fathers of Townsville. His great grandmother, Catherine Colvin, arrived in Townsville alone in 1864, when there were only three white women in the settlement. His grandparents, St John and Cecile Robinson, created Townsville's Mt St John Zoo in the early 1900s, at that time the largest private zoo in the world.

In the 1940s Cliff, along with his brothers and sisters, was involved daily in the feeding and care of the animals, and it was at the age of about six or seven years that he started sketching. The zoo was subsequently taken over by Wirth's Circus as a resting place for their animals but was eventually closed down in 1966.

"Living at the zoo was a great experience. We kind of grew up isolated in the wild with the animals. There was no electricity or running water.

"That's where I first took my sketch book so that I could sketch the animals, especially the crocs sunning on the banks of their enclosures, they wouldn't move for hours."

Cliff has worked as a ringer in Queensland and in the Kimberley region of Western Australia, and spent three years with the Department of Main Roads based at Marble Bar in the Pilbara region, the hottest place in Australia.

Roughrider Tom Cannon in the 1960s.

—Photos courtesy Kerry Kendall

When he was about seventeen years old he headed south to study art at the Newcastle arm of the East Sydney Technical College, but after a year he went back to the bush.

In the early 1970s, while working in London as a barman and cook (and attending art lectures at the Tate Gallery and the National Gallery), he started experimenting with burning his images onto wood.

"I saw an electric soldering iron in a shop window and it reminded me of the black fellows I'd seen in the Kimberley, heating up wire to burn into their shields and boomerangs. Canvas and oils were expensive, but the soldering iron was only five quid and I practised on offcuts of wood. The smell of turps used to get to me too.

"I sold them on the fence at Hyde Park. I was doing Africa at the time, mostly action drawings of lions, giraffes and zebras."

He then returned to Australia, working as a professional barramundi fisherman on the Daly River in the Territory for a couple of years, as well as hunting buffalo in the off season, a period which Cliffy regards as the best time of his life.

Nowadays he lives on the outskirts of Townsville, creating his burnings which, because they are so true to life and accurate in detail, are in high demand throughout the outback.

Top: R.M. Williams in the 1980s, from a photo by David Seeto.
Centre: Cliff working on 'Fluffy Catches a Scrubby' about 1998.
Above: 'Boiling the Quarts, Dotswood station, Queensland.

Kalarji or Clargie Saltmere

Camooweal, Queensland

I first met blacksmith Deal Adams in 1994, and he pointed out two photographs of Clargie Saltmere in the book *The Border and Beyond* by Ada Miller, which clearly showed him wearing long necked spurs. Deal told me that he had made those spurs back in the 1940s.

When I finally met Clargie he said the spurs had been given to his father, Jack Saltmere between 1940 and 1945 on Alexandria, apparently made by Deal at that time They have heel bands angled slightly to fit the heel and the 75 millimetre curved necks have been brazed onto the heel band, rather than each spur being forged from one piece of metal. The rollers, one 15 point and one 11 point, have been hand cut with fairly blunt points. There is a groove filed on each side of the neck at the bottom about 8 millimetres from the join to the heel band.

Clargie, now caretaker at the Camooweal Racecourse, is a former ringer and was head stockman at Rocklands station and Barkly Downs, Western Queensland.

Top: Clargie with his spurs, Camooweal, 2000. Centre: One of his spurs.
—Photos Don Corcoran

Bottom: Kalarji, head stockman on Barkly Downs, Queensland, about 1950.
—Photo Hoofs and Horns/Marie Mahood

Jack Sammon

Rydal, New South Wales

FORMER DROVER Jack Sammon has told much of his story in verse, included here with his permission.

THOSE DROVING DAYS

Do your thoughts ever unfold to those days of old
when cattle strung out on the plain,
as they slowly pass by with dust rising high
can you see those old drovers again?
Or the ringers you knew from times long ago who
had shared your campfire's blaze?
Do you ever ponder or allow thoughts to wander
Back to those droving days?

Have you awoke in a fright on a dark stormy night
and your thoughts flash back through the years,
to those nights on the route when the storms were about
you rode around Territory steers?
Did your heart miss a beat when those steers hit their feet
and rushed off camp with a roar?
With sounds of horns clashing and dry timber crashing
you gallop around them once more.

'Droving Days'

—Photo Jacqueline Curley

Do you ever think back to that trip on The Track
when you took stores into Marree,
across the dry desert land all covered with sand
for as far as the eye could see?
When all was in drought with no grass on the route,
You battled to get the mob through.
But you got them there with a few head to spare,
by using the tricks that you knew.

And remember the days, when you rode in the haze
of dust rising up from the plain,
or nights in a camp with a swag that was damp,
you shivered in cold winter rain.
Do you still miss the sound as you camped on the ground,
Of horse bells on the night air?
Or the whispering breeze as it drifts through the trees,
at times you wish you were there?

Can you imagine again the tug of the rein
as you race to steady the lead
on a good horse beneath with the bit in his teeth
that was well bred and built for speed?
Or recall a bad colt that could buck and bolt
when you tried to put up a ride?
All that actually hurt when you bounced off the dirt
was mostly only your pride.

Now the years have rolled on and the drover has gone
from those stock routes out in the west.
We've all settled down and got jobs in town
with a mortgage and all of the rest.
Though it's often said that the life that we led
Was not what it's made out to be,
I know it was rough at times things were tough
but the life that we led was free.

By the 1960s the droving era in the north of Australia was fast drawing to a close. Paved all-weather roads were being built throughout the north, enabling large transports to travel further out over what previously been nothing more than rough bush tracks.

With the advent of the road trains the practice of walking cattle from stations in the north came to an end, as they could now be shipped in a fraction of the time it took to walk them to the nearest railhead. Although some droving of cattle did continue, work got harder to find and most drovers were forced to sell their horses and plants and find alternative occupations.

Quite a few drovers left the bush and settled down in towns, some like myself, finding jobs in mines and working underground, with nothing left to show for the life we lived, save our memories and maybe an old pair of spurs hanging on the wall.

Rusty Spurs

There's a pair of spurs hanging on a nail out in the shed,
The straps are dry and cracking and the metal's rusty red.
My father gave them to me when he taught me how to ride
and well do I remember how I strapped them on with pride.

Those old spurs bring back the memories of days so long ago
to times of droving cattle where the western rivers flow,
where I used to ride on night watch when stars were shining bright,
I rode around the cattle just beyond the fire's light.

We lived for months away from home out on the great stock route,
walking cattle slowly in from the stations further out.
Though days were long and life was hard, the saddle was our throne
as kings of our domain, we answered to ourselves alone.

But we didn't feel the winds of change blowing our way so fast,
soon the drover and his plant was a memory of the past.
For contractors with big machines were building roads of tar
they pushed their way across the plains and made a vivid scar.

Now big trucks in the wet or dry could tackle outback roads,
By night and day they rattled out to pick up bovine loads.
Yes, the drover's days were numbered as trucks came out our way,
For trips that took us months to do they now travel in a day.

Although we tried to struggle on the trucks were here to stay,
So like all the other drovers I gave the game away,
When I sold my plant and horses for anything I could,
I caught a train that headed south to leave the bush for good.

I've settled down in town and hung those spurs up in the shed
Now I wear a miner's lamp, working underground instead.
But at times when I see those spurs my mind goes drifting back
To droving big Gulf bullocks down the dusty Leichhardt track.

Jack later wrote to me about his ringing days:

"I did my first droving trip when I was about eleven. I was on school holidays when Mick Home took me with him with a mob of fats from Alderley station to the trucking yards at Dajarra, a short trip of six days. I only helped with the dinner watches and dog watch but to my way of thinking I was a full time ringer.

When I was around fourteen I did another trip from Alderley to Dajarra when my father was not able to get a drover to take the bullocks. My younger brother and myself went with him using the station plant and when we trucked the cattle he paid us one man's wages between the two of us. I bought a new Silver Spur hat and a pair of R. M. William's boots with my share.

When I went ringing and running camps on stations I did some short droving trips with station plants as well as giving drovers a few days starts and watches when they took delivery from me. One year I did a trip with Johnny Stewart from Rocklands to Tanbar with two thousand cows and calves, a trip of over four months.

I also did a few trips in charge of cattle from Alexandria station to Marion Downs and a few trips from Lorraine to Kajabbi. I gave up droving and ringing at the end of the 1978 season."

A typical road train.

—Photo Jacqueline Curley

When I left home to start work my father gave me his old three inch swan neck spurs with the advice that I should never wear them when riding a colt, never hang them off the saddle till dinner camp and if I was not game to put them on first thing in the morning don't wear them at all.

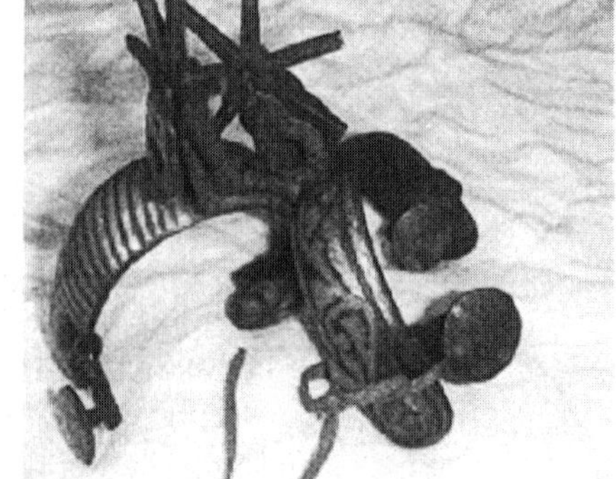

I bought a pair of Wave Hill spurs from Jack Britt for £10 when I was ringing at Forest Home in 1965 but lost one when I was head stockman on Delamere a few years later. Old Bill Tapp also lost one of his so we tossed up for it and I lost the toss.

Included is a photo of a pair of spurs that the late Bob Lewis gave me. Bob was a Texas cowboy and cowboy poet who worked on some of the bigger ranches in Texas before they were cut up and fenced. He told me that he bought them from an old spur maker in Mexico back in 1947 for $2. The silver inlay was fashioned by melting down a silver dollar coin.

The Bob Lewis spurs.

—Photo Jack Sammon

Bruce Simpson

Caboolture, Queensland

Bruce Simpson, poet, author, former drover and saddler, is highly respected by his contemporaries and has the experience to speak with authority about the droving days, a way of life that will never again occur in Australia.

These times are well presented in his book *Packhorse Drover* which details the routines of the drovers and ringers, men who worked hard and played hard, as did their counterparts in the previous century. Bruce writes about life on the road, of humourous and dramatic events, of the character types, including the cooks or 'bait layers', and of min min lights, rushes and smashes.

Included is the tragic story of the shooting of Palmer Brushe on Alexandria station in the Northern Territory in the 1930s. Snowy Baker, who was a horse breaker on Alexandria, had a relationship with an aboriginal girl there and was intensely jealous. While he was away from the station he was told that another man, Matey Cotters, was sleeping with the girl. Baker, mad with jealousy, strapped on his revolver and rode into the homestead that night.

Baker always wore long-necked spurs that dragged on the ground and jingled as he walked. Cotters, who had the girl in his room, recognised the sound and ran from his room, bursting into Palmer Brushe's quarters at the far end of the barrack style building.

Palmer Brushe who was the windmill expert on the station and a good friend of Snowy Baker, was sitting on the bed yarning with Frank Sweeny, another employee. Cotters slammed the door shut behind him and raced out the back door. Baker was not far behind roared out, 'Come out you gutless dingo, or I'll shoot you through the door.'

Palmer walked toward the door intending to calm Baker down, when Baker fired two shots through the closed door, instantly killing Palmer.

Baker kicked open the door and burst in, reeling back when he saw the man on the floor. He then walked up to the homestead and handed the revolver to the manager, saying, 'For Christ's sake take this. I've shot my best mate.'

Snowy Baker was subsequently sentenced to a long term in Fanny Bay gaol but was released from the gaol, with all other prisoners, when Darwin was bombed by the Japs in 1942. Cotters then decided it was time to leave the Territory and Baker also dropped out of sight.

On a more humorous note, Bruce gives a good account of a trip into Normanton by a bunch of ringers, including Bruce, for the annual rodeo and races in 1949.This a great story and typical of the way that hard working men relax after months in the stock camp or on the road droving.

Another good tale is Bruce's first encounter with a min min light, in 1945. "Min min lights were often seen in the early days east of Boulia, Queensland, near the site where the old Min Min pub once stood. The light remains a great mystery of the outback and still has scientists baffled."

The incident happened on Gallipoli, an outstation on Alexandria station. After delivering a mob of herd bulls there Bruce and his mate, Cecil Rose, called in to have a yarn with the pumper. In those days many of the stations employed men who lived at remote bores, maintaining the diesel engines that drove the gear to raise water from the bores. These men ensured that there was always sufficient water available for the cattle using the troughs and generally only had human contact when supplies were brought from the station, or a stockcamp was working that area.

This particular pumper "had a wild look in his eyes, the loneliness had obviously got to him". While having a mug of tea the pumper, looking over Bruce's left shoulder said, "A min min took me dorg y'know." He then went on to say, "It would have took me too, y'know, only I talked it out of it."

Cecil Rose, who by then had choked on his tea, said in a strangled voice, "You talked to it?" "Yair,' said the pumper, "it's friendly like now; comes up and has a yarn to me every night." Bruce and Cecil later agreed that the pumper "had gone troppo, the sooner we're out of this the better."

Later that night they both saw a bright moving light to the south, which they watched until it disappeared after about a half an hour. They agreed that they would tie up a horse the following night and investigate the light.

Bruce then gives an eerie account of his attempt to find the light when it appeared the next night and comments that of the three min min lights he has seen since, none left the impression that the first one did.

In *Packhorse Drover* Bruce also refers to Fred Gutte, blacksmith on Wave Hill station, who made and sold the famous Wave Hill spurs, and knew Deal Adams, blacksmith and spurmaker on Alexandria in the Northern Territory in the 1940s.

Read also Bruce's *Hell, Highwater & Hardcases,* another insight into life in the outback, each book including much of his poetry.

In 1997 Bruce published *In Leichhardt's Steps,* a carefully researched account of explorer Friedrich Wilhelm Ludwig Leichhardt and his two expeditions in Australia prior to his disappearance during his last trip in 1848.

This book includes a logical assessment of what probably happened to Leichhardt's party and the text is interspersed with Bruce's stories and comments, based on his knowledge of the bush, the country traversed, and the day to day problems that would have been faced by Leichhardt.

Other titles by Bruce include *The Territory Rouseabout and Other Humorous*

Beetaloo and Tanumbrini stations. I also assisted Kevin Paterson with general stock inspection duties on Helen Springs and with travelling stock, dipping at No. 7 bore.

"Wave Hill was my next appointment. In 1964 I was promoted to district stock inspector, which meant that I worked from Moola Bulla station in the west, to Top Springs at the start of the Murranji track.

"During the years 1965 to 1969 I managed Legune station, Ellendale and Humbert River stations. Station life was becoming very uncertain and in late 1969, after moving to Adelaide, I became a life assurance agent for the Temperance & General Mutual Life Society.

"This change of work led me to becoming established in Darwin and because of my ability to work with ordinary people in the suburbs I became an endorsed candidate and member of the Country Liberal Party in the new Legislative Assembly.

"I did not go into Parliament for the money – in fact my earnings dropped significantly when I entered Parliament. I spent twelve and a half years working with Territorians to achieve with them, their hopes and aspirations for a quality life in the north. Still, there are assets and infrastructure needed to bring us into line with the high living states in the east, but the Country Liberal Party achieved, and stayed in office for twenty six years working for Territorians.

"I am pleased with my own contribution while in Parliament, such as the establishment of roads and bridges, and the creation of the Gregory National Park as some examples of my personal political achievements.

"As the first Minister for Tourism we secured Royal Brunei Airlines, Malaysian Airlines and other infrastructure such as the Ayers Rock Airport and the construction of a major tourist village there, (now Yulara).

"My five years as the Tourism Minister saw the tourism budget grow from half a million dollars to $13 million with representation offices established throughout Australia and then all over the world.

"My connections with my pastoral background and particularly the men I worked with have always stayed strong.

"I recall the instruction and advice given to me when I started as a new chum kid at Humbert River station. "No spurs".

"Charlie Schultz didn't believe that young jackeroos and ringers should wear spurs and I didn't wear them in the first three years of my rural education. I found out that there were many ringers not capable of wearing spurs responsibly and as my life in the bush rolled along, I realised that spurs were mostly effective to get your mount away from danger in an emergency situation, such as getting away from a charging bull.

"When I did buy spurs they were off the rack, R. M. Williams, but I quickly traded them in when Neil Dudgeon gave me a pair of Wave Hill spurs. He asked me to hang on to them for life and I am sorry to say that in the early 1960s, Pic Willetts traded me a well-bred chestnut mare, with LTR branded on the near thigh, for the Dudgeon spurs. Pic later swapped the spurs to drover Bill Cussens and I often thought about buying them back from Bill but I didn't get the opportunity to make him an offer before he died.

"Interestingly the mare I collected from Pic in the early 1960s ultimately went to Legune station where the owners, Bill and Annette Sullivan, bred from her one of the best Territory racehorses to grace silks in Darwin and throughout the Top End.

"Just returning to the Fred Gutte spurs – if you left your horse at speed to throw a bull by the tail in the bush, the spurs would sit tight on the R. M. Williams boots and never budge.

"It is now quite some years since I worked on stations and sadly the old timers are moving away from the bush and the pastoral industry is a ghost town of personal memories.

"Being at the cutting edge with the Schultz family, the Underwoods, the Quiltys and the Duracks gave me a special feeling of belonging in an era of tremendous change. I worked with fantastic men who were the stock inspectors of the century, eg David Napier, Jack Travers, Kevin Paterson, Ernie Rayner and Naish Gainley.

"No bush story would be complete without congratulating Australia's great Aboriginal stockmen and women for their contribution to the pastoral industry in Northern Australia. In those days aboriginals rode the outback cattle runs with confidence and pride. Sadly those days are gone.

"Now the days of the Murranji Track are just about forgotten, but we battle on and hope to catch up with our mates at the next bush race meeting."

Top: Certificate Of Registration for Roger's TXT brand, Humbert River, 1966.
Above: Roger Steele (on left) with gun ringer and jockey Les Humbert at the official opening of the Durack monument, near Timber Creek, Northern Territory, on 1st September, 2000. This tribute to the Durack family is on the Victoria Highway, about 10 km east of Timber Creek at the turnoff to Bullita.
—Photos courtesy Roger Steele

Allen Strudwick

Uralla, New South Wales

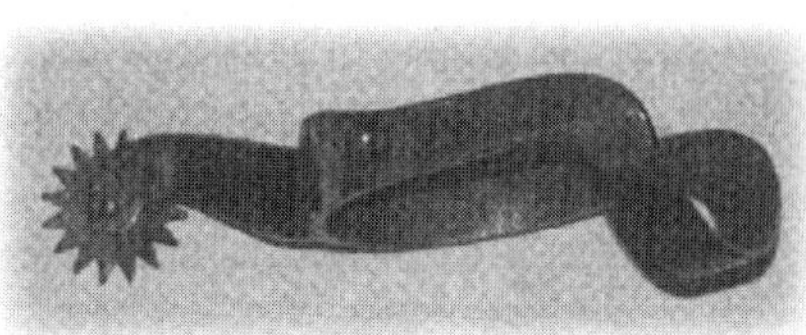

THE UNUSUAL SPUR at right is one of a pair on display at the Australian Stockman's Hall of Fame in Longreach, Queensland. One of them is engraved on the metal understrap, *Won by Allen Strudwick, Buckjumping Champion, Mt. Dutton Bay Rodeo, 1948.*

I found that they had been donated to the Hall of Fame in 1994 by Allen Strudwick, who, when I contacted him, suggested that Stan Morgan, the former secretary of the Rodeo Association at Mt. Dutton Bay, which is on the Eyre Peninsula in South Australia, could probably give me more information about them.

Stan Morgan and his Rigid spur design are dealt with in the section dealing with 'The Spur Designers.'

Allen Strudwick was born on 30th September 1929 at Tumby Bay on the Eyre Peninsula, South Australia, and brought up on the family farm at Edillilie.

After leaving school he worked as a tally boy at the Edillilie grain stacks and recalls that they had six inches of rain one summer, before the roofing could be put in place. The top six layers of bagged grain had to be progressively stood up so they could dry out.

I asked Allen about the weight of bagged grain and he supplied the following interesting information;

"There were 3 bushels of grain per bag, with the weight of the different grains being: Oats, 40 pounds per bushel, 120 pounds per bag; barley, 50 pounds per bushel, 150 pounds per bag, and wheat, 60 pounds per bushel, 180 pounds per bag.

"The bags were always heavier, because bag fillers (a hand-held funnel-shaped implement)

Left: Allen at Mount Dutton Bay Rodeo, South Australia, 1947.
—Photos courtesy Allen Strudwick
—Top photo Jenny Wilson/Australian Stockman's Hall of Fame

were used to get extra weight into each bag, usually an extra 10 to 15 pounds of grain.

"The wooden beams, or anchors, for the roof of the grain stack, were put in at 20 bags high, and a further 3 layers of bags on top of this, to bring it to 23 bags high. I would estimate there would be 300 to 400 bags per layer, multiplied by 23, would give 6,900 to 9,200 bags

"The engine driven elevators couldn't reach the top of the grain stack, so a high pole, or 'whip', was erected with a pulley at the top, and a cable through the pulley. A horse was taken from the waggon team, and used to pull the bags of grain up to the last layer. The horse had to pull up and then hold while the bag was taken off – if the horse went too far you had a burst bag of grain, (not good)".

When his two brothers, Roland and Mervyn, returned from the war, a farm was purchased and Allen worked, and then share farmed there. This property adjoined the Government Soldier Settlement Scheme at Wanilla, where the land was cleared and sown down to pasture before it was fenced up into individual farms.

In the early 1950s Allen purchased a block of country twelve miles west of Cummins on the Eyre Peninsula. It was fertile land but split up by salt lakes and lacked permanent water, and he subsequently sold it to his father. There was an old pioneer's cottage on this block where Allen and his brother lived while they cleared and farmed the land, and this cottage was later moved to the Koppio Museum by members of the local Historical Society.

At about this time there was a general movement of farmers to northern New South Wales where Allen had previously travelled and been impressed by the abundance of water there. When he was offered the management of a property in the Furracabad Valley, Glen Innes, which provided a much needed house, he felt it was 'an opportunity too good to miss'.

Allen decided to move to New South Wales by driving his four year old Massey Harris 744D tractor, (powered by a Perkins 6 cylinder diesel motor), towing a three ton four wheeled trailer, with all his worldly goods, including a portable two stand shearing plant and tools of trade.

He left Cummins on the 17th March 1958 and arrived at his destination in the Yooroonah area, east of Armidale eleven days later, averaging about 120 miles each day. The tractor is still in use on Rowena.

Allen ready to leave Cummins, South Australia, heading to the Glenn Innes district, New South Wales, in 1958.

He travelled through Whyalla, Port Augusta, Peterborough, Broken Hill, Wilcannia, Cobar, Nyngan, Nevertire, Warren, Gilgandra, Coonabarabran, Gunnedah, Tamworth and Armidale. Somewhere north of Yunta, South Australia, in the early hours of the morning, a willy willy stripped all the blankets off the bed which he had set up in the trailer. He had a very early breakfast that morning to get warmed up again.

In October 1958 he returned to South Australia to marry his fiance, Betty Isabel Ashman, in the Cummins Methodist Church. They had their honeymoon travelling back to the Furracabad Valley. After their six year commitment at Glen Innes, they sold a property they had bought at Yooroonah and purchased their present farm, 'Rowena', on the Kingstown Road west of Uralla.

For the past twenty years Allen has been involved with the New South Wales Farmers' Association, serving as secretary of the Kingstown branch for twelve years, as the Uralla District Council Chairman for three years, and as a delegate to the Annual Conference held in Sydney for over twenty years.

Photo taken in 1948 when Allen won the Buckjumping Championship at Mount Dutton Bay Rodeo. From the left, Allen Strudwick, Keith Traeger, Duncan McKenzie and Roland Strudwick.

Jack Sullivan

Ord River, Western Australia

JACK SULLIVAN WAS BORN in 1901 of a European father and an Aboriginal mother on Argyle Downs station in the East Kimberley division of Western Australia. His Aboriginal name was Banggaiyerri and he worked on the cattle stations of the region as a stockman and teamster. Like most bushmen of the day he could handle any job, be it yard building, fencing, cooking, horsebreaking or droving.

In his late twenties Jack 'came over to the white side'. Half castes, or 'yellow fellers' were generally accepted as white men, and Jack was certainly regarded as a competent man. In 1973 he met anthropologist Bruce Shaw, who had a close acquaintance with Aboriginal Australians living near Kununurra, in the East Kimberley.

Bruce Shaw recognised Jack as one of the few remaining identities of the region, and began recording Jack's reminiscences, resulting in the publication in 1983 of *Banggaiyerri, The Story of Jack Sullivan, as told to Bruce Shaw.*

This is a first hand account of the way of life on the cattle stations of the Kimberley over a seventy year period. Jack details the routines on the stations, many of the identities of that time, both black and white, speaks of spearings and shootings, and of Aboriginal beliefs and customs.

The photograph is of Jack when he was head stockman on Argyle Downs station in the 1940s, working for Eric Durack. His spurs, or 'hooks' as they were often termed are clearly visible, as is the holstered heavy calibre revolver used for shooting cattle when necessary.

As Jack said, "That forty five revolver would bring a bull down, it was nearly as good as a forty four rifle. If you were a head stockman you had to carry that in case of danger. Your man might get gored or a bull knock him

Jack Sullivan.
—Photo Walkabout Magazine/R Bean

over when you cannot get there to protect him, and you had to pull out a gun and shoot that bull."

Jack makes many references to the use of pistols, or 'squirts', on the stations:

"They used to have those old-time Mausers too, different from the Luger automatic, all covered in by a wooden pouch which clipped on as the stock to make it a long gun, a rifle."

No doubt many of these, along with Luger pistols, found their way to the Australian outback after World War One.

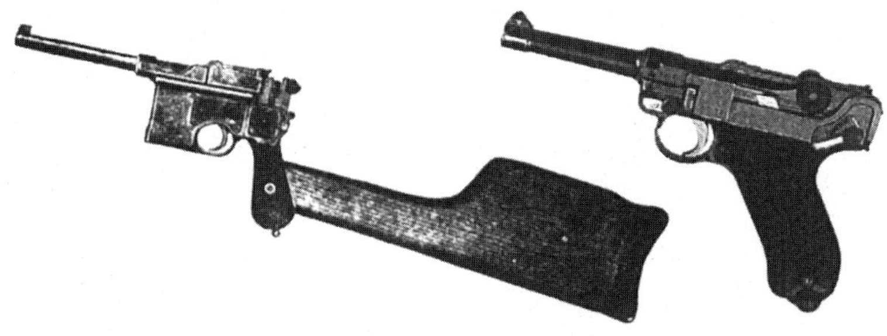

The upper photograph is of a Luger pistol. Below it is a Mauser pistol like the one Jack described, and the wooden holster which serves as a detachable stock. This pistol was referred to as the 'Broomhandle Mauser' because of its unusually shaped grip.

—Luger photo Don Fraser. Mauser photo Don Corcoran

Guy 'Woolly' Thomas

Aberdeen, New South Wales

GUY THOMAS WAS BORN in Narrabri, New South Wales and went to Nutwood Downs in the Northern Territory at the end of 1973, while Tony Clark was manager and Tom Kerwin was the head stockman.

When he arrived, as a sixteen year old with long hair, he was given two choices by Tony Clark – 'Agree to have a haircut, or have it forcibly removed'. Guy took the first option, but the nick-name of 'Woolly' stayed with him.

In early 1974 he went back to New South Wales to attend Yanco Agricultural College in Leeton. From 1975 to 1977 he worked on both Nutwood Downs and Helen Springs, which was managed then by Tim Doran, with Jack Wheeler as head stockman.

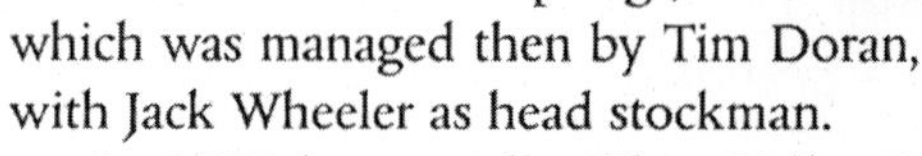

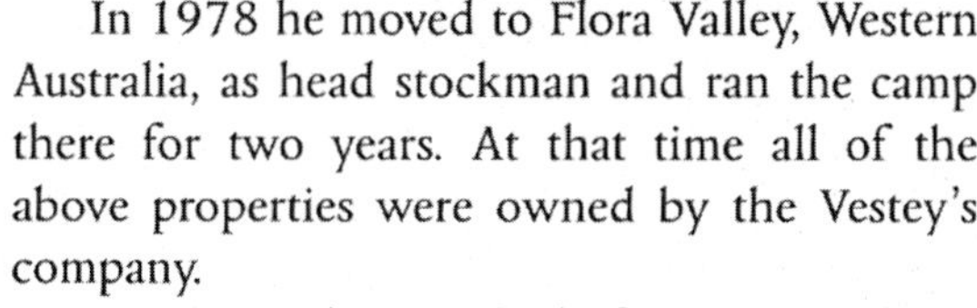

In 1978 he moved to Flora Valley, Western Australia, as head stockman and ran the camp there for two years. At that time all of the above properties were owned by the Vestey's company.

In 1980 he worked for Consolidated Pastoral Company, or Hunter Pastoral Company as it was then known, managing Lana Downs, at Winton, Queensland until 1983, then Hunters Vale, Ellerston, New South Wales, until 1987.

For the next five years Guy worked as a farrier in Tamworth, and at present is the manager of East Rossgole station, Aberdeen, owned by MBT East Rossgole Pastoral Company, a position he has held since 1992.

Because of his interest in blacksmithing and farriery, Guy has collected numerous spurs, and is interested in all things connected to horses.

While living in the Hunter Valley, he has also become involved in breeding, training and trialing Border Collies.

Top (upper): Spurs found by Guy on Kirkimbie station, Northern Territory. They are similar in style to Wave Hill spurs but have the necks brazed onto the heel bands. Lower: Another pair of Guy's spurs, found on Flora Valley station.
—Photos Don Corcoran

Above: Guy with friends, 2000.
—Photo courtesy Guy Thomas

Grant Unsted

Berry Springs, Northern Territory

GRANT UNSTED was born in Sydney and left school in 1959, working for a couple of years on properties in Queensland, including Tooloon at Charleville and Coongoolah South near Cunnamulla. He next went to Willeroo near Katherine in the Northern Territory for three years in the early 1960s, while Jack Pender and then John Barnes were the managers.

From there Grant went into drilling, first for Mines Branch of the Northern Territory Administration, and in the 1970s in his own business, Bynoe Drilling. From 1981 he has concentrated on water boring for the rural, horticultural and domestic market.

Grant purchased three pairs of Wave Hill spurs from 'Ma' Hawks at the Top Springs store in the Territory, in 1961, for £3 a pair. The store had excess stock of Fred Gutte's spurs, who by then had left the Territory and was living in Adelaide.

Photographed by Kim Corcoran, the pair of Grant's spurs shown above are mismatched, as seen by comparing the 'point' at the bottom of the neck of each spur where it joins the heel band. I have been in contact with Grant and he has another mismatched pair, indicating that when the spurs were separated many years ago, two odd pairs were created. Other examples of Fred's spurs have the 'point' removed with a flat file, although the side grooves can always be seen. This is dealt with in more detail in the section dealing with Fred Gutte, 'The Blacksmith Spurmakers'.

Above: Grant at Willeroo. The neckstrap with hobbles and a horn-saw on the saddle were standard gear in any stock camp in those days. The Vestey's Willeroo brand of the 1950s, ZTQ, had by then given way to Bryce Killen's WKT brand.

—Photo courtesy Grant Unsted

Right: Horseplay at Ingaladdi Waterhole, Willeroo, 1962. Grant (standing) with Jack Pender. Grant is wearing a Smith and Wesson .45 calibre revolver while Jack has a .455 Webley, used usually for shooting injured cattle and scrub bulls.

—Photo Ernie Rayner

Hans van Hees

Scone, New South Wales

Hans van Hees, below, was born in Holland and grew up at his grandfather's riding school. He began riding at the age of three and has been involved

with horses all of his life. With 75 mounts stabled at the riding school, there was always gear to be repaired and he soon developed leatherworking skills, making his first Western saddle by the age of fourteen.

After working in many countries as horse trainer, cowboy, stockman and saddlemaker, Hans settled in Australia in 1970. He specialises in high quality custom made western saddles, built to fit horse and rider and makes his saddles one at a time, including the trees.

Hans is also a maker of braided horse gear and gun leather, teaches saddlemaking and leatherwork at the Hunter Valley Institute of Technology and lectures occasionally at the University of Newcastle.

Here are some unusual spurs from Hans' collection:

A blacksmith made spur (right) of Australian origin, crafted of brass and iron, with a neck of twisted design.

Initially a flat heel band was made from iron, with riveted buttons. Two pieces of iron were twisted together to form the neck and flattened where the rowel is fitted. The neck, with 'wings', was then attached to the heel band and brass rods added for decoration.

There is no rowel pin – the rowel is fixed and was never intended to roll. Certainly, judging from the workmanship, the maker could have fitted the rowel in the conventional way had he so wished.

A very unusual pair of folding spurs (left), professionally made, probably about 1900. They are of nickel steel, each with two iron pins and a spring in the neck, and with iron studs.

— Top photo courtesy Hans van Hees

A pair of brass box spurs (right), marked for the left and right boots. Box spurs as can be seen have a shaft, within the heel band, designed to fit securely into a metal 'box', set in each boot heel. They do not require straps, are easily removable, and were usually used by the military and sometimes by police. Most box spurs found are of solid nickel or nickel plated iron, rather than brass.

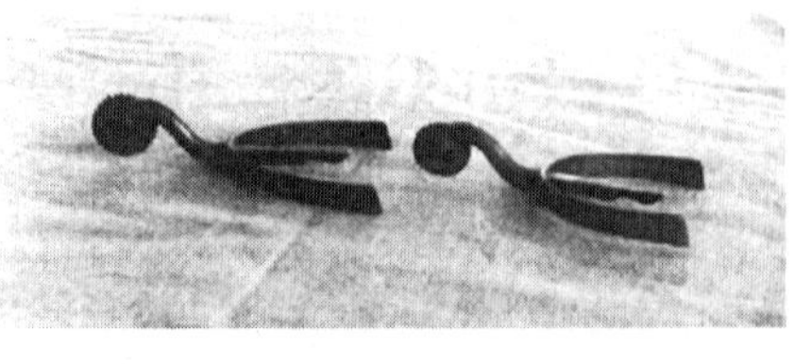

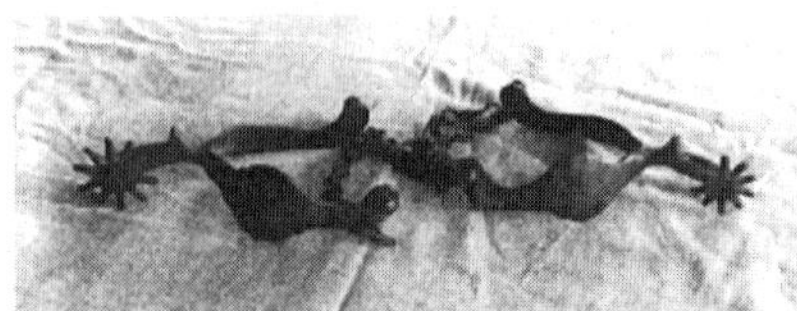

A pair of solid brass Californian style spurs (left), retailed in Australia during the 1920s.

Jack Watson

Northern Territory

Jack Watson, Manager of Victoria River Downs from 1894 to 1896, was well known for his outlandish behaviour. He was nick-named 'The Gulf Hero' after he had rescued a Chinese sailor who had fallen overboard from a lugger off the Carpentaria coast.

When the sailor was attacked by a shark Jack who was a passenger on the lugger, dived into the sea and drove off the shark with a knife.

The following is taken from notes compiled by Darrell Lewis:

As well as his wild exploits and harshness towards the Aborigines, Watson was inclined to be 'flash' or eccentric in his dress. In 1896, Mounted Constable Willshire, the officer in charge of the Gordon Creek Police Station wrote: 'Just fancy meeting in the bush wilderness a fashionable amateur with Mexican spurs and a footballer's jersey on...' (Willshire, W. 1896. *Land of the Dawning.* Page 76).

Above: Jack Watson.

— Photo courtesy Jan Cruickshanks

—Top photos Don Corcoran

From all accounts it is clear that Constable Willshire was no friend of the Gulf Hero and seemed to defame him at every opportunity, an attitude reciprocated by Watson.

The reference to the Mexican spurs is undoubtedly accurate because the following is the exact text of a letter from Watson, dated 20.7.1891, to his brother Ned who was then in San Francisco:

> I want you to get me from 'Frisco the biggest pair of Mexican spurs that 'Frisco can produce and a smaller pair. I expect the enclosed will cover the price and ex' you will know how to go about the job better than I do. Send them when you get them care Applin Brown & Co Palmerston have them properly booked and get receipt from the ship as things go astray sometimes.

This letter is in the possession of Jan Cruickshank, Watson's grand-niece.

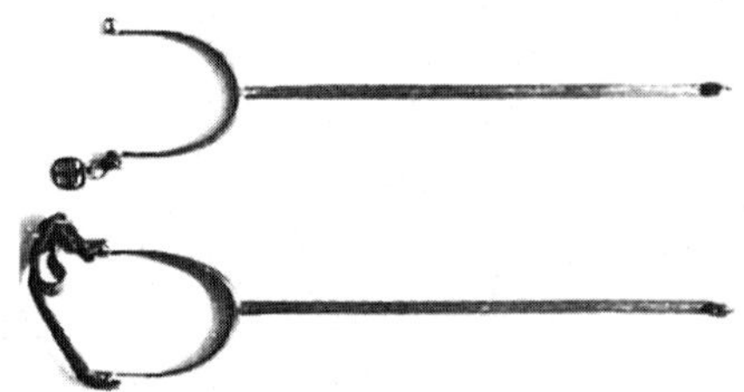

The spurs shown here, which were also his spurs and are still in the Watson family, are certainly *not* the Mexican spurs. Watson must surely have had their necks lengthened to 39 centimetres as a joke. Except for the longer neck they are identical in style to the Holdsworth, Macpherson & Co. spurs as shown in their catalogue elsewhere in this book.

Perhaps one day the 'Mexican 'Frisco' spurs will be located, but it is possible he was wearing them when he drowned swimming across the flooded Katherine River in 1896. Newspaper reports put April 1st, 1896 as the date of death, while the Watson family Bible records his death as March 24th, 1896.

Jack Watson's extended spurs.
—Photo Darrell Lewis

Rodney Watson

Mount Isa, Queensland

Rodney Watson was born in Camooweal in 1931 and his grandmother, Florence Emily Conroy, was the eldest daughter of one of the early pioneering families. She was only six years old in 1890 when the family came to Camooweal, which had only been gazetted as a town in 1883. This little girl became a much loved and respected identity in Camooweal, Florence Emily Watson, known to all in the town as Auntie Floss.

Lilian Ada Miller's book, *The Border and Beyond,* is a detailed history of this frontier town, the surrounding country and beyond.

Up to the age of 29 years, Rodney was ringing around Camooweal and the Territory, and droving for Larry and Johnny Darcy, Sid Biondi, Boy Beaumont, Bill Cussens, Mick Cussens and Eric Rankine, and during that time he also did ten trips with Pic Willetts. In addition he was head stockman on Nutwood, Elsey, Tanumbrini and Mataranka stations in the Territory.

In 1960, Rodney paid £600 for his own droving plant which he bought from drover Sid Howard. The plant consisted of 45 horses, 8 packsaddles, 6 sets of pack bags, 2 pairs of 6 gallon water canteens, 6 riding saddles, camp ovens and associated gear.

When he finished droving in the middle '60s he went contract mustering in the Territory on Hodgson River, Hodgson Downs and Legune stations.

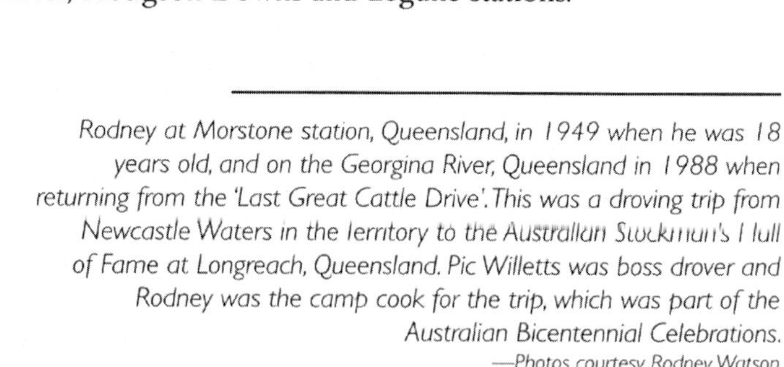

Rodney at Morstone station, Queensland, in 1949 when he was 18 years old, and on the Georgina River, Queensland in 1988 when returning from the 'Last Great Cattle Drive'. This was a droving trip from Newcastle Waters in the Territory to the Australian Stockman's Hall of Fame at Longreach, Queensland. Pic Willetts was boss drover and Rodney was the camp cook for the trip, which was part of the Australian Bicentennial Celebrations.

—Photos courtesy Rodney Watson

When he was fifteen years old Rodney Watson was working for drover Bill Cussens and bought his Wave Hill spurs when they were camped there, waiting to take delivery of a mob of cattle bound for Morstone in Queensland.

"Fred made my spurs (left) while we were there, using old shovel blades for the rollers, for a cost of thirty shillings. Each spur was made from one piece of steel.

"Fred was a wheelwright and made wagons for the donkey teams to cart wood for the bakers. He was a very nuggety man wearing old trousers and a blue singlet and didn't have much hair."

"At one stage, Jimmy Rigeroho, a ringer who worked on Brunette Downs, gave me a pair of forged short-necked spurs. They had been made on Brunette by Roy Wolfe, who was there in the late '30s or early '40s, but have since been lost."

THE NORTHERN TERRITORY OF AUSTRALIA

Stock Routes and Travelling Stock Ordinance 1954-1955.

FORM OF AUTHORITY GIVEN BY AN INSPECTOR.

To: (Name) Rod Watson

I, Roger Michael Steele

appointed under the Stock Routes and Travelling Stock Ordinance 1954-1955, as Inspector, do hereby authorise you to travel the Wallamunga Bullock mob no less than (49) Forty nine miles per week.

Reason being, Cattle coming from Drought affected areas, poor condition.

Signature: Ron Steele

Date: 30/5/64

Place: Wave Hill Stn

I have shown here some copies of documents from Rodney's droving days in the 1960s.

The form at right is signed by Stock Inspector Roger Michael Steele, who was later to serve twelve years in the Northern Territory Country Liberal Party Government, as a Darwin and Katherine Member of Parliament, Parliamentary Speaker and Cabinet Minister.

Roger, a founding member and former Chief Executive Officer of the Australian Stockman's Hall of Fame at Longreach, Queensland, currently lives in Darwin and is actively involved in tourism and political matters.

The following photographs show dockets from stores along the stock routes from Wave Hill to Dajarra in Queensland. These store owners, colourful characters in their own right, were a great backstop to the drovers. In many cases they gave goods on credit to the drovers as they took their plants west to take delivery of mobs, and again when they were returning with the cattle, often not receiving payment until months later when the drovers were paid.

As Bruce Simpson also says in *Packhorse Drover*, when writing of the drovers leaving Camooweal to pick up mobs in the Territory:

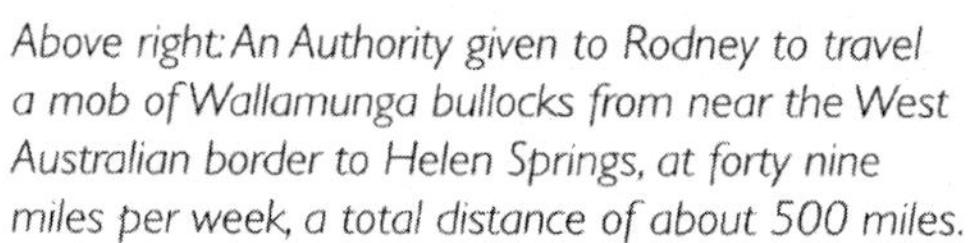

Above right: An Authority given to Rodney to travel a mob of Wallamunga bullocks from near the West Australian border to Helen Springs, at forty nine miles per week, a total distance of about 500 miles.

When the drovers had sorted out their plants and shod all their horses, they headed out to pick up the mobs they had been offered. The trip out to take delivery could take over six weeks, and very often the Camooweal storekeepers—Tom Cronin, son of Camooweal's founder, and Joe Freckleton—would stand the drovers the cost of tucker and horseshoes until they returned.

At left is a docket from Sid Hawks' store at Top Springs, Northern Territory, which was where the Dry River, Wave Hill and Auvergne Stock Routes meet the Murranji Track.

I recall buying revolver ammunition there in the early 1950s and talking to Sid Hawks who, I believe, as a young man had won the Stawell Gift footrace in Victoria.

The docket below is from Max Schober's store at Elliott, near Newcastle Waters, Northern Territory. Clarrie Pankhurst tells the following story of Max Schober in *The Boss Drover and His Mates:*

He has been a wonderful bloke Maxie; he stuck to all the drovers no matter who they were. Mick Cussens was coming back with a mob from Limbunya one time and he picked up more rations from Schober's. Maxie was in Darwin so Mick never paid him for either lot. On Mick's trip the next year he called in to stock up with more rations and Maxie tackled him.' He said in his heavy broken English, 'Hey Mick Cussens, you never paid me last year.

'No,' replied Mick, 'you robbing old bastard. Look at the prices you charge.'Max, insulted to the core expostulated, 'You call me a robbing old bastard. I'm not a robber, I stick to you drovers all the time. I buy for one shilling, I sell to you for two shillings. I make one per cent.'

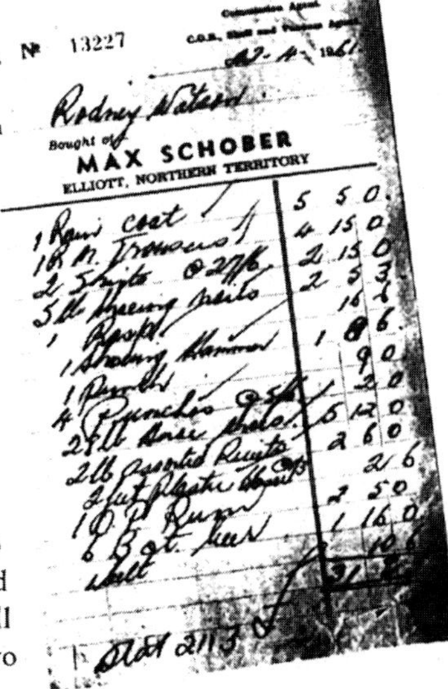

A № 13227

Rodney Watson

Bought of MAX SCHOBER

ELLIOTT, NORTHERN TERRITORY

On the next page is a docket from the Rankine River Store on the Barkly Stock Route. It was here I was with drover Larry Darcy loading some supplies onto the packhorses when he decided to buy a real luxury, some butter. Butter was sold in tins, and when opened was kept fresh for a while by carrying it in a wet hessian sack in a pack bag. It got rancid, or 'cheesey', after a time, but certainly none of it went to waste.

I also remember that on the maps in those days the store was shown as Ranken Store, and the river was the Rankine River. Similarly Barkly was often spelled as Barkley or Barklay.

R. E. CARTER
RANKINE RIVER STORE, N.T.
Nº 11086

Below is a docket from the store at Urandangie, just over the border in Queensland, about ten days out from Dajarra where most of the mobs coming in from the Territory were put on the rail.

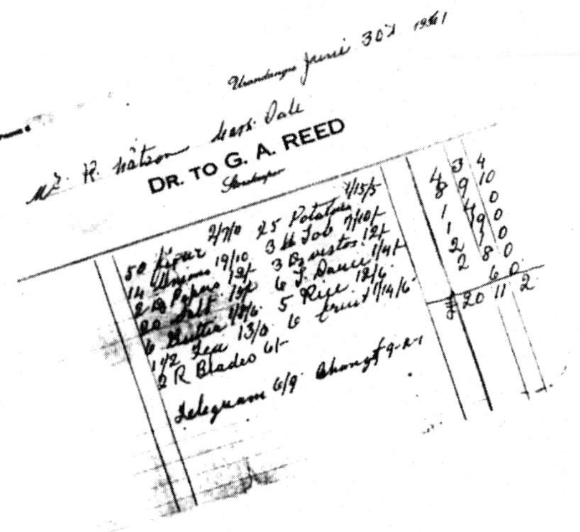
Urandangie June 30th 1961
Mr R. Watson
DR. TO G. A. REED

Rodney Watson as a young ringer on the Diamantina River, late 1940s.

Accidents can happen!

Rodney Watson took this photo at Newcastle Waters about 1963. He was on his way with Moola Bulla cows to Eva Downs when these piccaninnies walked over to the dinner camp to play with the donkey, which Rodney had picked up earlier on the trip.

Photos Rodney Watson.

Scotty Watson

In 2003 while in Alice Springs I met Scotty (Stephen Rennie) Watson and he told me that he had been droving for about 50 years. He did his first trip down the Murranji as a young ringer in 1948 and over the next ten years, as boss drover, took mobs down the Murranji from Limbunya Victoria River Downs, Waterloo and Moola Bulla.

Scotty was the overseer on Moolooloo in the late 1960s and also said he worked much of his droving years out of Beetaloo station.He moved the last big mob off Beetaloo, to Hamilton Downs, in the 1950s.

He bought his Wave Hill spurs from Fred Gutte, at Wave Hill, in the 1950s and stamped his initials SW on the necks.

While talking about spurs he told a story about Alex Grant, who was an Overland Telegraph linesman, based in Daly Waters, and who had finally retired in 1948 after working his whole life for the PMG. As a retirement gift he was presented with a pair of solid silver spurs.

Scotty died in 2005 and his daughter Gail Watson provided the photographs.

Scotty Watson, about 1954.

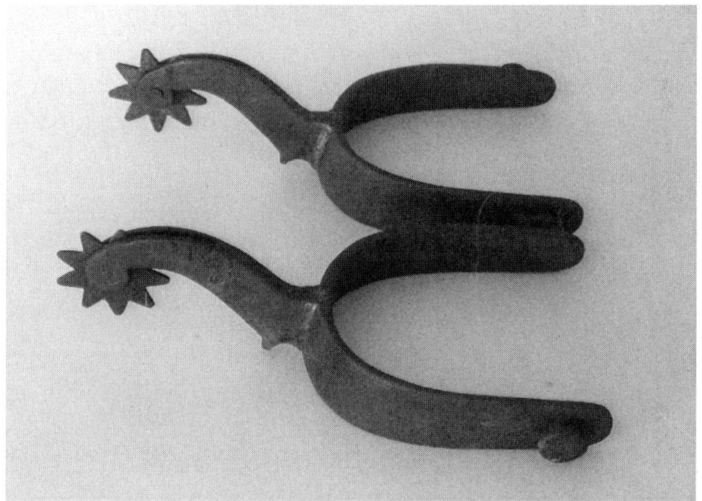

Scotty Watson's Wave Hill spurs.

Pic Willetts

Camooweal, Queensland

NOEL 'PIC' WILLETTS took delivery of his first mob on the road in the early '50s, lives in Camooweal and is an active supporter of the Drovers' Camp Association.

Pic was in charge of the 1988 'Last Great Cattle Drive'.

His spurs, which are of light spring steel with necks about 60 millimetres long, were purchased about 35 years ago. The rollers, not original, "have been changed many times".

In 1967 he was the last drover to take a mob down the Murranji track with 1400 mixed bullocks, from Auvergne and Newry stations in the Northern Territory. They were for delivery to Walgra station, south of Urandangie, just over the Queensland border. This was a trip of about 950 miles (1600 kilometres), taking about 15 weeks at 63 miles (105 kilometres) per week.

On spurs Pic said, "I prefer spring steel spurs, forged spurs are too heavy. I like straight necks with the roller kicked up a bit, just put the toe down and out and lift the horse from under. When riding buckjumpers I hung on with the spurs hooked underneath."

Pic told me an interesting story about a pair of Wave Hill spurs he once owned. He originally swapped these spurs from Roger Steele, who was then the Stock Inspector at Top Springs, for a chestnut LTR mare. (LTR was Ray Lewis' brand).

Later on Pic broke in six colts for drover Bill Cussens, who took a liking to the spurs. Another exchange took place, with Bill making up a set of bronco gear for Pic as a swap for the spurs.

Bill Cussens died about six years ago and the spurs and his whip were

Top: Pic in 1988 on the 'Last Great Cattle Drive'. This classic photo was taken near Tandyidgee Bore on Newcastle Waters by Coral Beebe of Ucharonidge station. Above: Pic's spurs.
—Photo Don Corcoran

placed on his coffin during the service. I am hopeful that one day I will be able to track down these spurs to photograph them.

At the time of writing Pic, and co-author Merice Briffa, have just published a book titled *Wind On The Cattle, Recollections Of Fifty Years Of Droving,* told by Pic the way it happened, with emphasis on the working and handling of big mobs of cattle on the road. These were tough days and the boss drovers were tough men.

I have included here some text and a poem from former drover, Jack Sammon of Rydal, New South Wales.

> On a recent visit to the little border town of Camooweal, in Western Queensland, I called in to see an old droving friend who I had not seen for years, now retired after working as a drover for over fifty years. We sat out on his veranda and talked of the days when the droving industry was at its height, when tens of thousands of cattle walked down the stock routes every year and we talked of the men who drove them, most who now have passed on.
>
> As we talked memories came back to me of a trip I took with my father when I was about ten or eleven, he and a cattle buyer called Jack West took me out along the Barkly and Wave Hill stock routes inspecting cattle that were for sale. At night we often camped with the drovers that were walking cattle down the stock routes, many of whom are mentioned in this poem.

Visions From The Past

I stopped to pay a visit, as the sun was going down,
To a friend now living in a little border town.
He's the "Piccaninny Drover"; Noel Willetts is his name,
Who for over fifty years had followed the droving game.

While sitting on his v'randa 'midst old and dusty packs,
That hung there with his camp gear and saddles on the racks,
Old Pic was telling stories of the days that have gone by,
When he was droving Wave Hill bullocks through the Murranji.[1]

As we were reminiscing at the closing of the day,
Sights and sounds of the town just seemed to fade away,
I pictured mobs of cattle walking down the dusty tracks
And those long forgotten drovers with wagonettes and packs.

Along the Barkly stock route came Jack Britt and Old Jack Gill
Behind a mob of bullocks they brought in from Wave Hill,
They're followed by Bill Cussens with twelve hundred 050s[2]
And Norm Stacey with a mob from where the Wickham flows.

Tom Lewis was at Wendy, he'd been quarantined a week,
Ben Benson with the Alroys was camped near Moonah Creek,
Jack Carroll with the VCTs[3] was nearing Lake Nash dip,
And George Man Fong with Newcastles had started on his trip.

Walter Cowen with the Rocklands was on the road again,
Mick Horne was in Dajarra loading Helens on the train,
Ray Turner with his chooks and goats was near the Rankine Store
And Sid Howard with the Cresswells was passing Pidgin Bore.

The Bulls Heads[4] were nearing Walgra, Doug Scobie's in the lead
With Eric Rankine close behind, holding back on feed.
Mick Bonning was at the 'Dangie[5] and Pedwell's at Brunette
And Jackson was at Avon he'd not started his mob yet.

There was Keith O'Keeffe, Jack Laffin and also Luke McCall
As well as many others whose name I can't recall.
Those visions pass on by me as the evening shadows dance,
While sitting on the veranda, completely in a trance.

But thoughts were interrupted by the sound out on the road,
As one of Cleary's transports with high and swaying load,
Came rattling in with cattle from across the Barkly plain,
Where those old forgotten drovers will never ride again.

©Jack Sammon 2001

1. Murranji, name of thick scrubland that the stock route went through.
2. 050, Ord River Station cattle brand.
3. VCT, Rocklands Station cattle brand.
4. Bulls Head, Victoria River Downs cattle brand.
5. The 'Dangie, the township of Urandangie.

relic spurs

OLD SPURS, found in the bush or anywhere, are of great interest. For example, the single nickel steel spur at right was picked up by Rodney Watson on the old racecourse at the Rankine Store, on the Barkly Stock Route, Northern Territory, about ten years ago.

This was the venue for the Rankine Races, held there by the Alexandria, Brunette and Creswell (or ABC) Race Club from 1922 until 1948, when the race meeting was moved to Brunette Downs. This spur, which is 'Prince Albert style', has probably been lying there for over fifty years.

Similarly the old pistol and spurs shown at left could no doubt tell some stories. The pistol, which is a Colt Model 1878 double action revolver, either .44 or .45 calibre, was found near the old Norwood township, which is the site of an old Cobb & Co. staging post on Bett's Creek in Northern Queensland. An alert ringer riding there dismounted to investigate when he heard a horseshoe strike metal. The old spurs were found elsewhere.

I am hopeful that one day an equally observant bushman on Manbulloo, near Katherine in the Northern Territory, will find a Colt Model 1917 'New Service' .455 calibre revolver, identical to the pistol at right.

I purchased this pistol personally from R. M. Williams at his Prospect store in Adelaide in the early 1950s for £15 and used it for many years in the bush. When I joined the New South Wales Police Force in 1957 I thought it appropriate to pass it on to a mate as the Police Department, who issued me with a useless .32 calibre Browning semi-automatic, would not have been impressed had I kept the Colt.

Subsequently it was lost in an incident with some troublesome cattle on Manbulloo, on the eastern side of the King River north east of Cowai waterhole.

Manbulloo workers, keep your eyes open around Cowai – you might find this revolver in a limestone crevice!

The small, heavily rusted spur at left, with a short neck and originally a horizontal roller, shown was found by Darrell Lewis at one of two locations reputed to be where twenty three Aborigines were shot dead after killing a trooper who rode into their camp. This occurred in 1893, at Collins Creek on Rosewood station in the Northern Territory.

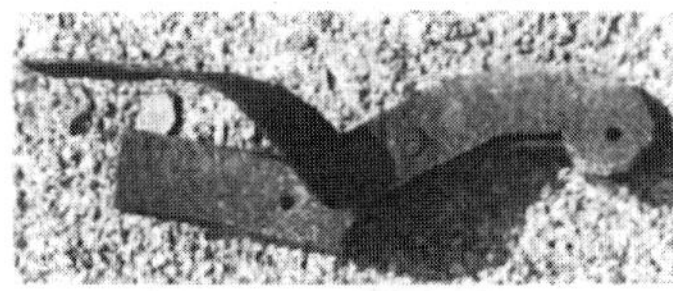

Similarly, the spur at left roughly cut out of heavy sheet iron, was photographed by Darrell Lewis at the site of the old Mount Bundley homestead, near Adelaide River in the Territory.

The spur at right was also found by Darrell Lewis in 2010, at a site where M. P. Durack and a man named Walter Okes had started drilling for oil in 1920. It is in W. A. near the eastern end of the White Mountain Range, on country used by Mistake Creek. He picked it up on a shale and spinifex flat about 150 metres from the original bore hole.

Colin Ferguson of the Rodeo Saddle Shop in Cloncurry, Queensland, sent the photo of the spur at the right which he found "along the Cloncurry River Anabranch in an area where there used to be an old blacksmith's shop".

The old spur at left was found in a paddock at Millmerran, Queensland and has an Australian 1949 halfpenny as a roller, with only two teeth filed. It is almost certainly a Buermann spur. (Refer *Cowboy Bits and Spurs*, Joice I Overton, page 98.)

August Buermann Manufacturing Company, of Newark, New Jersey, U.S.A. was making spurs from the 1868 until it was acquired by North & Judd Manufacturing Company, of New Britain, Connecticut, in 1926. This spur, courtesy Warren and Kay Skewes' Bar-S-Dot Museum, Moonbi, N.S.W. was originally donated by Leo Benjac of Leyburn Queensland.

At right is an unmarked spur, purported to be a gooseneck of R. M. Williams manufacture, however no spur of this design has been found in R. M. Williams catalogues. Courtesy Warren Skewes, Bar-S-Dot Museum, Moonbi, N.S.W.

A relic heel spur, of New South Wales Police issue, about 1840 or 1850, which was dug up in the grounds of the old Police Station at Scone, New South Wales in the 1930s. The heel spur pre-dated the box spur design, -- the spike, inside the heel band, was hammered into the boot heel and the heel band was secured by screws or nails on each side.

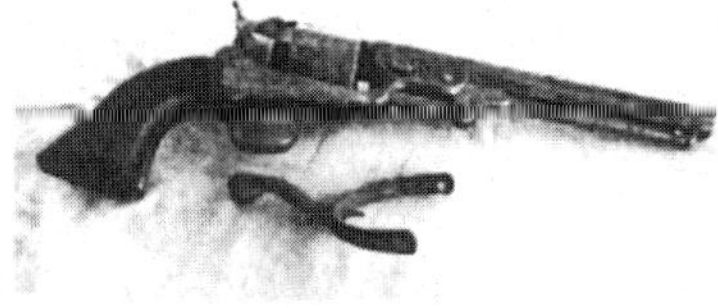

The old Scone Police Station now houses the local historical museum. The spur is shown with a New South Wales Police issue Colt Model 1951 .36 calibre revolver, courtesy Hans van Hees.

—Photos in order in which they appear: 1. Kim Corcoran; 2, 3. Don Corcoran; 4, 5, 6, Darrell Lewis. 7. Col Ferguson. 8, 9, 10, Don Corcoran.

Details of the photographs on this page can be found, clockwise from the top left, on pages 146, 135, 138, 53.

Details of the photographs on this page can be found, clockwise from the top left, on pages 104, 163, 143, 205, 10.

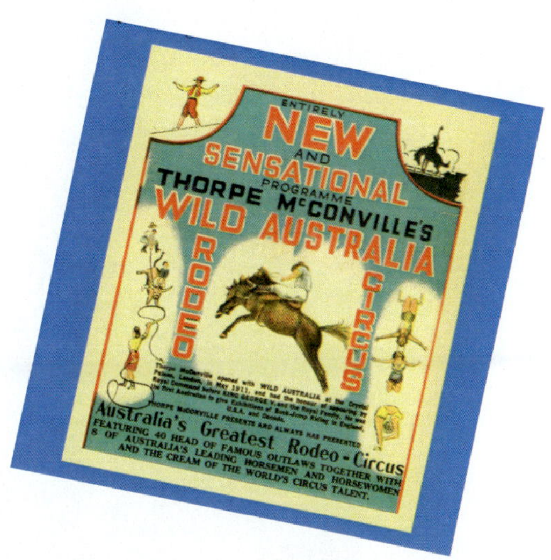

Details of the photographs on this page can be found, clockwise from the top left, on pages 10, 97, 113, 128, 35.

Details of the photographs on this page can be found, clockwise from the left, on pages 58, 85, 85, 37.

the blacksmith spurmakers

IN THE EARLY AGES the blacksmith must have reigned supreme among the craftsmen of the day, coming into being with the discovery of iron as a workable metal about 3000 years ago. Here was a man, equipped with a forge, anvil, hammer and tongs, who made fire his servant and was able to make or repair all things needed for war, agriculture and day to day living.

The motto of the Guild of Blacksmiths, chartered in the seventeenth century in England, was 'By Hammer and Hand all Arts do Stand'.

Photographs of blacksmiths and blacksmiths' shops are few and far between, in part due, no doubt, to the limitations of cameras from the 1860s and the fact that the blacksmiths' shops were usually poorly lit to allow the smith to more easily monitor the colour of the metal while forging.

This group of three photographs is from the Australian Investment Agency Collection and is reproduced courtesy of Darrell Lewis. The photo below is captioned 'Wave Hill staff, 1922' and that at right is labelled 'Two donkey teamsters from Wave Hill Depot, Smithy & Staff, August 1923'.

The picture below bears the caption 'Bush waggonette built at Blacksmith's shop. Wheelwright Bray Blacksmith Gaynor 25-6-21. Manbulloo Station'.

Darrell makes the following comments about these photos:

Top: The smithy at Brigolong, Victoria, around 1910. The names of the blacksmiths are not known.
—Photo courtesy Jill Bowen/Australian Stockman's Hall of Fame

All three blacksmiths are very short powerful-looking men and could almost be one and the same. The two from Wave Hill, especially, could be the same bloke and I suspect they are. A man called Tommy Wakelin was blacksmith at Wave Hill in 1920–21, but he was on Victoria River Downs for most of 1923, so the caption 'Two donkey teamsters….' could have the wrong date or, more likely, it could actually be at VRD. In the collection listing, the photo is under the heading Wave Hill, but this could be a mistake. The two teamsters are said to be 'from Wave Hill Depot' which suggests that they were not at Wave Hill when the photo was taken, but rather were from there. I'd lay my money it being at VRD and the smith being Tommy Wakelin. Tommy was in the Victoria River country from at least 1895 and in 1909 was attacked by Aborigines in Jasper Gorge. He left VRD in December 1923 and on 4th January 1924 was drowned while trying to cross his packhorses through floodwaters at the King River crossing.

While researching blacksmiths I have found many variations in the spelling of their tools, depending on which country and what period.

Vyce can be vice or vise, the hammer handled chisel can be termed a set, sett or sate, a flatter may be called a flattener, swage is also referred to as swedge and the hardie sometimes becomes a hardy.

Top: Gordon Blackwell at his forge in the grounds of the Hawkesbury Agricultural College, Richmond, New South Wales about 1985.

—Photo courtesy Jill Bowen/Australian Stockmen's Hall of Fame

Right: J. B. Edney and Son, of Wagga Wagga, New South Wales, about 1900. This smithy also housed a gunsmith.

—Photo courtesy John Swinfield

Deal Adams

Belmont, New South Wales

In 1994 I wrote a letter to the Australian Stockman's Hall of Fame newspaper asking if anyone had a pair of Wave Hill spurs they were prepared to part with. I had swapped a pair from ringer Roly McPherson for a bullwhip while working on Willeroo in the early 1950s. They were subsequently lost and I was looking for another pair for sentimental reasons.

Soon after the letter was published I was telephoned by Dan 'Deal' Adams who lived at Belmont, north of Sydney, and who told me he made spurs on Wave Hill when he was there about 1936.

I went over to Belmont to meet him and found that his wife Annie was the sister of Larry Darcy who I had been droving with in the 1950s. I had a number of interesting yarns with Deal and Annie before we moved overseas to live and Deal died about July 1996. He was called Deal throughout the Territory because of his enthusiasm for playing cards.

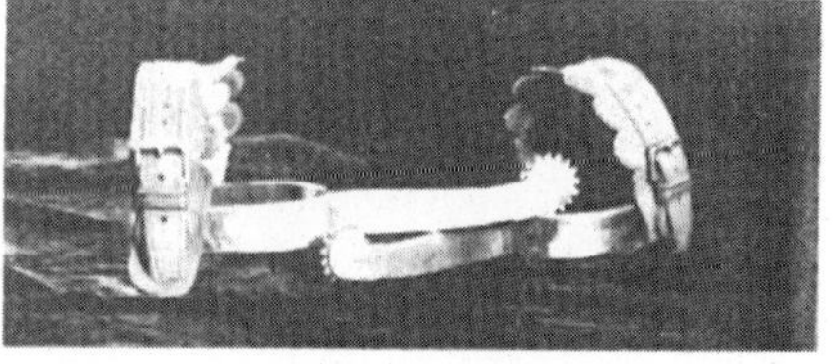

At our first meeting Deal showed me a pair of long necked stainless steel spurs which he had recently made and said that these were in the style he made when at Wave Hill. They had long straight necks, about 15 centimetres, curving up slightly where the roller is fitted, are not angled to fit the boot heel, and are intended to be worn as shown in this photo, with the neck curved upwards.

At the same time he showed me Ada Miller's book, *The Border and Beyond,* pointing out two photos of Clargie Saltmere, formerly head stockman at

Top: Deal and Annie Adams in the 1990s.
—Photo courtesy Annie Adams
Above: Deal's stainless-steel spurs.
—Photo courtesy Deal Adams

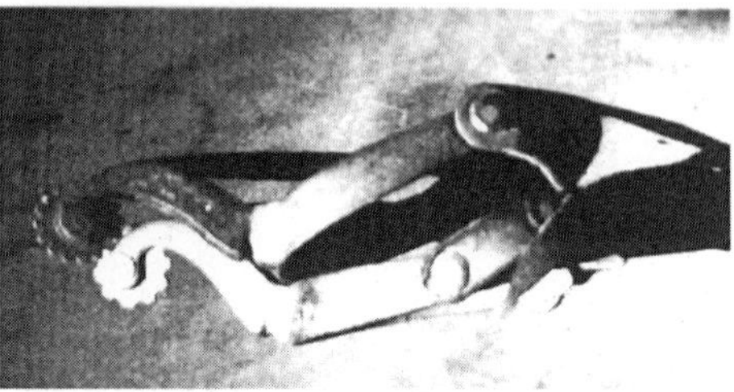

Rocklands, wearing spurs with long curved necks. Deal said that he had made those spurs in the 1940s, and although most of his spurs were straight necked he had made a few goose necks over the years.

Deal told me he had qualified as an engineer many years ago (his certificate was displayed on his lounge room wall), and when I met him he was working part-time on the construction of ultra light aircraft near Belmont. He made the point that he had started off making wagonettes and the like and was now involved in building aircraft.

In his book *Packhorse Drover* Bruce Simpson made the following remarks about Deal Adams, who he met in 1944:

> At morning smoko I met Deal Adams. I soon learnt that Deal was a rather extraordinary individual. He was a jack of all trades, and master of them all—a good ringer, capable saddler and a builder of horse drawn vehicles.
>
> After smoko I strolled over to the blacksmith shop where Deal was busy with an electric welder. I watched him for a while, then when he pushed the mask up to inspect a weld, my curiosity got the better of me.
>
> 'What's this going to be, Deal?
>
> 'This,' said Deal, grinning at me, 'This is going to be a rubber-tyred wagonette for the stockcamp.'
>
> I was impressed, and showed it.
>
> 'What are they using at present?'
>
> 'They're carting the gear around on a big dray I made for 'em.'
>
> 'You made it. What about the wheels?'
>
> He looked surprised. 'I made them too, but it's a bit heavy to pull; this will be as light as a feather.

Top: Clargie Saltmere's spurs.

—Photo Carmel Williams

George 'Poddy' Aiston

Birdsville Track, South Australia

Mr G. V. Bell of Dulkaninna Station on the Birdsville Track wrote to me of 'Poddy' Aiston, a retired policeman, who made spurs.

A further letter, published in the Australian Stockman's Hall of Fame newspaper in September 2000 from Reg Arthur of Charleville, Queensland stated:

> George 'Poddy' Aiston was a policeman stationed at Mungerannie Station on the Birdsville side of Mulka from 1912 to 1924. His wife was the governess to Mr and Mrs Bill Crombie's children. On retirement from the police force, George Aiston purchased Mulka from Jim and David Scobie.
>
> I first met the Aistons in 1942 while working for Don Scobie who was droving off Clifton Hills to Lake Lettie station outside of Marree.
>
> Don Scobie was the son of Alex Scobie of Scobie whip fame who was then living at Ooroowillanie on the Marree side of Mulka. But to be quite honest, I cannot remember George Aiston ever making spurs or hearing anyone ever mentioning him making spurs, although no doubt he had a blacksmith's shop and could have quite easily knocked up spurs between 1924 and 1942."
>
> Mulka, (although a station in it's own right) got droughted out probably in 1934 which was the year the Birdsville Stock Route was closed to cattle. In 1942 Mulka was a wayside store for travellers and drovers and as George Aiston had the lease on the government bore (£50 a year) he could and did charge travelling stock a penny a head for water."
>
> George Aiston was famous for his anthropology writing and photography and was honorary consulting anthropologist to the Australian Institute of Anatomy in Canberra. He died in Broken Hill in 1944 after being airlifted out of Mulka by the Royal Flying Doctor Service."
>
> His immense collection of firearms dating back to 1700s and also his Aboriginal artefacts were presented to the South Australian and Canberra museums by Mrs Aiston on her retirement from Mulka in 1954.

William Stewart Arnold

Charleville and Quilpie, Queensland

INFORMATION FROM Pat Stemm at the Waltzing Matilda Centre in Winton, Queensland about a blacksmith named Arnold led me to Alec Arnold of Southport, Queensland. Alec told me that his father, William Stewart Arnold was a blacksmith, working at Thylungra station west of Quilpie, and Adavale near Charleville in the 1920s, later moving into Quilpie.

Alec, who was born in 1928 at Adavale, told me about his father:

"He was a cranky old bugger, there were six boys and four girls in the family and we all had a turn swinging the fourteen pound hammer for him. If we missed, he didn't!

"He was a wheelwright as well, and had a big round metal plate that he used when working on wheels. It had fire underneath and all us kids used to stand around the plate to pour water on the steel tyres, when he was shrinking them onto the wheels. We all had bare feet and every one of us got burnt at one time or another.

"My brother, Thomas Victor, couldn't get on with him and left home, he was away for fourteen years. My father died of pneumonia in 1946 aged 74 and was blacksmithing until he was 73 years old."

Alec remembers him making all sorts of spurs, sometimes using pennies for rollers but to date I have not been able to locate any Arnold spurs.

In later correspondence Alec told me:

"When on Thylungra station where he was blacksmithing he used to do a lot of horse shoeing and all repairs to wagons for droving trips. He would go to outlying stations to do all types of work for them for weeks, then back to Thylungra. I wasn't born then, my sister told me this.

William Stewart Arnold at his wedding, 21st June 1913, at Adavale.

—Photos courtesy Alec Arnold

"Then we moved on to Adavale and I was born shortly after. I would not know how long Dad had been there before we moved to Quilpie as I was only five when we left. From three years old I had a pretty fair idea of what went on. He used to make the ploughshares for the old Chinese farmers to plough their little garden plots.

"Then it was time to pack up for Quilpie, we had a fair load on the old Ford truck. You never got too many miles an hour out of the old truck. Anyway we made it there and then there was the big job of unloading. I had to keep out of the way as I was only five. It did not take Dad long to get things set up.

"Later Dad turned the old truck into a wagonette, the first horse drawn vehicle to have rubber wheels in the district, which was so much better to handle in the wet weather. We had to get the big plate brought to Quilpie by heavier truck for using to put the rims on the wooden wheels of the wagons.

"At one stage he did repairs on the old metal boat which was used to get the mail through Cooper Creek in the floods.

"When Dad made the goose neck spurs, the shank with the roller on it used to look like a goose's neck, about six inches long.

"When we were at Quilpie Dad used to catch yellow-bellies in the Bulloo River and we'd carry them home in the galvanised washing tub. We also had a pet emu that kicked like a mule, my brother and I used to yoke it to a buggy to cart water to the house. We lived in an old tin house with tin walls, it was hard living."

Top: William Arnold fishing on the Bulloo River, Quilpie, about 1938. Above: Alec with Hazel in Southport, about 1950, before they were married.

Barry Blain

Camooweal, Queensland

KEITH LUSCOMBE of Pittsworth, Queensland has a pair of forged spurs made in Camooweal in the early 1960s by Barry Blain, who ran the Caltex garage there. These were made from car springs and styled after Fred Gutte's spurs which by then were no longer being made, as Fred left Wave Hill about 1957.

They are beautifully made, each spur from a single piece of steel, and differ from the Wave Hill spur in that the heel bands curve down where the studs are fitted. They are angled to fit the boot heel, and have necks about 63 millimetres long with 16 point rollers.

Bill Dinnie

Strathdickie Smithy, Proserpine, Queensland

WHILE RESEARCHING William George 'Weary' Lade of Proserpine I contacted Bill Dinnie, blacksmith and spurmaker, who knew Weary and made spurs for the rodeo committee in Proserpine to be used as rodeo trophies. Bill mentioned that at one stage there were four Dinnies, Bill, his two brothers and his son Andy, listed on the Federal electoral roll of Dawson, as blacksmiths.

The following is text from a letter Bill wrote to me regarding his method of spurmaking:

"I am enclosing photos of three pairs of spurs that I made for the rodeo committee as a memorial trophy for the bareback ride. I must have made about fourteen pairs altogether. We had to do a lot of handwork in those days getting all the scratches out before having them chromed. Now, with buffing equipment and compounds it would make the job much quicker.

Top: Barry Blain spurs.

—Photo Don Corcoran

"I made my first pair of spurs when I was thirteen years old, that would be fifty eight years ago, splitting and opening one piece of steel for each spur, which was the method that the blacksmith on Wave Hill used later to make his spurs. I made two pairs last year, one with the shanks welded on, they went to a station in Cape York and the second pair were for a local chap who had been to the Stockman's Hall of Fame and bought back photographs of Wave Hill spurs.

"I made them from a Holden coil spring, first straightening out a section and annealing it in lime powder. Heat to cherry red and cool slowly is the recipe. Next step was to saw about 120 millimetres down the centre then flattening the bar to about 22 millimetres thickness, using a flatter and striker. Then I cut off the required length leaving enough for the shank.

"I used to make straight shanks or goosenecks, to whatever length or style the customer preferred. For rowels I used old crosscut saws or shovel blades, roughing out a circle with a cold chisel and filing it to size. Then using a carpenter's file I would file in the teeth, often ending up with one tooth smaller than the rest. Once I got one right I kept it for a template. In those days we called them rollers until a learned chap told us they were rowels!

"We did not have power in the old bush shop so had to take spurs to the local garage to have holes drilled. Apart from the forge the only machine we had was a grindstone worked by a treadle.

"During the late war years we were using emery wheel dressers. This was a tool, with a handle approximately 300 millimetres long, with a fitting which had about six toothed wheels, interspersed with washers. While the grinder was in motion the toothed wheels were moved from side to side across the surface of the wheel, taking out any hollows or glaze in the process. The toothed wheels

Top: Bill at the forge, about 1980. Above: Inside the shop, 1980s.

—Photos Bill Dinnie

had up to eighteen teeth, were 1½ inches in diameter with a ¼ inch hole in the centre and were made of good quality steel. They made excellent rowels, and from then on I used them almost exclusively in the spurs I made. Later dressers had wheels with a ½ inch hole in the centre so I adapted the rowel pin, making it larger in diameter to accommodate the bigger hole.

"When I made spurs for the rodeo on the Mexican pattern, I did not use the emery dresser wheels for rowels, but made them 1¾ inches in diameter with ten teeth which somebody nicknamed cartwheels. Some I made 2 inches with more teeth, as shown in one of the photos. When we were first making these by hand it used to take 3 or 4 hours to finish one pair.

"My son Andy, who is also a blacksmith, made cartwheels and did a very fine job on them, making at least thirty pairs all up. He helped me a lot with the spurs.

"When cutting with a hacksaw you had to be very careful as the blades were so brittle you only had to drop one and nine times out of ten it would end up in two pieces or more. They were made from pure carbon steel, with no tungsten, and when sawing you had to keep your arm, and the blade, dead straight to avoid breaking them. It wasn't until after World War II that we were able to get the flexi-back and similar blades which are the norm today

"To save a lot of cutting we used to favour old Winchester barrels, round ones for preference, because of the hole down the middle there was less to cut.

"Once the wings had been cleaned up, mostly on the side of the grindstone, they were heated and bent over the horn. I always used a short piece of pick handle to bend them, so as not to leave hammer marks. The only time I used a hammer was after the wings were opened, I would place them across the horn, with the shank up, and hit down on the end of the shank to get a good shape at the end of the cut, the inside of the heel band. After the wings were bent I would forge the shank to whatever style was required.

"The advent of electric welding and bench drills made it so much easier, the

Top: A wall in the shop on which brands were burnt to see how they looked
—Photo Bill Dinnie

wings could be bent and the shank welded on after. I mostly used ¼ inch cup head bolts for the studs, a little bit of filing got rid of the square under the head. The studs used in my early spurs were brassed, or brazed in. The holes were counter sunk and the studs driven in. An old brass buckle was filed, borax was melted and crushed to a powder, mixed with the filings and sprinkled on when the parts were made quite hot. Afterwards, where the neck of the stud fitted into the heel band, it was cleaned up with a file and looked good. One thing in those days was the excellent selection of files available.

"Over the years I have made lots of repairs to spurs, the most common being that the rowel had worn through the pin and dropped out. You were then faced with the job of getting out the two halves of pin most times mashed up by the owners trying to knock them out with inadequate tools. Another repair job, although not so frequent, was where the shanks were very thin where the slot for the rowel was and the rowel would wear through one side of the shank and be left hanging down. When the Willoughby spurs were made I often had to get the rowel screw out for the owners.

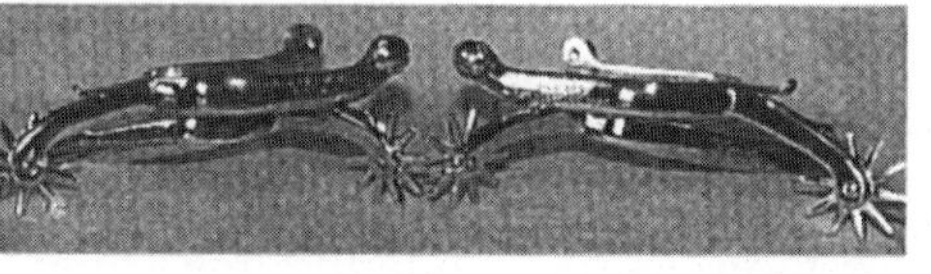

"Spurs were used a lot in those days, I have seen them worn thin on the underside, where they fitted the heel, as sharp as a knife. We were taught to use spurs sparingly, mainly just a tickle now and again. Sometimes you would sink them in if a beast broke from the mob and you had to turn it back.

"My brother Dave was the first ever blacksmith's apprentice under Weary Lade at the sugar mill. Up till then smiths came up through the ranks as strikers serving many years before qualifying. My youngest brother Angus was also an apprentice blacksmith serving his time under Dave at the mill. My son Andy was apprenticed to me in my shop."

Bill provided the following observations about blacksmiths, their tools, and the eventual demise of their craft.

Top: Trophy spurs made by Bill. Above: One of Bill's cartwheel rowels (left) and a toothed wheel from an emery dresser.
—Photos Bill Dinnie

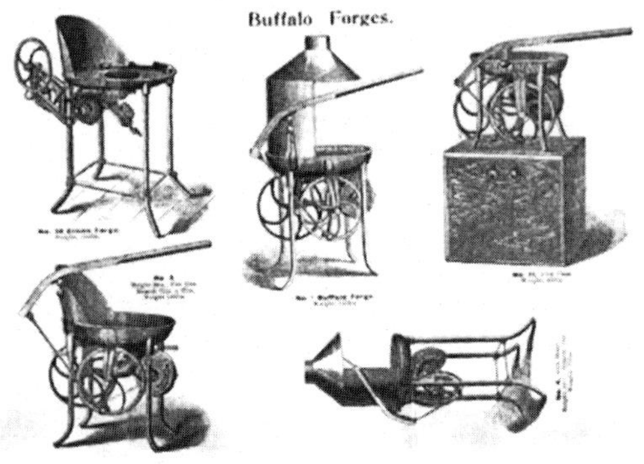

From the beginning of the Iron Age the craft of working and shaping iron came into being, with primitive tools, basically a rock held in one hand, pounding a heated lump of iron on a large rock. Eventually iron tools were developed, chiefly a hammer and a large block of iron to serve as an anvil.

From those smoky aeons of time a trade or craft was born which was to endure for many centuries, with the skills and secrets of shaping hot iron into a desired form being handed down from father to son. Charcoal, in the main, was the principal fuel used, with the air blast being supplied by many means, chiefly bellows, in their many shapes and forms. Blacksmithing, a tribute to man's ingenuity and perseverance, developed many implements and machines as well as an ongoing improvement in the quality of iron.

Many sayings originated around the forge: 'Strike while the iron is hot', 'Too many irons in the fire', and 'Go at it hammer and tongs', to name a few.

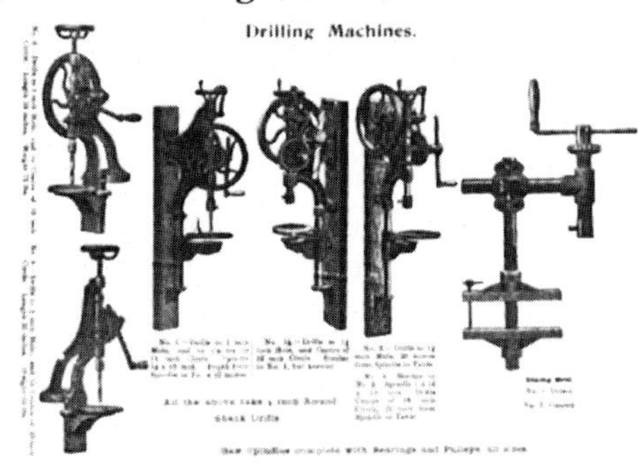

Every township had one smithy, often more, depending on size. The village blacksmith commanded a great deal of respect and the shop was a favourite place for people to collect while the smith shaped huge chunks of iron. The flying sparks seem to enchant some people.

The smithy was constructed of whatever material was available, stone, brick, slab or corrugated iron, with a chimney or vented ridge. The two most important pieces in the 'shop' were the forge and the anvil. The air supply for the forge was mainly by bellows, but later a geared blower was made, which by turning a handle caused a fan to rotate inside a casing, giving a good blast of air. It took up little space compared to bellows where there was also the risk of puncturing the leather with pieces of iron.

Top: A page from an early Buffalo Forge catalogue.
Above: Some early drilling machines.
—Courtesy Darrell Lewis

The majority of the bellows were made of cast iron with steel gears – one of the principal makers was the Buffalo Forge Company of Buffalo, New York, U. S. A. They also produced various post drills with different sized steel bits, which made the job of putting neat holes in exactly the right place very easy.

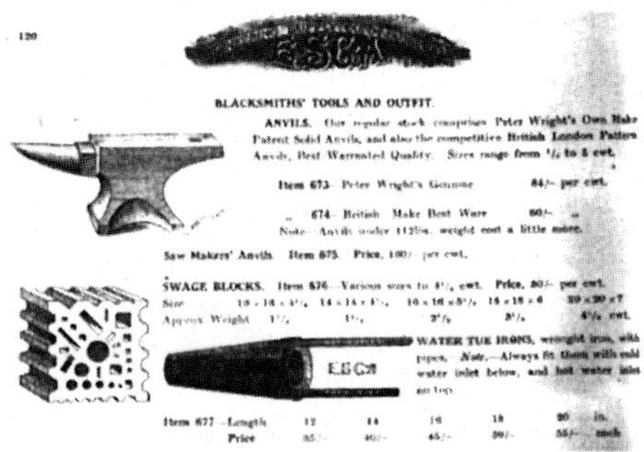
120

BLACKSMITHS' TOOLS AND OUTFIT.

ANVILS. Our regular stock comprises Peter Wright's Own Make Patent Solid Anvils, and also the competitive British London Pattern Anvils, Best Warranted Quality. Sizes range from ½ to 5 cwt.

Item 673—Peter Wright's Genuine 84/- per cwt.

" 674—British Make Best Ware 60/- "

Note—Anvils under 112lbs. weight cost a little more.

Saw Makers' Anvils. Item 675. Price, 100/- per cwt.

SWAGE BLOCKS. Item 676—Various sizes to 4½ cwt. Price, 80/- per cwt.

Size	[illegible]	[illegible]	[illegible]	[illegible]	[illegible]
Approx. Weight	[illegible]	[illegible]	[illegible]	[illegible]	[illegible] cwt.

WATER TUE IRONS, wrought iron, with pipes. Note.—Always fit them with cold water inlet below, and hot water [illegible] on top.

Item 677—Length	12	14	16	18	20 in.
Price	35/-	40/-	45/-	50/-	55/- each

A page from a 1924 E.S.C.A. (Engineering Supply Co. of Australia), Brisbane, catalogue.

—Courtesy Bill Dinnie

The anvil, usually about two hundredweight, has the horn or beak at one end, then a small flat surface known as the shelf or table, then the face which is the main flat surface. At the opposite end to the horn, referred to as the tail, there is a small round hole known as the pritchel hole or punching hole, and a much larger hole called the hardie hole. The hardie hole was square to accept the shank of the hardie, which was shouldered with a cutting edge. It was an easy job for the smith to cut a heated piece of iron simply by placing it on top of the hardie and hitting it with a hammer.

Other pieces which make use of the hardie hole include the bottom swage and bottom fuller. The swages have various sized half round impressions which are used with the top swage to enable hot metal to be brought to a round shape. The top and bottom fullers are the opposite to the hardie, being used to groove, draw out, or 'set' rounded corners.

Hot sets were basically a chisel on a wooden handle which the smith held over the mark on the hot iron. The striker then struck it smartly on the top to cut it through. The top fullers and top swages had handles and were used in the same manner, with the striker doing the hitting.

The better quality anvils were made by an English firm, Peter Wright, who also produced very good leg and T bar vyces.

A flatter is a tool shaped like a hammer head, but with an accurate flat surface at one end and a crowned end at the other that can be struck with a heavy hammer. It is used for dressing the hot iron to give a good flat finish and take out hammer marks.

A water tub was necessary, usually a wooden cask cut in half and holding about twenty gallons of water, sometimes known as the butt, slack tub or bosh. It had many uses, mainly quenching to harden and temper, to sprinkle on 'green' coal to stop the fire spreading, or to cool either side of a heated section so a sharp corner could be bent. It also made a handy repository for tongs around the edge. Green coal is coal which is fresh, and has not yet been changed by the heat.

Some shops had a lime box which held powdered lime to anneal hard steel, although most just relied on ashes. It was the insulating qualities of ashes, and lime, which allowed the heated steel to cool very slowly, leaving it in a workable softened state. Another thing the old smiths were aware of was that if carbon steel was left to soak too long in the fire the fuel absorbed the carbon from the heated steel. Today, this process is known as decarburising, or carbon migration.

A leg vyce was usually fastened to a short post in the shop to allow access all around. Various sized sledge hammers were used and a striker, often a man learning the trade, assisted the smith.

Some of the larger shops had swage blocks, tyre rollers, upsetting machines, straightening slabs and post drills. Outside the shop was usually a grindstone and invariably, leaning against the walls, were all sizes of tyre rims from wooden wheels.

Swage blocks were made in various sizes from cast iron and had numerous shaped half round, vee, and half hexagon impressions around the edge, whilst in the middle was an assortment of squares and rounds which were handy for punching and forming the heads on anvil tools. Alldays and Onions of Birmingham, England, and Carron, Iron Founders of Falkirk, Scotland, made excellent swage blocks.

Tyre rollers were geared, pyramid type rollers, used to curve the tyres for various sized wooden wheels. Upsetting machines saved cutting and shutting a tyre by allowing the smith to take a short heat, (about a six inch section of the rim), putting it between the jaws, and then turning a big wheel, geared to one of the jaws, which would compress, or upset, the heated portion which could then be hammered down.

The straightening slab was a large cast iron slab weighing several hundredweight with several holes drilled through it, and was used for straightening, curving, twisting and untwisting large jobs around pins inserted in the holes of the slab. It was for work which could not be done on the anvil, such as wagon axles, circle plates and turntables. These slabs were not very common, being found only in some of the large shops.

The invention of the internal combustion engine sounded the eventual knell of this once flourishing trade. The two world wars probably contributed as much as anything, as well as modern technology phasing out the work once performed by the smith. Oxy and electric welding put into the hands of ordinary men made a big impact. About 1920 would have been the peak of the craft and from then there was a gradual decline.

In this electronic age many people visualise the blacksmith as a man holding a horseshoe, a job which amounted to only a small part of his labour. Horseshoes are made now without feeling the touch of a hammer. The process consists of bars of concave iron going through an induction furnace, being clipped off and curled around a central mandrel with levers, and small rams pushing on toe clips and punching nail holes, all while still red hot, a case of technology replacing muscle.

Some old timers would still have fond memories of the village blacksmith, reliving the time they sat around and watched him work, and nodding approval when he completed a job.

Alas, the disciples of Tubal Cain have now joined the ranks of coopers, riveters, tailors and many other honourable tradespeople. As a matter of interest, Tubal Cain was known as the first artificer in metals.

An anecdote as to why the smith taps the anvil between blows is told in legend thus:- In the distant past the devil used to be shod. He always picked out the same old smith and never paid. Consequently the time came when the smith decided to put an end to it. He prepared a chain, wrapped it around the anvil stump and clenched it with a rivet. When the devil came in, the smith, with his back to the devil, picked up his hoof, wrapped the chain end around the ankle and as quick as a flash whacked a rivet into the chain to hold it. The smith then left, while the devil cursed and ranted, but was never able to get free. Symbolically, all smiths tap the anvil between blows to keep the chain secured so the devil cannot escape.

The photos on this page show Bill in the smithy in June 1997, when he handed the business over to his son, Andy.

—Courtesy Seven News

For those wishing to see what a blacksmith's shop really looked like, Bill Dinnie, along with other volunteers, has set up a realistic smithy, with many of Bill's original tools displayed, in the Proserpine Museum, on the Bruce Highway.

There is a box of rasps and other shoeing gear in the foreground, as well as a hitch ring which Bill made to show what they looked like. As Bill said, every second awning post in any town had one.

The Blacksmiths Shop, Proserpine Museum.
Photo Bill Dinnie.

Gulf Spurmaker

Georgetown, Normanton, Croydon, Queensland

NOEL WILLIAMS, of Camooweal told me of an old timber-cutter and blacksmith who used to work around Georgetown, Normanton and Croydon in the Gulf country of Queensland during the 1930s and 1940s. Noel cannot recall his name, but he had a travelling sawmill and workshop, pulled behind a horse-drawn waggon, cutting timber for gates and making metal buckets for wells.

The spurs he made were straight necked, the heel bands and necks being about 25 millimetres in depth, with large rollers. The heel bands were shaped in the forge and the necks were then welded on in the forge. For studs he used the rivets which were used at that time when making iron water tanks.

Fred Gutte

Wave Hill, Northern Territory

FREDERICK WILLIAM GUTTE is certainly the best known of Australia's outback spurmakers. Born in 1889 at Tarcowie, west of Peterborough, South Australia, he worked as a blacksmith and farrier for his father Charlie, and took over the business when Charlie and other members of the family moved to Port Pirie.

Fred and other blacksmiths who had some mechanical flair provided help to early motorists in those times, though his niece is quoted as saying, "This was just a hobby for Fred, he was always a blacksmith at heart." He closed the shop, probably at the end of 1943, and went to the Northern Territory as a blacksmith for the Vestey company, starting at Manbulloo station near Katherine, in April, 1944 and he remained in their employ for the rest of his working life.

red photographed at Caltowie.

—Courtesy Betty Burns

Teresa Donnellan in her book *Tarcowie, Place of Washaway Water* has numerous references to the Gutte family. Fred was a noted accordionist and Tarcowie was said to be 'a home of harmonious blacksmiths'.

This photo of the Gutte family shows Fred with his parents, brother, three sisters and niece taken outside the family home at Tarcowie about 1912. From left to right they are Oliver Charles Gutte, Alice Kotz with her daughter Melva, Florence Lemm with her hand on her father, John Charles Gutte, Fred, leaning on the chair where his mother Mary is seated, and Myrtle Larsson.

Mrs Betty Burns of Adelaide, the daughter of Myrtle Larsson, remembers Uncle Fred well. He lived at Goodwood, Adelaide, with her parents when he returned from the Northern Territory in the late 1950s. Eventually he set up a small forge and, amongst other things made small spurs for her sons and a basket ball ring for her daughter.

Mrs Burns sent me the photo of Fred taken at Caltowie (previous page), and later wrote, "Fred would have been about forty years old when his mother died. He had a keen eye for the ladies and was very particular in his appearance. He was engaged in his younger days to a schoolteacher but nothing came of that."

Mrs Kay Cavanagh of Victoria, the daughter of Melva Kotz, provided the photo of Fred, right, taken in the late 1950s or '60s in Adelaide when Fred was living at Goodwood.

From comments made by the people who knew Fred he was a quiet man, well liked and respected, and was certainly a master blacksmith. He made

—*Photo of Gutte family courtesy Geof Gutte, grandson of Oliver Charles Gutte*

his spurs over a period of eleven or twelve years, from about 1945 until 1957 or 1958.

I have examined many of Fred's spurs, from Rodney Watson's made in 1946, to those of the mid 1950s. They are all basically the same style, with only minor variations. It seems that he developed the design while at Manbulloo, where he made his first pair, moving to Wave Hill soon after in 1946. This observation is further supported by Bill Hamill's comments later in this section, about Fred experimenting with old spurs at Manbulloo and his belief that one type of spur should be made which was suitable for everyone.

Fred's spurs were called the Wave Hill spur and were made to fit snugly on the heel of the Cuban heeled elastic sided riding boots worn by the majority of drovers and ringers at that time. From my own experience I would best describe Fred's spurs as being "at one with the boot."

Being hand forged from whatever mild steel was available at the time, different pairs were not necessarily identical although each spur of a pair was carefully matched. The rollers varied, and although the studs were often hand made he sometimes used tank bolts. The length of the neck or depth of the heel band was likewise variable.

Fred made his spurs to fit different boot sizes and an examination of many of his spurs confirms this. The inside width of the heel band, measured from side to side where the studs are fitted, varies from 77 to 87 millimetres. Similarly, the neck measurement, taken in a straight line from the roller pin to the top of the neck where it joins the heel band, varies from 60 to 80 millimetres. Original Gutte rollers studied have 7, 8, 9, 11 or 16 points and diameters from 37 to 42 millimetres.

As Len Hill has described, the heel band and neck of each spur were crafted from one piece of steel.

The 'trade mark' which distinguishes Fred's spurs is the grooves, filed with a round file at an angle on each side of the neck, at the base where it joins the heel band. These grooves created a projection or 'point' which can be seen in most of the photographs of his spurs.

These 'points' are more pronounced on some spurs and the mismatched pair shown on page 134 (Grant Unsted's spurs) shows the degree of variation.

Sometimes Fred would file the grooves on each side of the neck only, and at other times he would also draw the round file across the underside of the neck. This would join the side grooves and accentuate the 'point', as can be seen on Grant Unsted's spur on the right hand side of the photo on page 134 and also on George Booth's spur on page 23.

By contrast the 'points' on Blue Ellis' spurs, page 67, are not so evident as is also clearly illustrated here in these three photographs of Peter LeDuff's spurs. It can be seen that Fred has used a flat file on the underside of the neck, removing the 'point', but always leaving the distinctive side grooves visible.

The close up photos of the neck also demonstrate that Fred finished the ends of the rowel pins with a flat file, or with the hammer, making them flush with the surface of the neck. Screws were never used.

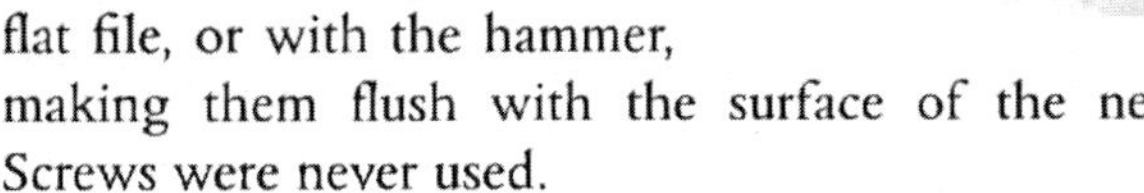

Without exception all authentic Gutte spurs I have examined have straight heel bands, rounded at the end where the strap studs are fitted. They are never turned downwards, as are, for example, the Barry Blain Wave Hill copies on page 162 and some of the modern copies currently being retailed.

Nor did Fred bend the neck of the spur toward the horse, as in the Willoughby design and many other rodeo spurs where there is a definite difference between the left and right spurs. Looking from above the neck of the Wave Hill is perfectly straight, so either spur of a pair can be used on either boot, as can be seen in the photograph below.

Bill Hammill was head stockman on Manbulloo station and was there when Fred arrived in the west season of 1945. The following extract from Bill's book, *Don't Trot the Bullocks*, details his recollection of Fred.

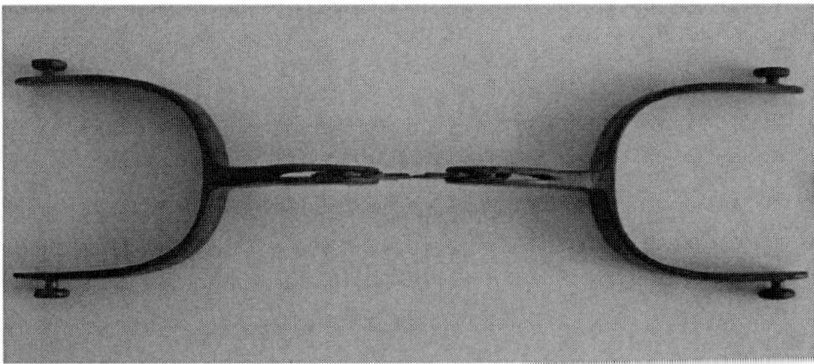

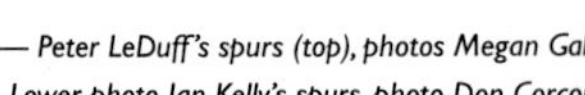

— Peter LeDuff's spurs (top), photos Megan Gal
Lower photo Ian Kelly's spurs, photo Don Corcor

Fred and Spurs

"Another character at Manbulloo was a blacksmith named Fred Gutte, who manufactured the Wave Hill spur, which was well known in the 50s and 60s in the Kimberley, the Northern Territory and Western Queensland. Fred came to Manbulloo in the late 40s [Bill has confirmed in recent correspondence that both he and Fred arrived at Manbulloo in April, 1944.—Don C.] while I was head stockman there. Born in South Australia, he grew up in a small town on the Murray River [Fred was born at Tarcowie, west of Peterborough in South Australia.—Don C.]. His father had been a blacksmith and Fred had followed the same trade. His mother had died when he was a youngster [Fred's mother died on 4th February, 1926, when Fred was 37 years old.—Don C.] and he and his father carried on the business for many years. The work was mainly among the farming people of the time, sharpening and repairing farming implements, repairing wheels on buggies, wagons and drays and shoeing farm horses. When his father retired Fred carried on the business on his own and cared for his father as well.

"After his father's death he decided to get out and see a bit of the world. He told me a few of his experiences during the Depression of the 30s. On one occasion, he had walked out five miles (eight kilometres), shod eight draught horses in the day and received in payment a bag of vegetables that he carried home the five miles on his shoulder.

"One Saturday morning he received a big surprise. He was in town, wondering how best to spend a small amount of money he had in his pocket, when a customer he had done work for caught up with him and paid £3/12/6 ($7.25). He immediately bought himself a new suit for £3 ($6) which left him 12/6 ($1.25) for a bit of tucker and a few beers at about threepence (3c) a pot during the afternoon. However, on his way around town, he met his S.P. bookie and splurged with a three shilling (60c) bet. The horse came home at 25 to 1, and I could imagine his feeling, after starting the day with just sufficient coins in his pocket to make a jingle. 'Father and I lived like kings for a week,' he told me.

"When he got to Manbulloo, it was during the Wet season. As I had always been interested in that type of work and there was not much other work to be done, I spent a lot of time in the smithy shop and did quite a bit of striking for him. He did not mind passing on his techniques and I became quite handy at shaping a bit of iron or steel. It used to amaze me that Fred could do in about two taps what I used to do in about a dozen; he could almost make a bit of metal talk. To see him welding two pieces of steel was fascinating. He would get them at the right heat, dip them in a bit of sand and borax, lay them together and with one hit they were welded together forever. I used to try, sometimes successfully, but mostly without success. He used to refer to first heat and second red heat and so on, but I never became very adept at reading those heats. As far as I was concerned, it was cold before it went into the forge and red when it got hot.

"It was at Manbulloo that Fred became interested in spurs, as there was always a drover about wanting a spur repaired or altered or a set of rowels made. He admitted to me that he doubted he had seen a pair of spurs before he came to the Territory. He used to look at all the different types of spurs that were brought to him for repairs and confide in me that one type of spur should be made which was suitable for everyone. While I was assisting him, he experimented a little on old spurs, fiddling and reshaping them to fit the boot.

"One day he announced to me that, come Saturday, he was going to have a go at manufacturing a pair of spurs to his own design. Of course, I was not going to miss out on the first experiment, so I spent the day in the shop with him. That first pair did not have much in common with the later patented Wave Hill spur, but at least I was a witness to the first pair of spurs made by Fred.

A rocker arm broke on one of the old Packard motor cars that were the only vehicles on Manbulloo. One could not be found in Australia to replace it, so that was one of the only two vehicles off the road. Fred was a bit slack one day so he asked the mechanic for one of the complete rockers and he would have a go at knocking one up. He succeeded and as far as I know that rocker arm remained in the vehicle until it was pensioned off.

"He was transferred to Wave Hill Station shortly after this, and it was not long before he had perfected the ideal stockman's spur that fitted perfectly and snugly on the R. M. Williams Cuban heeled riding boot that was worn by 90 per cent of the stockmen and drovers in the North. Fred must have made hundreds of pairs during his time in the North. I have given my spurs to the Stockman's Hall of Fame, as my Yamaha does not really require them during a day's muster.

"Fred was a big man and he had a hearty appetite as some of the stockmen of the time could tell you. Ten minutes before the tucker bell, Fred could be seen heading towards the feed bag and as the first gong went Fred had a foot inside the door. Any other employee who was ten minutes late usually saw Fred having his third helping of goodies, that should have been their first helping.

"To see him in the bush, one would never think that romance would have ever been in his make-up, but I met him in Adelaide when we were on holidays. He knew the town pretty well and he took me to a few outings at night, where he had a wonderful time, usually dancing the night away with all the bright young things. He was well over 15 stone (95 kilograms), but I was told he was a wonderful dancer and as light as a feather on his feet. Never judge a book by its cover.

"I once borrowed him from Wave Hill when I was managing Ord River, to do up the donkey wagon wheels and a few other jobs. When he finished I told him I would book him on the plane the following week, to return to Wave Hill.

"'Don't do that, Bill,' he implored 'I've got about a ton of scrap picked out from your rubbish heap that I want to take back.' Fred never missed out on a bit of scrap that could be made into spurs or brands for his private use He was given a truck and driver for his return."

* * *

Bruce Simpson in his book *Pack Horse Drover* says of Fred:

> Spurs were not used on every horse. However, all ringers owned a pair. The length of the spur neck was usually two and a half or three and a half inches (6-9 centimetres), longer than the English Cavalry spur, because stockmen rode with longer stirrup leathers and with legs forward. Blacksmiths played an important role in outback life. The smithy who made the famous Condamine bells from old saw blades was one; Fred Gutte was another. Fred was employed by Vestey's as a blacksmith on Wave Hill station in the Northern Territory. In his spare time he made and sold the famous Wave Hill spurs – acclaimed by horsemen throughout the North-West as the best spur ever produced.

Clarrie Pankhurst, in the book *The Boss Drover and his Mates* by Anne Marie Ingham says:

> I'd bought myself a pair of Wave Hill gooseneck spurs. There was a saddler and blacksmith named Fred Gutte at Wave Hill and he used to make spurs out of spring steel. He'd beat them out in the forge. Best spurs out, and if a drover didn't have a pair of these he was like the cockie on the biscuit tin, he just wasn't in it.

In 1950, Cecilia Senior wrote of Fred in an article, titled 'They're Racing at the Negri', which appeared in *A. M. Magazine:*

> Blacksmith Gutte, Territory craftsman, beat out a few pairs of his famous spurs, coveted trophies for the Blackfellows' Derby and the natives' rodeo events.

In the section 'The Horsemen', a pair of gold plated Wave Hill trophy spurs, won by Lloyd L. Fogarty, of Timber Creek, Northern Territory, is illustrated.

Fred Gutte died in Adelaide, in 1971, and was cremated at Centennial Park Crematorium.

An additional stone, engraved with the words 'Frederick William Gutte, Eldest Son Of Above, Died 20th Sept. 1971. Aged 82 Years', is attached to the headstone on his parents' grave in West Terrace Cemetery, Adelaide, position AYR E NORTH, Path 4, Plot 4, West, and implies that Fred's ashes are buried there, although this is not confirmed by cemetery records.

In 2005 I was contacted by Peter Cause of Cause Contracting Pty Ltd, based in Maleny, Queensland. Cause Contracting is a family business which has been building quality steel cattle yards across Northern Australia for over forty years. Their range of activity extends from the east coast, through Queensland and across the Top End to the Kimberley.

Peter had replaced the 'Old Station Yard' on Wave Hill with 'Cause's Yard', which is capable of handling 5000 head of cattle, in 2005. Over the years he had heard of the blacksmith Fred Gutte, and his legendary Wave Hill spurs, so he though it fitting to make and erect a sign on the site of the old blacksmith's shop, which had been near the original homestead.

The sign is made of 8 millimetre plate steel, and is 900 millimetres wide and 900 millimetres high. Peter chalked on the wording on the plate and then formed the letters with weld. As can be seen in the photograph, the sign, like the Wave Hill spurs, is intended to last for a generation or two.

Peter Cause's Sign, Wave Hill.
Photo Peter Cause.

THIS MARKS THE SITE OF THE OLD WAVE HILL STATION BLACKSMITH SHOP – HOME OF "THE WAVE HILL SPUR" MADE HERE BY FRED GUTTE 1946–56.

Isis Downs Blacksmith

Isisford, Queensland

IN SEPTEMBER 1999, Ralph G Proctor of Lilydale Victoria wrote to the Australian Stockman's Hall of Fame about his days as a young man in Queensland. Ralph was born in 1915 and from 1935 until 1939 worked on Isis Downs for Bruce Johnson, looking after the studs.

While there, he had a pair of spurs forged by the station blacksmith, whose name he cannot recall. Each spur was made from one piece of metal, the slot for the rowels being cut with a hacksaw.

"For each spur the blacksmith used a piece of mild steel, about 10 inches long, by 1 inch by $^{3}/_{16}$ of an inch, cutting it down about 6 inches with a hacksaw. He measured the width of my riding boot and shaped the heel band around the anvil horn while the steel was almost white hot. He shaped the neck upwards at the rowel end, in preparation to be cut with the hacksaw to fit the rowel.

"He cleaned and filled the rough patches inside the heel band with solder, finishing it off smoothly with a file. The studs were ready made rivets which he cut to length, tapered slightly, and tapped into a tight fitting hole, burring it over inside the heel band. He did not make the rowels but used bought ones, but we cut off the tips as they were far too sharp and dangerous if one tripped over. These spurs are made to be worn with the neck curved up."

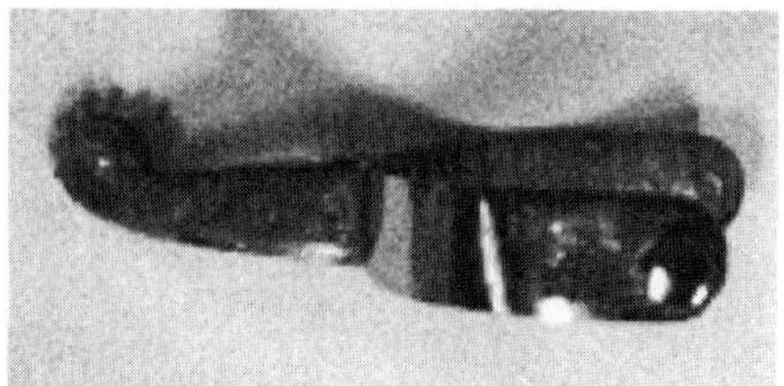

Top: An aerial view of Isis Downs taken about 1936.
—Photo courtesy Ralph Proctor

Above: One of Ralph's spurs, which were chrome-plated many years later.
—Photo Jenny Wilson/Australian Stockman's Hall Of Fame

Weary Lade

Proserpine, Queensland

I had first heard of Weary Lade's fancy spurs and rollers from Noel Williams in Camooweal. Noel gave me a couple of names to follow up and eventually I was able to locate Weary's nephew, Bill Lade in Proserpine.

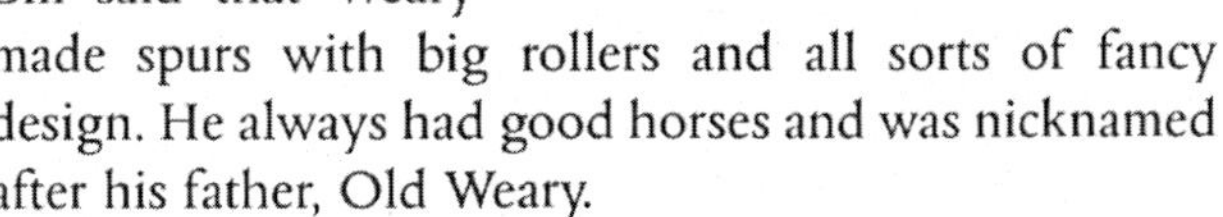

I learned that William George "Weary" Lade, was a blacksmith at the sugar mill in Proserpine and a pickup man at the local rodeos. He died in 1960 aged 46 years. Bill said that Weary made spurs with big rollers and all sorts of fancy design. He always had good horses and was nicknamed after his father, Old Weary.

Bill Dinnie, blacksmith of Proserpine, wrote that: "Weary learned the trade from his father Old Weary, who was an excellent smith. I remember Weary making spurs for some station hands and, like me, he often used the pieces out of emery dressers for rowels. The last pair that he made to my knowledge were for himself. He used to be one of the pickup men at the local rodeo and wanted a fancy pair for himself. He was lucky in a sense that the mill had a good machine shop.

"For his fancy spurs he used spring steel and the rowels were stainless steel about 2 inches (50 millimetres) in diameter and were a work of art when finished. Between every second tooth he made a saw cut and drilled a hole between each saw cut.

"With his earlier spurs, before using stainless steel, he would solder two rowel blanks together and then cut and drill them so that they ended up identical. It is so much easier to cut thicker material with a hacksaw rather than cutting them singly."

Bill Dinnie also told me that Weary always wore white jodhpurs, jacket, a small brimmed hat and high boots when riding in shows or as pickup man at rodeos, and a wide brimmed hat when working in the bush.

Top: Weary in the 1950s.

—Photo right courtesy Bill Lade. Photo left courtesy Bill Dinnie

Above: A sketch of how Weary cut and drilled his rowels.

—Courtesy Longina Phillips Designs

George or Mick Madigan

Quilpie, Queensland

In December 1996, Bryan Colquhoun of Flaxton, Queensland, wrote the following in the Australian Stockman's Hall of Fame newspaper:

> Do any of your older members remember the spurs made by George Madigan in the 1930s and '40s? George was a blacksmith on Mount Margaret in the Quilpie area, and there were a good many of his hand made spurs in south-western Queensland. I believe he favoured an axle from a T Model Ford as material for spurs.

I have spoken to a number of drovers and ringers who told me they knew of a Mick Madigan around Quilpie and Longreach in the 1940s but to date I have found no further information about this blacksmith.

Nick Magnoli

Victoria River Downs, Northern Territory

Nick Magnoli was blacksmith on Gordon Downs before he moved to Victoria River Downs on 19th August, 1955, where he stayed until 18th October, 1958. I understand that he began making spurs while at V.R.D. which were similar in style to Fred Gutte's spurs.

At left is a Magnoli spur, formerly owned by Jack Wheeler, head stockman on Helen Springs in the 1970s. The neck is brazed onto the heel band.

—Collection of Guy Thomas, Aberdeen, NSW. Photo Don Corcoran

Niel Sorenson

Injune, Queensland

Bruce Simpson told me in one of his letters that he had heard of a blacksmith spurmaker named Sorenson, at Injune, who made swan neck spurs which he stamped with his name. This information had come from a friend of Bruce, the late Rae Webster, who was a collector of spurs and who I later met at Bruce's home.

Rae did not have any examples of Sorenson spurs but a letter to the Australian Stockman's Hall of Fame newspaper provided the following information from Vic (Splinter) Chalk of Roma, Queensland, which he had gleaned from Bruce Sorenson of Injune.

> Niel Sorenson went to Injune from Western Australia in a wagon pulled by a black horse called 'Darkie' (Bruce didn't know the year). He set up a blacksmith's shop where he made spurs out of dog spikes from railway sleepers (very unusual material I thought). He also made other things as well and no doubt he would have shod horses etc.
>
> He spoke about a golden horse and when he died, people looked for this golden horse but it turned out he had a horse ornament tacked up above the front door of the shop and it was painted gold. That is all I can give you on his life in Injune but Bruce also told me he was buried in Roma Cemetery.
>
> So I contacted our Roma Town Council and they provided wonderful help and sent me photocopies of all information. He died at the age of 89 years in 1959 and his grave is position 084N at the cemetery. My wife and I went out to the cemetery and located a bare piece of ground, but no grave number, marker or headstone.

Roy Wolfe

Brunette Downs, Northern Territory

Rodney Watson of Mount Isa, Queensland has told me of Roy Wolfe who worked on Brunette Downs in the late 1930s or early '40s and who made spurs at that time.

Bruce Simpson in his *Hell, Highwater & Hard Cases* says of Roy Wolfe: 'Originally from Wellshot in Queensland, Wolfe worked in the Northern Territory. A very good man on a rough horse.'

I have included here a poem familiar to many of my generation from primary school days, Henry Wadsworth Longfellow's 'The Village Blacksmith', written in 1840. Longfellow was an American, born in 1807, a fact that surprises many people who believe he was writing about the typical British blacksmith, but he did have English ancestors and travelled in England often. It is interesting that after his death in 1882, his bust was placed in the Poet's Corner of Westminster Abbey, for his fame was almost as truly British as American.

Although there were quite a few claims by blacksmiths in both England and America who believed they were the inspiration for the words, it is most likely that the blacksmith's shop in Cambridge, Massachusetts, complete with a spreading chestnut tree, was the one he wrote about. The smith's name was Dexter Pratt, and Longfellow used to pass the smithy daily on his way to Harvard College, and often stopped to watch the smith at work.

The Village Blacksmith

Under a spreading chestnut tree
The village smithy stands;
The smith, a mighty man is he,
With large and sinewy hands;
And the muscles of his brawny arms
Are strong as iron bands.

His hair is crisp, and black, and long;
His face is like the tan;
His brow is wet with honest sweat,
He earns whate'er he can,
And looks the whole world in the face,
For he owes not any man.

Week in, week out, from morn till night,
You can hear his bellows blow;
You can hear him swing his heavy sledge,
With measured beat and slow,
Like a sexton ringing the village bell,
When the evening sun is low.

And children coming home from school
Look in at the open door;
They love to see the flaming forge,
And hear the bellows roar,
And catch the burning sparks that fly
Like chaff from a threshing-floor.

He goes on Sunday to the church,
And sits among his boys;
He hears the parson pray and preach,
He hears his daughter's voice
Singing in the village choir,
And it makes his heart rejoice.

It sounds to him like her mother's voice
Singing in Paradise!
He needs to think of her once more,
How in the grave she lies;
And with his hard rough hand he wipes
A tear out of his eyes.

Toiling,—rejoicing,—sorrowing,
Onward through life he goes;
Each morning sees some task begin,
Each evening sees it close;
Something attempted, something done,
Has earned a night's repose.

Thanks, thanks to thee, my worthy friend,
For the lesson thou hast taught!
Thus at the flaming forge of life
Our fortunes must be wrought;
Thus, on its sounding anvil shaped
Each burning deed and thought.

the spur designers

IP Australia is the Federal Government organisation which has the responsibility for examining and granting Australian patents, as well as administering the patents, trade marks and designs systems within Australia.

Until the 1960s applications for spurs were listed under *Class 39-7, Harness for Control*, which is a sub-set of *Class 39, Harness and Animal Power.* However, at the present time applications relating to spurs would be listed under *Group 44, Boots and Shoes.*

Research of IP Australia records, from 1904 to 1960, has gleaned the following information :

At no time did Deal Adams or Fred Gutte apply for a patent.

1904, W. H. Connelly lodged Application number 1561 for spurs and number 1562 for 'securing rowels to spurs'. No further detail of this application can be found.

Stan Morgan

Port Lincoln, South Australia, 1946

Stan Morgan applied for a Provisional Patent for the Morgan Rigid spur in 1945 and the patent was granted in 1948. Stan entered into an agreement with R. M. Williams to manufacture the spur, the arrangement being that he would be paid a 5 shillings royalty for each pair sold.

At about that time the Tom Willoughby produced his spur, which proved very popular and overshadowed the Rigid spur.

Stan believes that only about 50 pairs were manufactured, and perhaps 20 pairs sold. I have not been able to find any advertisements for Stan's spur in R. M. Williams catalogues or *Hoofs and Horns* magazines of that period.

The following is from the records of IP Australia, formerly the Department of Patents, Commonwealth of Australia, and by permission of Stan Morgan.

The Morgan Rigid Spur.
—Photo Jenny Wilson/Australian Stockman's Hall of Fame

Patent Specification 127,464

Application Date: 15th Sept., 1945. No. 23,320/45.

Applicant and Actual Inventor. Stanley Germain Morgan, of South Australia.

Assignee. Percival Lincoln Puckridge.

Complete Specification after Provisional Specification, Lodged 15th July, 1946.

Complete Specification, Accepted 15th April, 1948.

Complete Specification

"Improvements in and relating to spurs."

We, Percival Lincoln Puckridge, of Port Lincoln, State of South Australia, Commonwealth of Australia. Grazier, British Subject, and Stanley Germain Morgan, of Coulta, State of South Australia aforesaid, Grazier, British Subject, hereby declare this invention and the manner in which it is to be performed to be fully described and ascertained in and by the following statement:

This invention relates to improvements in and to spurs. Spurs have heretofore been made in a variety of shapes and these usually comprise a pointed star wheel or disc supported in a vertical slot in a member projecting from a U-shaped frame which is adapted to engage the heel or rear portion of the wearer's shoe or boot and is held to the shoe or boot by means of a strap or straps fastened to the U-shaped frame. To obtain added rigidity it has been proposed to provide an additional holding strap which is intended to engage around the front of the heel to hold the spur downwards in a more or less rigid fixture.

It is the object of this invention to so construct the frame of the spur that the said spur will be rigidly held to the wearer's boot and in this way ensure that the spur will move with the boot and be under better control.

According to our invention the rowel is formed in such a manner that it may be horizontally or vertically disposed and is supported in a slot in a member projecting from the spur frame which is adapted to fit around the back part of the boot immediately above the heel but this frame is formed so that the front portion of the spur frame is adapted to be disposed immediately to the front of the heel and this member bears against the underside of the sole at the junction of the heel to the waist portion of the boot, the rear part of the spur frame being so shaped as to accommodate the rear part of the boot and having connected to it a strap by which a forward pressure is given to the spur frame which pressure then holds the spur frame rigidly to the boot.

To enable this invention to be more clearly understood it will now be described in some detail with reference to the accompanying drawings in which:

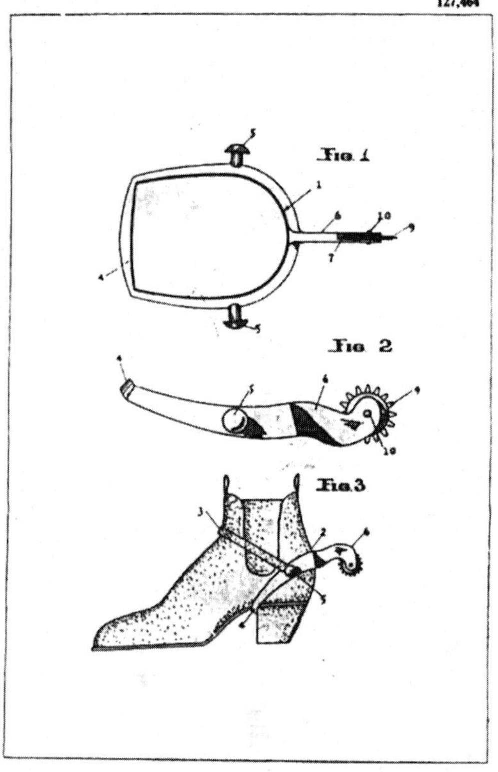

Fig. 1 is a plan of the spur frame and rowel.
Fig. 2 is a side elevation of the same, and
Fig. 3 is a side elevation showing the spur attached to the boot.

That portion of the spur frame which accommodates the boot is so formed that the rear part **1** is approximately the same configuration as that portion of the boot **2** to which it is held by means of a strap **3**. The forward part **4** of the spur frame is formed in such a manner that it may pass under the heel and be accommodated at the juncture of the heel and the waist. Attached to the external surface of this frame are studs or rivets **5** to which are attached straps **3** which may be passed over the forward part of the boot and by adjusting same the spur frame can be held firmly against the boot of the wearer.

An outwardly extending member **6** attached to the spur frame has formed in it a slot or groove **7** in which the rowel **9** is free to rotate about a pin **10**, said member **6** being of such a configuration as to hold the rowel **9** in its correct horizontal or vertical alignment when the spur is attached to the wearers boot. The forward pressure supplied by the adjustment of the strap **3** then gives a two point support to the spur frame, ensuring that the spur must at all times move with the boot.

Having now fully described and ascertained our said invention and the manner in which it is to be performed, we declare that what we claim is:

1. In spurs improvements wherein the rowel is supported upon a frame, said frame being adapted to fit around a boot in such a manner that said frame is supported at its one end by the rear of the boot, at its other end by the junction of the heel and the waist of said boot, and the said frame is supported by a strap intermediate the length of the frame, the said strap passing around the boot.

2. In spurs improvements wherein the rowel is supported upon a frame, said frame being shaped to fit around a boot in such a manner that said frame is supported at its one end by the rear portion of the boot immediately above the heel and supported at its other end by the junction of the heel and the waist of

the boot, and has a supporting strap detachably secured to it intermediate its length said strap passing around the boot.

3. In spurs improvement according to any preceding claim wherein the frame is formed of a curved portion at its rear to fit around the rear of the boot above the heel and has a substantially straight portion at its front to fit around the junction of the waist and the heel of the boot.

4. In spurs improvements constructed substantially as described and illustrated.

Dated this 22nd day of October, 1947.

Percival Lincoln Puckridge, and Stanley Germain Morgan.

By their Patent Attorneys,

Collison & Co.,

Fellows Institute of Patent Attorneys of Australia.

Witness—A. R. Donnell.

Born in Port Lincoln, South Australia, on 21st April, 1916, Stan grew up in the Mount Dutton Bay area on the Eyre Peninsula. His grandfather bought Warrow station in the late 1800s, trading as D. Morgan and Sons, and the Coffin Bay country was purchased by some of his sons in 1933 for £750. These properties were subsequently sold to the National Parks and Wildlife Service in 1976.

Stan was involved in running gymkhanas and then rodeos on the Eyre Peninsula from the 1940s into the 1950s, and acted as pickup man at these events. In 1956 Stan was on the committee which organised a rodeo at Cummins. A month later, using the same horses, they held the South Australian State Championship at Wanilla, riding under Australian Rough Riders Association rules, with the top riders of the day attending. Initially these events were arranged to raise money for a Soldier Settlers' Hall at Wanilla, a goal which was achieved within five years.

Stan told me of his interest in sailing.

"In 1967 I crewed with Joska Grubic on 'Adria' in the 1967 Sydney Hobart yacht race. I then designed my own yacht, *Iniquity*, and had it built of steel at Whyalla. She is 50 feet, with a 12 feet

Stan cruising in Iniquity, *1988.*
—Photo courtesy Stan Morgan

maximum beam and is a beautiful fast seaworthy boat. I sailed her in the 1983 and 1986 Sydney Hobart races and I am prouder of her now than when I owned her.

'The present owner took her to the Antarctic in 1992 and then did the Brisbane Osaka race, coming 4th in his Division. His last trip was south of New Zealand where he struck a 'bomb', which is a super freak storm that rolled them, with a minimum of damage."

Stan also sent me a photo of a saddle that he designed, shown below.

'I had this saddle custom built by Eddie Powell, now of Jimboomba, near Brisbane. It has 4 inch padded pig ear pads, all built into a Ralide tree. These pads are kept 2 inches clear of the thighs to allow the legs to swing forward when the horse bucks. The stirrup flaps are also kept well forward for that reason. Result, the perfect saddle.'

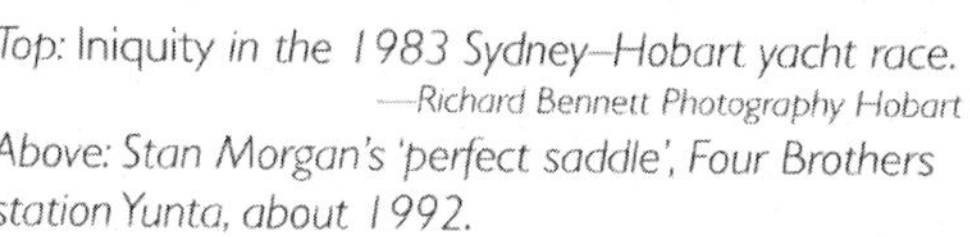

Top: Iniquity in the 1983 Sydney–Hobart yacht race.

—Richard Bennett Photography Hobart

Above: Stan Morgan's 'perfect saddle', Four Brothers station Yunta, about 1992.

—Photo courtesy Stan Morgan.

Hans Benson

Baralaba, Queensland, 1946

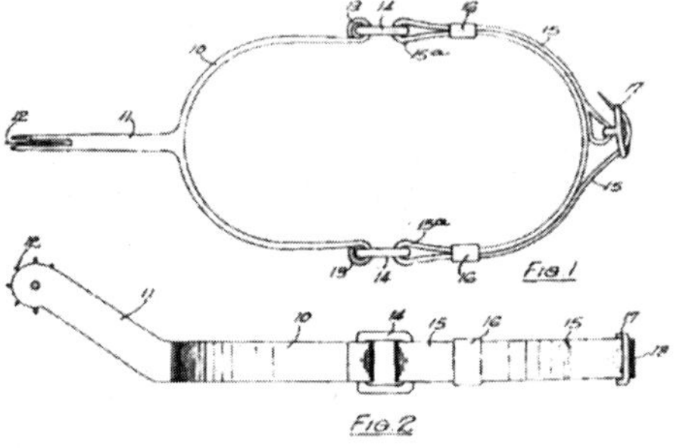

On the 16th April, 1946, Patent No. 121,365 was granted to Hans Benson, farmer, of Baralaba, Queensland, for an "Improved Spur".

A complete specification and drawing is on file, detailing "The object of this invention is to provide an improved spur which will be comfortable to the wearer, will not damage the wearer's boot and will be securely fastened to the boot."

Hans Benson's design eliminated the need for studs to secure the spur strap and instead has the ends of the heel band turned outwards to enclose a square dee link on each side. A single long strap is passed through the dee links and is buckled together over the instep to secure the spur on the boot. Metal keepers on each side, where the strap loops through the dee links, limit the size of the loops and hold the two parallel running sections of the strap together.

Basil Campbell McNairn

Pechey, Queensland, 1947

On the 19th February, 1947, Basil Campbell McNairn, farmer and grazier of Waratah, Pechey, Crows Nest Line, Queensland, lodged an application for a patent for his "Safety Spur Fastener". A complete specification was lodged on 10th November, 1947, but subsequently lapsed and no patent was granted.

Basil McNairn described his invention, "For the fastening of spurs to rider's boots, in the place of a leather strap over the instep, made of galvanised steel 1/16 inch thick, curved in the shape of the spur itself, with sliding cuts on each end."

The drawing attached to the specification shows a metal 'strap', with keyhole slots at each end designed to admit the head of the strap stud on a spur, and then lock into place, "thus making it impossible to lose spurs fitted with the Safety Spur Fasteners of which I am the inventor."

Tom Willoughby

Crookwell, New South Wales

Tom Willoughby was one of the founding members of the Australian Rough Rider's Association (ARRA) in 1945 and was a popular and legendary roughrider of the 1940s and 1950s.

Tom's brother, Greg, of Eton, Queensland sent me this photo of Tom, and wrote the following:

"The spurs were designed by Tom in 1946 and made and sold by R. M. Williams of Prospect, South Australia. They were designed primarily with rodeo in mind but were very popular with campdrafters as well as for general stock work.

"They were a very snug fit on an R M. Williams riding boot and had two sizes of rollers. These could be changed with a screw that once tightened would not come loose.

"Tom first started rodeoing around 1938-9 and in 1945 was an inaugural member of the Australian Rough Riders Association (ARRA) which is now called The Australian Professional Rodeo Association, (APRA). He served as president for three years and was always on call as an advisory member. He retired from rodeo in 1956 with eleven Australian titles and the only rider to have held an Australian title in each rodeo event and to hold four titles simultaneously.

"Tom was a judge for many years after his retirement but unfortunately had a bad accident in later life and passed away in February, 1992."

The following is an extract from a tribute to Tom, which appeared in the *APRA Rodeo News*, written in 1992 by Peter Poole.

> There were ten boys and four girls in the Willoughby family, and riding horses was a way of life that they became accustomed to at a very early age.
>
> All the boys took part in rodeos, and it was Tom, with brothers Kevin and Les, and a cousin Allen, who begin to make a name for themselves on the circuit of shows, rodeos and gymkhanas.
>
> Tom was first to join the ARRA in 1945 and held badge number 34. Two years later he was named the All-Round Champion, a feat he was to duplicate in 1951. To this day he is the only contestant to win a National title in the then five major events, and also at one period or another finished the season as the top money winner in all the major contests.

> In 1951 the hard fought tussle for the All-Round Championship was between Tom Willoughby and Kevin McTaggart. This was eventually decided at the National Titles at Rockhampton held in late September.
>
> Kevin McTaggart had drawn Sheik, a tough Springsure (Queensland) outlaw, who could be bad news in the chute. Kevin got a bad start and was bucked off, but Tom had his own problems. He drew Wombi, a stout bronc who had bucked him off at this same rodeo in 1949.
>
> Wombi was seventeen years old and had never been ridden to time, with a string of victories that had surpassed the 500 mark. When Tom called for the gate, it seemed everything was forgotten in a display of arena action that had quickly built up to a crescendo of uncontrolled excitement.
>
> When the whistle finally blew it was duly noted that the rider had lost a stirrup iron right at the conclusion of the ride. The subsequent loss of points could cost him the National title, plus the strong possibility of not being the 1951 All-Round Champion.
>
> A storm of protest erupted as it was as it was obvious to everyone that the time signal had been given very late and this was most sportingly supported by Kevin McTaggart, as this would cost him the major award at the end of the year. The judges conferred, and they recognised that the time had been exceptionally long and thus made no penalty for the loss of the stirrup iron. Tom Willoughby was the new champion.

More recently I spoke to Tom's brother, Jack Willoughby of Coffs Harbour, New South Wales, who was involved in the early design of the Willoughby spur:

"About 1939 Tom and I were breaking in horses around Trangie and Narromine, Tom was older than me by about fifteen months. The spurs I had then were fairly heavy with long necks and I took them into a blacksmith wheelwright, just out of Trangie on the Narromine road, and got him to shorten the necks and bend them towards the horse. Both Tom and I used to ride in the rodeos and my idea was to be able to spur without turning the toe outwards. That was the beginning of the Willoughby spur.

"Soon after that I joined the Army and when I next saw Tom, about 1943, he had developed the under strap, and the triangular dees for the top

Jack, aged 84 years, with a horse he broke in for his daughter, Townsville 2002.

—Photo courtesy Jack Willoughby

Willoughby Spur

Patent Design

Price 47/6

- **Necks bent towards the horse.**
- **Patent triangular loops to keep spurs rigid.**
- **Special screw for quick change of rowel if spurs required for ordinary stock work.**

SPUR DESIGNED AND PRODUCED BY TOM WILLOUGHBY

Order from

WILLOUGHBY SPURS BOX 1500, G.P.O., ADELAIDE

strap, so the spur wouldn't ride up your legs while you were spurring a horse or bullock.

"By then he had them made and under patent. Tom and I were great mates and we knew each other's every move, particularly when handling young horses. Tom tried a number of times to get me back into the rodeos, but after the war I had started a young family and had the commitments that go with that responsibility."

Research at IP Australia confirmed that Tom applied for a provisional patent on his spur design on 28th May, 1951 but a full patent was never granted. This certainly would have been because his spur was already in production and a patent will only be granted when the invention has not been publicly disclosed in any form, anywhere in the world.

Above left: An advertisement from Hoofs and Horns *magazine, August, 1951.*
Above right: A well-worn pair of Willoughby spurs, with the Australian Rough Riders Association Constitution, By Laws and Rules, *1952.*
—Photo Megan Galvin

contemporary spurmakers

TODAY IN AUSTRALIA, highly professional spurmakers are making a wide variety of spur styles, often specially to order, servicing local and international markets.

The market place in Australia is limited and very competitive. Perhaps at some time in the future these craftsmen will create a society or guild, such as Australian knife makers have done, to establish standards of excellence and to promote their work, in this country in particular. I would suggest also that custom spurmakers engrave or stamp an identifying number or mark on their spurs, which will clarify the identity of each craftsman in the years to come.

Many of the spurs now being retailed in Australia are manufactured cheaply overseas and in no way match the quality of workmanship available here.

In the USA there are hundreds of contemporary spurmakers, their products attracting a very high level of investment by collectors. I anticipate that over the next few years there will be an increased interest in this field in Australia.

Australian Bits & Spurs

Toowoomba, Queensland

TERRY MACKIN, of Australian Bits & Spurs, manufactures all of his products in Queensland providing three styles of spur including a Wave Hill style. Special orders are available on request.

—Photo Megan Galvin

Leo Benjac

Leyburn, Queensland

LEO BENJAC started making spurs for bull riders in 1967 as a hobby and at present manufactures about 250 pairs a year for selected saddleries in Australia and overseas, as well as dealing direct with riders.

He makes about six basic styles which have been developed over the years by consultation with campdrafters and rodeo riders, and in 1983 designed a lip around the inside of the heel band to fit between the heel and the boot to stop the spur from slipping. From time to time he holds courses in spurmaking at his factory in Leyburn.

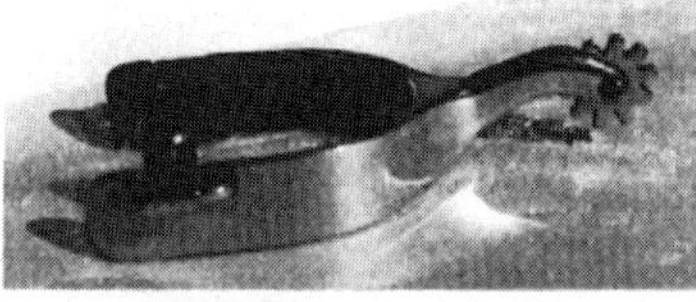

Most of his spurs are now produced from stainless steel plate, with the heel bands being cut by guillotine and then formed by hand, using special jigs. The necks are cut from 3/8 inch or 5/16 inch plate by laser, then welded onto the heel band.

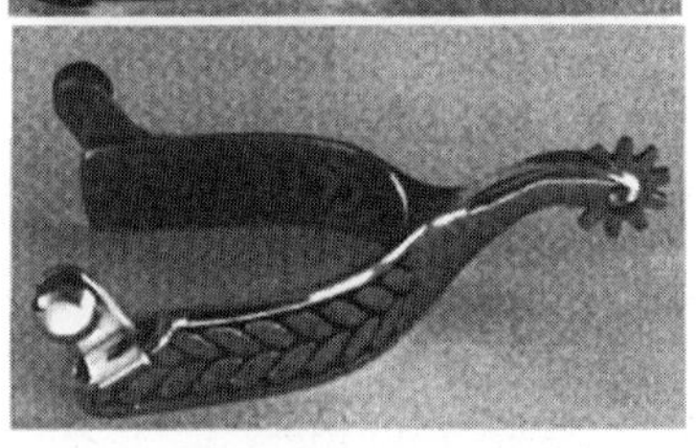

He also uses spring, or tool steel, from Sweden, cutting the necks and heel bands by hacksaw, although fancy styles of heel bands are cut by laser. More recently he has been making titanium bits and spurs, in particular for polocrosse players.

Leo's spurs – four of which are shown here – are stamped inside the heel band with one or both of the following marks: LEO, inside a crown and/or MADE, inside a map of Australia.

—Photos courtesy Leo Benjac

Lyle Davidson

Scone, New South Wales

LYLE DAVIDSON, spurmaker of Scone, the horse capital of Australia, made his first pair of spurs while still at school.

Some examples of Lyle's work are shown here. All spurs are made totally by hand.

—Photos courtesy Hans van Hees

"K" Bits & Spurs

Narangba, Queensland

Rod and Karyn Kaye, of "K" Bits & Spurs, Narangba, sent some photos of their spur-making process showing:

The heel-band before bending around the die (right); the neck being fitted on to the heel-band (left); polishing the spur (right); and the finished spur (below, left).

The silver work on the 'Kendra' spurs is by Annie Wieden of Jandowie, Queensland.

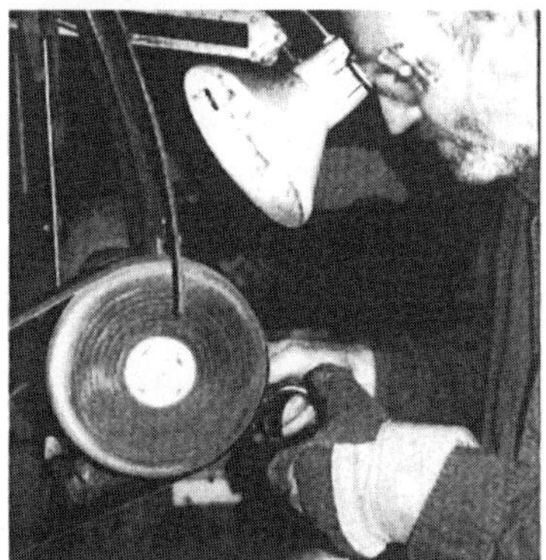

A boilermaker by trade, and an experienced horseman, Rod started making bits as a hobby about nine years ago and now produces a wide range of bits and spurs, making anything a rider requests.

Rod and Karyn set up their own business four years ago, and travel from Victoria to Western Queensland attending Campdrafts, Cutting, Reining and Western shows to sell their products.

On the right are more examples of Rod's work. The top pair were made for a tall, long-legged rider.

—All photos courtesy Karyn Kaye

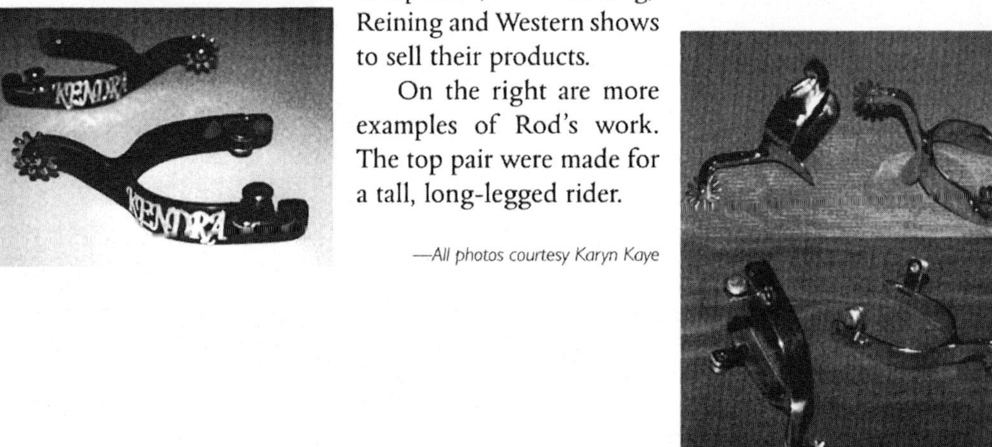

Ken Martin

Winton, Queensland

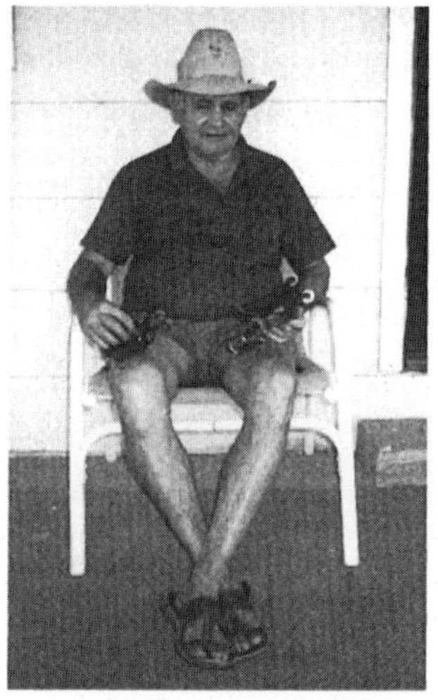

While in Winton I heard from Bernie and Richie Searle at their general store of a former ringer, Ken Martin, who made spurs and sold them locally. We finally tracked Ken down and found that he had been brought up on the road, his father Glen Martin was a drover in Western Queensland, the Northern Territory (mostly on the Eastern side) and in New South Wales.

Ken has worked on Durham Downs on the Cooper, ran the camp on Springvale for three years and was at Mount Windsor for seven years. In 1969 he went to Mount Bundey in the Territory, shooting and domesticating buffalo. He also worked at Mount Ringwood with Cecil Teece and for Abe Teece on Goodparla.

These photos by the author (above) show Ken and two of his spur styles.

To make his spurs Ken uses spring steel that is manageable, so it doesn't spring back when bending the heel band cold on the anvil.

"I use a harder and thicker steel for the neck, cutting it to shape with a hacksaw or angle grinder; using the first neck as a pattern to shape the second neck, and cut the slot for the rollers with the angle grinder. I then weld the neck onto the heel band and use ready made rollers. There's just too much work in making them by hand.

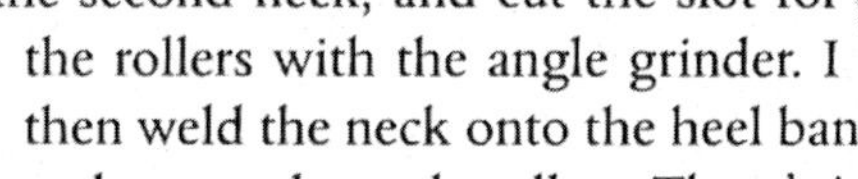

"I shape the necks from the rider's point of view, you don't want to spur a horse more than once to get him moving."

Ken also makes bronc spurs for rodeo work,and knows a bit about rough riding as shown in the photo at left, taken at the Condamine rodeo in about 1964. The horse did not fall backwards and Ken did stay on for the ten seconds..

—Photo at left courtesy Ken Martin. Spur photo Bill O'Brien.

Ken J Miller

Boonah, Queensland

KEN MILLER AND HIS WIFE Jo-Anne run their 50-acre Quarter Horse stud, 'Loriner', the home of stallions Roc's Excellence and Little Smart Doc, near Boonah, training and showing their own horses. They have established their business, Ken Miller Bits & Spurs, over a ten year period, and two examples of Ken's custom spurs are shown here. They are made of stainless steel, with 'rope edges'.

—*Photos courtesy Ken Miller*

Alan Morris

Lowood, Queensland

ALAN MORRIS, a blacksmith artisan living at Lowood, has won the Dame Mary Durack Outback Craft Award, Blacksmith Category, with spurs forged in the traditional manner. Alan made a pair of spurs for me while I was living overseas and photographed some steps of the process, as shown here.

1. The bar stock was made by forge welding layers of mild steel, iron and one layer of spring steel in the middle. The bar stock is then marked off in equal proportions for each spur.

2. The bar stock is heated and cut with a 'hot set', (a hammer-handled cutting tool).

3. The material is fullered using

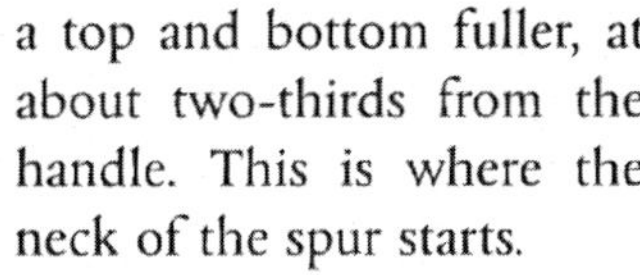
a top and bottom fuller, at about two-thirds from the handle. This is where the neck of the spur starts.

4. The neck portion is drawn out.

5. Shows the finished length of the neck of the spur.

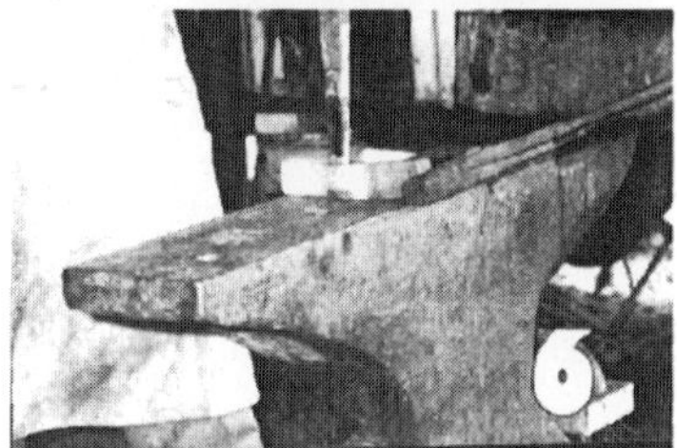

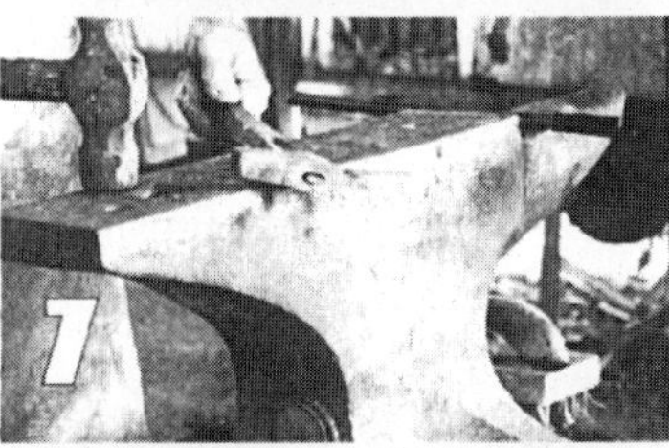

6. The yoke (or heel band) of the spur is formed by 'slot punching' where the branches of the yoke will separate from the neck.

7. Shows the punch through the metal and the round soft edge of the slot.

8. A hot set is used to split the material – first from one side half way through, then finished off from the other side.

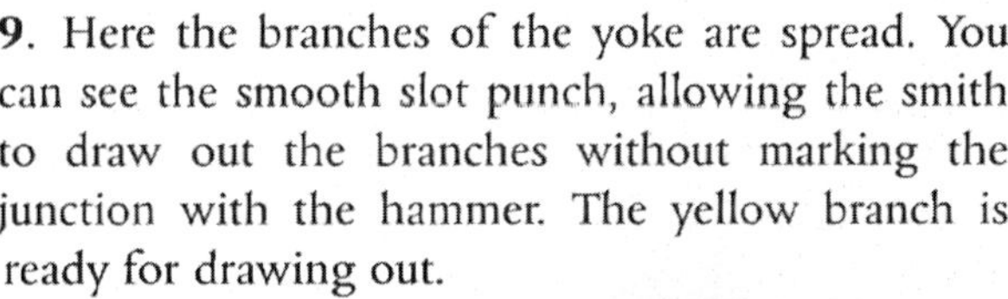
9. Here the branches of the yoke are spread. You can see the smooth slot punch, allowing the smith to draw out the branches without marking the junction with the hammer. The yellow branch is ready for drawing out.

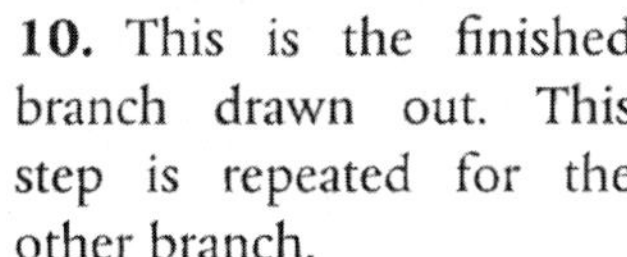
10. This is the finished branch drawn out. This step is repeated for the other branch.

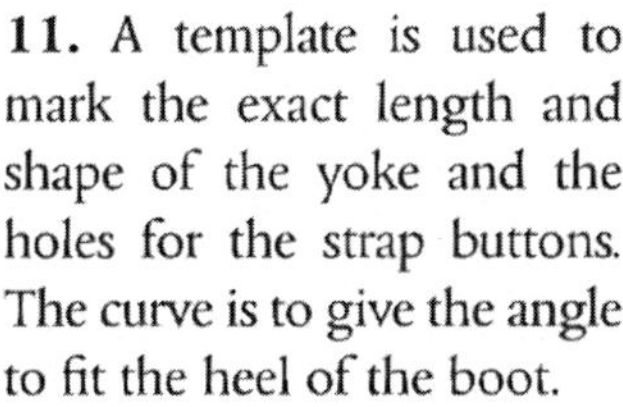
11. A template is used to mark the exact length and shape of the yoke and the holes for the strap buttons. The curve is to give the angle to fit the heel of the boot.

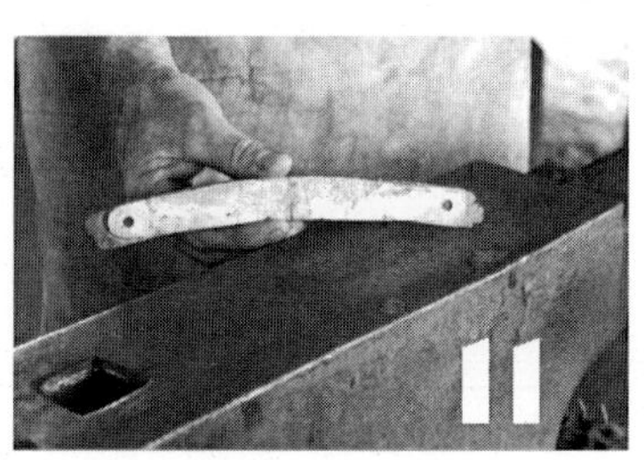

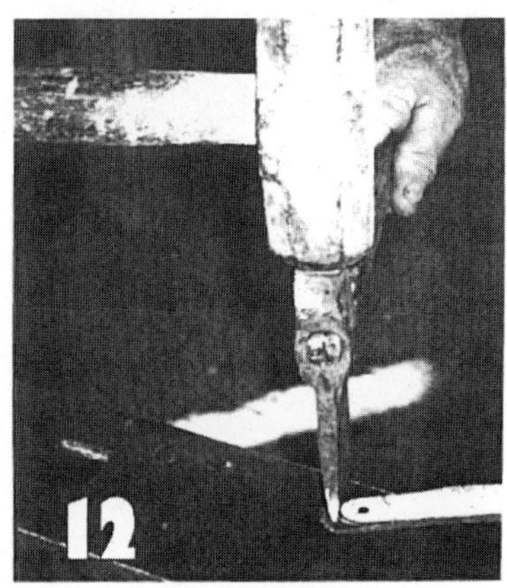

12. The excess is cut off.

13. The neck is then drawn out to give length and width.

14. The neck is rolled up and forge welded to produce suitable material in the neck to accommodate the rollers. The spur at the left hand side of the anvil is completed, the other one is ready for its first forge weld. This completes the basic forging. Next follows grinding and polishing to size and finish.

15. The material is cut out for the roller slot. The holes are drilled for the roller pin.

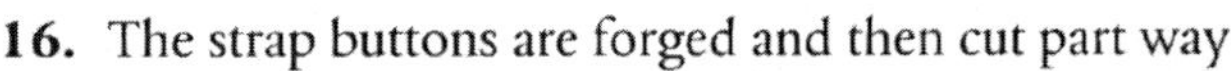

16. The strap buttons are forged and then cut part way through with a hot set. This leaves a handle to put the button back in the fire.

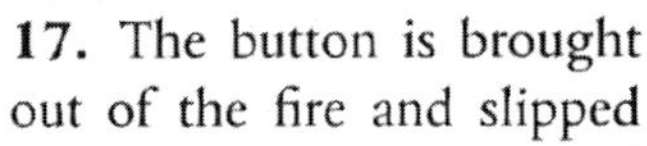

17. The button is brought out of the fire and slipped into a bolster; the handle is twisted off and the head is formed with a hammer. A finished button can be seen on the anvil. The buttons are then threaded and the holes in the yoke are tapped to accept the buttons. At this stage all polishing is completed. The spurs are then etched to bring out patterns in the stock from the welding of different types of steel, as explained in Point 1.

18. The finished spurs.

—All photos courtesy Alan and Alison Morris

Kevin Perks

Charters Towers, Queensland

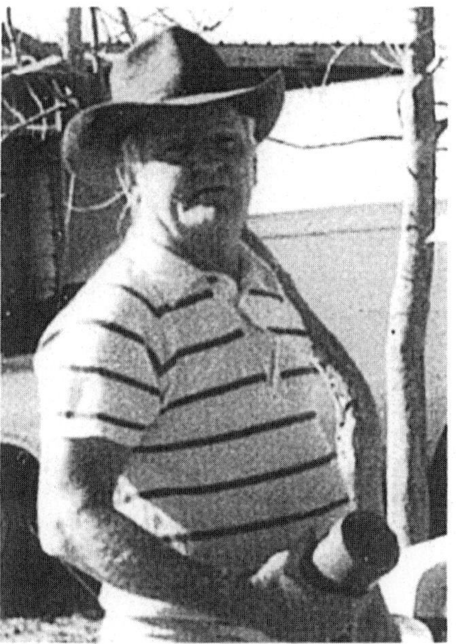

KEVIN PERKS, at right, was ringing for many years in Queensland, around Charters Towers and Maryborough, and later in the Northern Territory. He was also a cook for the road camps of The Department of Works in the Territory, and made spurs, knives and pocket knives as a hobby.

When he retired to Lochwall station, Charters Towers, he spent most of his time making knives, which were in great demand because of the quality of his workmanship.

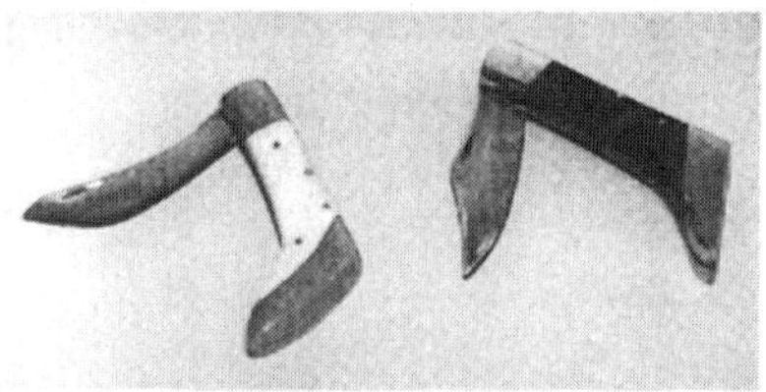

His brother, Mick, also a former ringer, was well known for the unique forks he made, twisting and weaving number eight fencing wire intertwined with brazing rods, resulting in very popular gold and silver barbecue forks up to 55 centimetres long.

The spurs shown here were made on Douglas station, near Hayes Creek Roadhouse in the Territory. Kevin had a small forge and bent the heel bands hot, favouring Land Rover springs as material, and in this case he riveted the neck on from inside the heel band.

Sadly, the Perks brothers died in 2000, Mick in his eighties, and Kevin in his seventies.

Top: A pair of Kevin's knives.

—Knives photo Kerry Kendall, other photos courtesy Alan Davis

Robert Toole

Narangba, Queensland

ROBERT TOOLE was born and raised in Cooma, New South Wales and started riding poddy calves at the shows and mini rodeos there in 1976. Over the last twenty four years he has competed in rodeos all over Australia, as well as in Canada and the United States.

Robert is now self-employed in his own business, Silver Steel Spurs, making custom spurs and trophy spurs for all rodeo events, and is a silversmith and engraver. In 1988 he had the opportunity to work with Master Engraver and Spurmaker, Jerry Veldez, in Billings, Montana, U.S.A., invaluable experience for setting up Silver Steel Spurs in 1997.

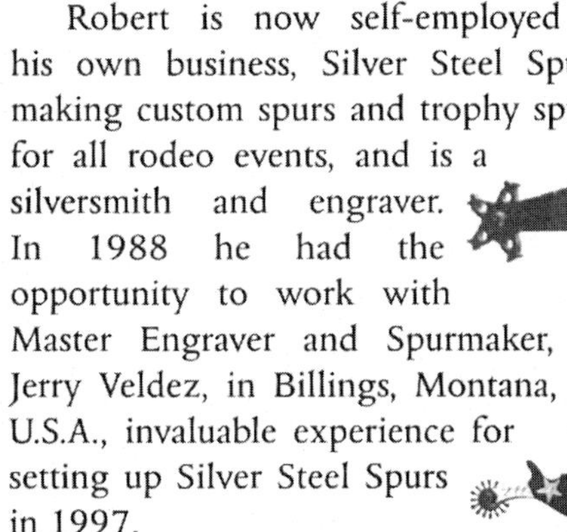

In 2000 and 2001, his Australian Professional Rodeo Association rodeo career peaked when he won the Australian Saddle Bronc Rider title at Rockhampton and Toowoomba in Queensland.

Top: Robert on Rough Going, Beaudesert, Queensland, in 2000 and (above left) the APRA Rookie Bronc Rider Trophy, 2001, made by Robert.
—Photos Mike Kenyon, Wellers Hill, Qld

Above right: Two other styles made by Robert.
—Photos Robert Toole

Trevor Young

Warwick, Queensland

BORN IN BUNDABERG, Queensland, in 1951, Trevor Young made his first spurs for rodeo riders in the 1970s and by 1976 was working full time as a silversmith and traditional hand engraver. He designs, creates and hand engraves every piece by himself.

Much of his work has been making gold and sterling silver trophy belt buckles as well as well as trophy cups, bits and spurs. He prefers to make individual and custom pieces and in correspondence wrote: 'People must realise that engraving tools and techniques have remained unchanged for hundreds of years. The engraver is truly as unique as the skill he has endeavoured to master. Today, because of automation, the engraver and his skills are unrecognised except by those who know and appreciate fine craftsmanship'.

Two of Trevor's custom pairs.
—Photos courtesy Trevor Young

spurs from other countries

WHILE LIVING OVERSEAS I took the opportunity to collect spurs where possible, in most cases from antique or second hand shops. I did not find any rarities but thought it worth including some photographs here.

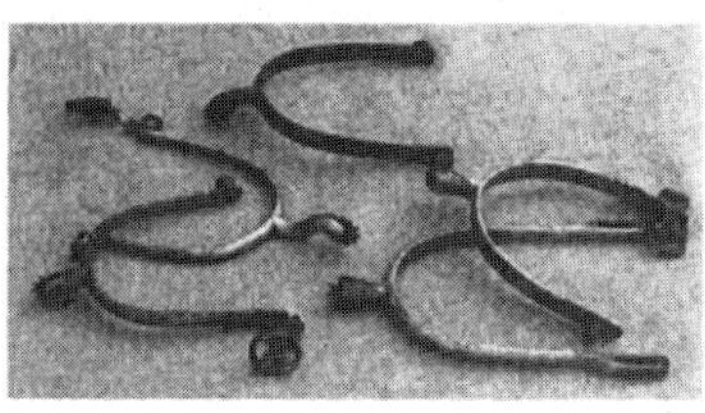

Five single spurs from Portugal are shown at left. The area where we lived was essentially a farming and donkey community and although we travelled extensively in Portugal we did not see horse shows or events such as are frequently held in Spain.

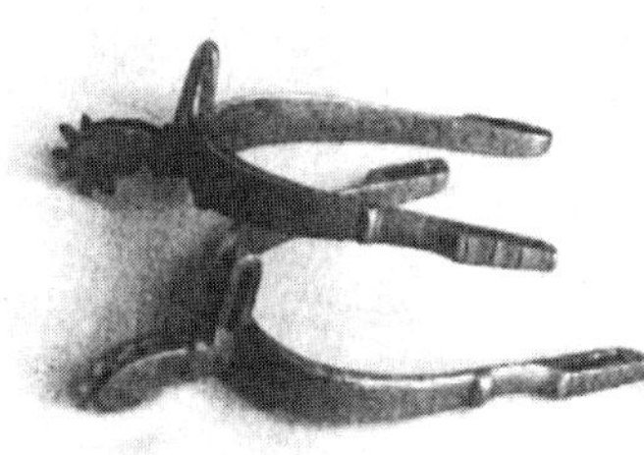

The pair of brass spurs at right were displayed in the Santa Luzia bar-restaurant in Manteigas, Portugal, where we lived for two years. 'Nossos caros amigos', our dear friends, Luis and Fernanda, gave them to us as a memento of our stay there.

The pair of Spanish spurs on the left are a modern style, manufactured in Huelva, in the south west of the country. They were purchased south of Seville, in Jerez de la Frontera, the home of the Royal School of Equestrian Art and the world famous Andalucian horses.

Every May Jerez hosts the Feria del Caballos, the Horse Fair, perhaps the most spectacular and colourful event we have ever attended. It is interesting that many Spanish riders use a single long strap to attach their spurs to the boot, threading it through the loops or slots in the spur, rather than the spur being fitted with strap studs or buttons.

The two pairs of English spurs at right are typical of that country, those on the left being military style box spurs, the short bar inside the heel band fits into a 'box' in the heel of the boot, eliminating the need for straps.

The 'brocante', or second-hand shops of France yield an interesting assortment of spurs, like those above left, some of them with heel bands spread to accommodate the very bulky early cavalry boots.

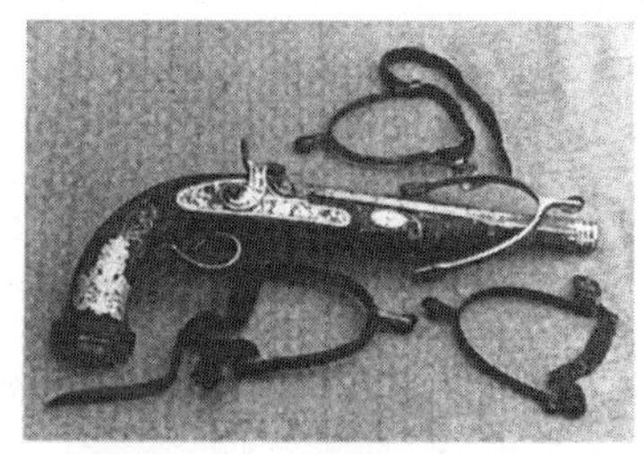

The antique shops of Turkey were the most interesting we found, with many treasures, including this very ornate pistol from the Ottoman period, and some spurs from the early 1900s.

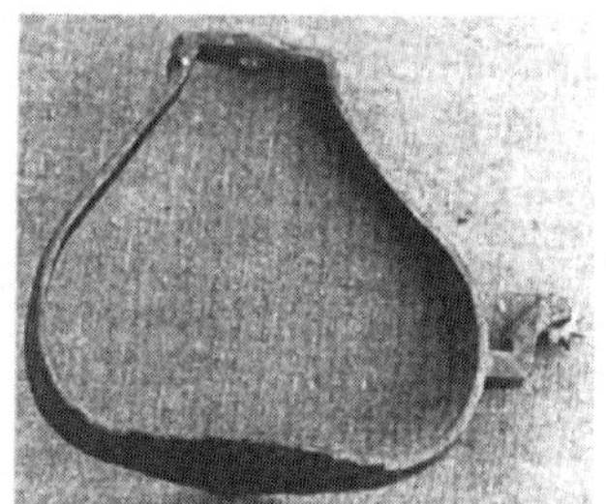

Most of our time in Greece was spent in the Cyclades Islands, where horses are not common and donkeys are still used as transport and beasts of burden. The closest I came to finding spurs was this stirrup incorporating a spur (left).

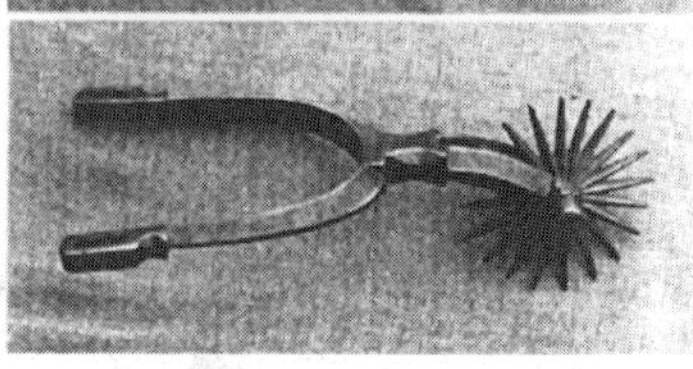

Two examples of Spanish Californian spurs (below right), purchased in England at the London Arms Fair.Also purchased in England is this typical Mexican spur (left). Like the Spanish styles, they have slots for the straps rather than studs or buttons.

The savage-looking spur below was purchased in Marrakesh, Morocco, and is said to be typical of those used by the Tuareg tribesmen of North Africa.

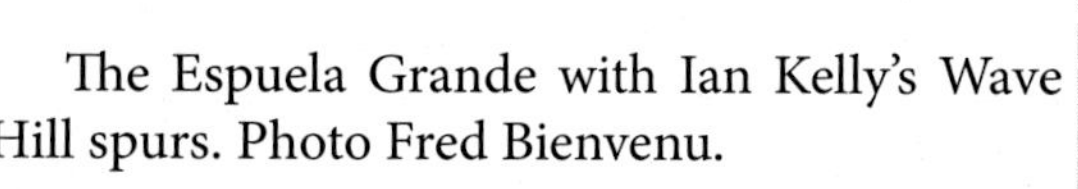

—Above photos Kim Corcoran

The 'Espuela Grande', or 'Great Spur' of the Spanish conquistadors. Photo by Fred Bienvenu.

The Espuela Grande with Ian Kelly's Wave Hill spurs. Photo Fred Bienvenu.

Spurs from the collection of Hans van Hees
Scone, New South Wales

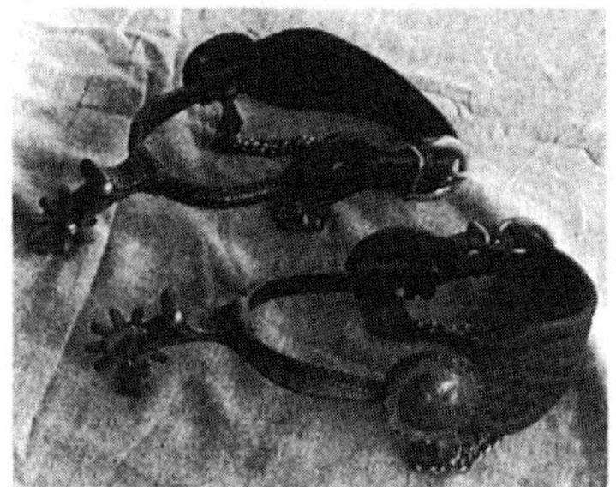

Double mounted silver inlaid Californian ladies' spurs (left), made by Garcia, of Elko, Nevada, U.S.A. in the 1920s. Note the jingle bobs attached to the rowel pins.

The earliest form of Bull-N-Bronc spur (right) produced by Garcia, they are sterling silver overlaid and originally belonged to Denver Dixon, a Wild West performer from the U. S. A. who came to Australia in the 1920s and 1930s. Denver gave them to his friend, the late Mick Roche of Sydney, N.S.W. who in turn, passed them on to Hans van Hees.

At right is a pair of Mexican made silver inlaid 'Gal Leg' spurs.

—Photos Don Corcoran

Spurs from the collection of Viv Carter
Murrurindi, New South Wales

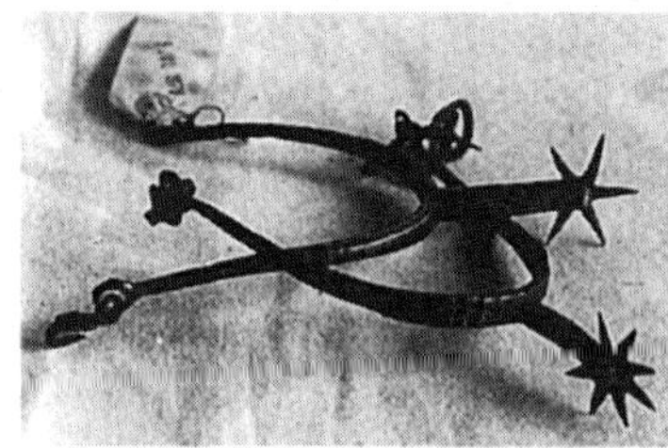

At left and right are European spurs, circa 16th Century.

The photograph below shows one of a pair of solid silver Japanese style spurs.

—Photos Viv Carter

retail catalogues and advertisements

WHEN RESEARCHING the history of spurs and many other fields of interest much information can be gained by studying early catalogues and advertisements.

For example, the R. M. Williams Angle Heel spur of the 1950s and 1960s incorporates the principle of the Wave Hill spur and in the 1920s and 1930s many saddleries stocked American made Mexican and cowboy style spurs, cowboy bridles, stirrups and even tapaderos (stirrup covers) as well as the standard English lines.

The 1935 Walther & Stevenson catalogue show a Lady's Guard Rowel spur — the guard pushes back exposing the rowel only on contact with the horse, so as not to scuff boots when walking or get hooked on dresses, particularly when riding side saddle.

1990 R. M. Williams Catalogue, Prospect, South Australia

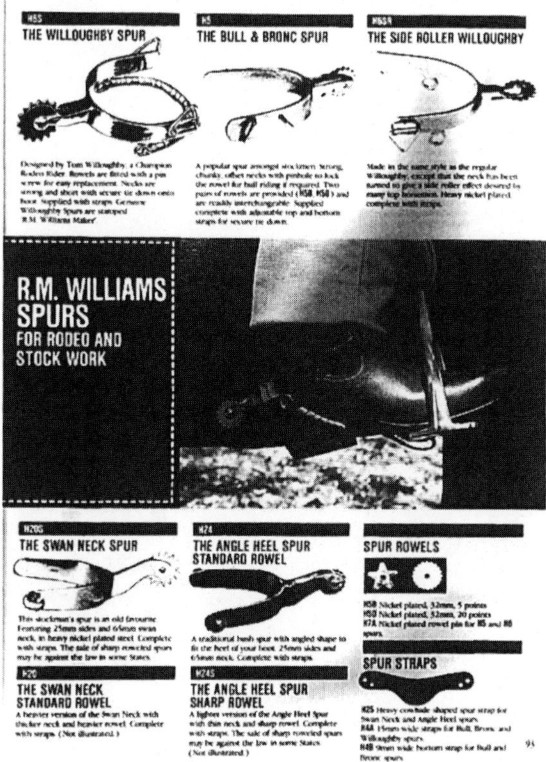

1987 Hoofs and Horns Advertisement

Three pages from a 1968 R.M. Williams Catalogue Prospect, South Australia

1967 L. Uhl & Sons, Catalogue No. 40, Brisbane, Queensland

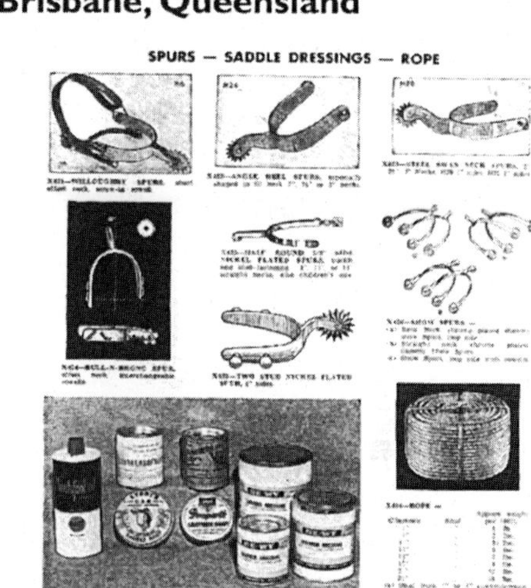

R. M. Williams 1954 Catalogue Prospect, South Australia

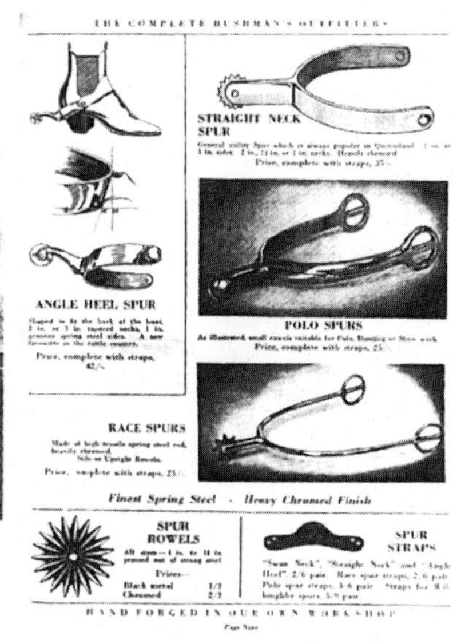

1950s Hoofs and Horns Advertisements

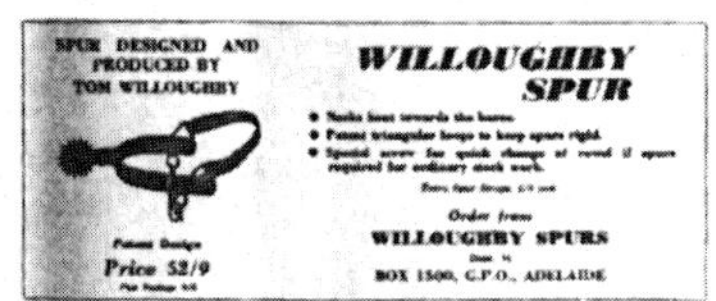

SPURS

Best Quality, N.P. on Irons Spurs with half-moon straps.

Straight Neck—

	To 2in.	2½in	3in. neck	
⅜in. side	5/-	5/3		pair
½in. side	6/-	6/6	7/-	pair
⅝in. side	7/-	7/6	8/-	pair
¾in. side	8/-	8/6	9/-	pair
1in. side	10/6	11/-	11/6	pair

Swan Neck—

⅜in. side	5/-	5/6		pair
½in. side	6/6	7/-	7/6	pair
⅝in. side	7/6	8/-	8/6	pair
¾in. side	8/6	9/-	9/6	pair
1in. side	11/-	11/6	12/-	pair

Best Quality N.P. on Steel Spurs, with half-moon straps.

Straight Neck—

	To 2in.	2½in	3in. neck	
⅜in. side	8/-			pair
½in. side	9/6	11/-	12/-	pair
⅝in. side	10/6	12/-	13/6	pair
¾in. side	12/6	14/6	15/6	pair
⅞in. side	14/-	15/9	17/3	pair
1in. side	16/-	18/-	20/-	pair
1¼in. side ..	21/6	23/6	25/-	pair

Swan Neck—

⅜in. side	8/6			pair
½in. side	10/-	11/-	12/-	pair
⅝in. side	11/-	12/-	13/6	pair
¾in. side	13/6	15/6	16/6	pair
⅞in. side	14/6	16/6	18/-	pair
1in. side	17/-	19/-	21/-	pair
1¼in. side ..	22/-	24/6	26/-	pair

STRAIGHT NECK SPUR.

Nickel plated on Iron Spurs, English made, with straps, To 2in.
Straight Necks, ⅜in., side .... 4/3 pr.
Swan Neck, ⅜in. side .... 4/3 pr.

SPUR ROWELS.

⅜in., ½in., ⅝in., ¾in. .... 4d. pr.
⅞in., 1in., 1¼in. .... 6d pr.
Mexican .... 1/- pr.

SWAN NECK SPUR.

SOLID NICKEL SPURS, with straps, half-round sides, heavy to 2in. straight or swan neck.
Price .... 7/- pair
Ditto, 2½in. neck. Price 7/6 pair
Ditto, 3in. neck. Price, 8/- pair

POSTAGE PAID ON SPURS.

TOM THUMB SNAFFLE.

N.P. on Iron, plain 4/3
N.P. on Iron, with Ring in mouth 4/9

ORDINARY BRADOON.

3in. and 3½in. rings, N.P. on Iron, 7/16in. 1/6
As above ½in. 2/-
3in. and 3½in. ring, N.P. on steel, 7/16in. 5/9
As above ½in. 6/9
3in. and 3½in. rings, Solid Nickel 6/9
RACE BRADOON, N.P., on steel, 3⅜in., Ring ⅜in. 7/6
PONY BRADOON, N.P. on Iron. Price 1/6

LOOSE RING SNAFFLE.

Pol. Iron, Medium, 2/-; Heavy, 3/-; Extra Heavy, 3/9.
N.P. Iron, Medium, 2/9; Heavy, 3/-; Extra Heavy, 4/-.

WILSON SNAFFLE.

Pol. Iron, Buggy, 1/6; Spring Cart, 2/-; Van, 2/3.
N.P. Iron, Buggy, 1/9; Spring Cart, 2/3; Van, 2/9.

G. J. SCHNEIDER, 387 GEORGE STREET, BRISBANE

1945 G.J. Schneider Catalogue, Brisbane, Queensland

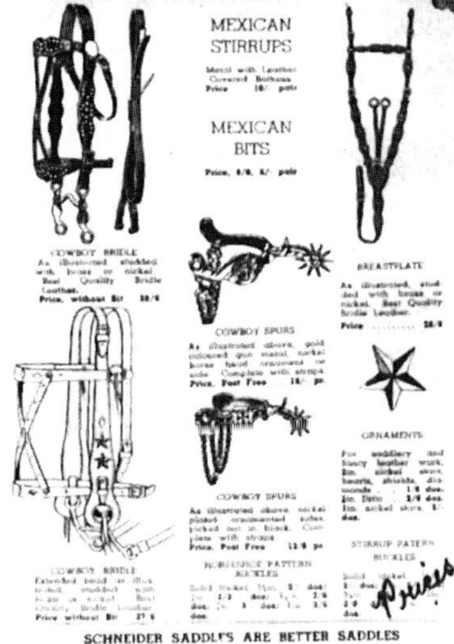

1941 L. Uhl & Sons Catalogue, Brisbane, Queensland

MEXICAN SPURS

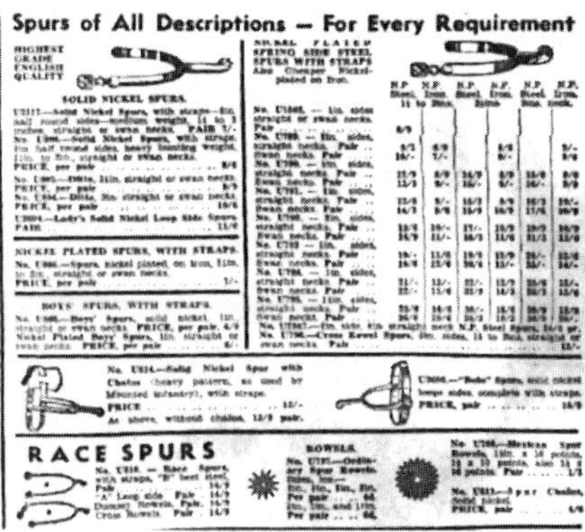
Spurs of All Descriptions – For Every Requirement

SOLID NICKEL SPURS.

NICKEL PLATED SPURS, WITH STRAPS

BOYS' SPURS, WITH STRAPS

RACE SPURS

1938 John Brush Catalogue, Sydney, New South Wales

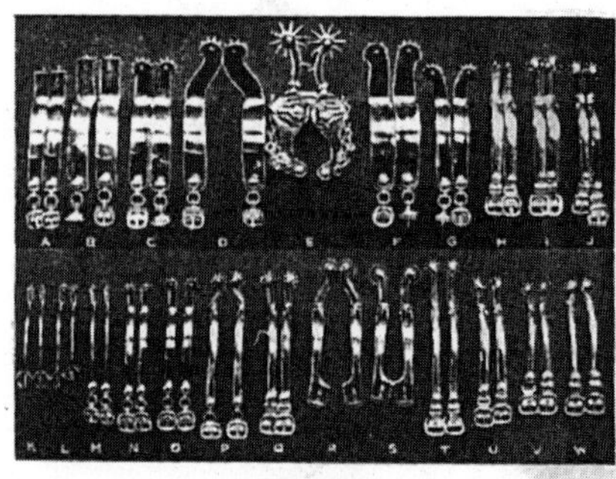

SPURS

A.	in. Side N.P. on Steel, Cross Rowels	13/-
B.	in. „ „ „ „ „ „	16/-
C.	in. „ „ „ „ Ordinary „	15/-
D.	in. „ „ „ „ „ „	16/-
E.	Gunmetal Texas Spurs	20/-
F.	1in. Side N.P. on Steel, Ordinary Rowels	19/-
G.	in. „ „ „ „ „ „	13/-
H.	in. „ N.S. Cross Rowels	8/6
I.	in. „ „ „ „	8/6
J.	in. „ „ Ordinary Rowels	7/6
K.	Wire Side Loop Side, Ladies, Cross Rowels	12/6
L.	„ „ „ „ Race	12/6
M.	„ „ N.P. on Steel Race, Cross Rowels	8/6
N.	in. Side N.P. on Steel, Ordinary Rowels	8/6
O.	in. „ „ „ „ „ „	8/6
P.	in. „ „ „ Iron „ „	6/-
Q.	in. „ „ „ „ „ „	6/-
R.	N.S. Bobs, Ordinary Rowels, Swan Neck	9/6
S.	N.S. Bobs, „ „ Droop Neck	9/6
T.	in. N.P. on Steel, Ordinary Rowels	10/6
U.	in. N.S. Ordinary Rowels	9/6
V.	Boys' N.S. „ „	5/6
W.	„ N.P. „ „	4/6

All with Straps—Post Free.

JOHN BRUSH,	BUTLERS & BRUSH,
371 George St. (near King St.)	432-4 Queen St. (opp. Customs House)
SYDNEY	BRISBANE

1935 Walther & Stevenson Catalogue, Sydney, New South Wales

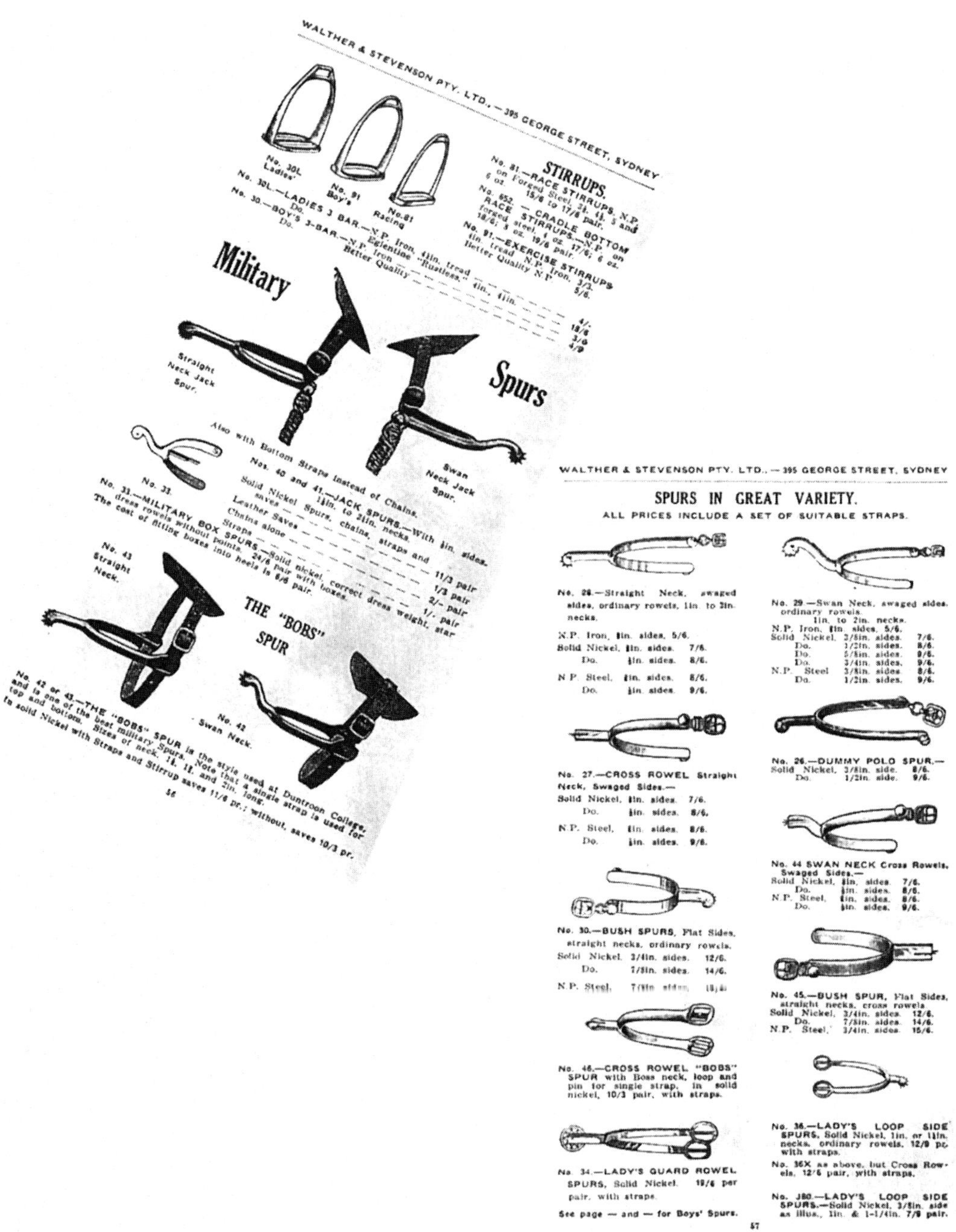

WALTHER & STEVENSON PTY. LTD., — 395 GEORGE STREET, SYDNEY

No. 30L Ladies' — No. 91 Boy's — No. 81 Racing

STIRRUPS.

No. 81.—RACE STIRRUPS, N.P. on Forged Steel, 3¼, 4¼, 5 and 6 oz. 15/6 to 17/6 pair.

No. 652. — CRADLE BOTTOM RACE STIRRUPS.—N.P. on forged steel, 4 oz. 17/6; 6 oz. 18/6; 8 oz. 19/6 pair.

No. 91.—EXERCISE STIRRUPS 4in. tread N.P. Iron, 3/3. Better Quality N.P. 5/6.

No. 30L.—LADIES 3 BAR.—N.P. Iron, 4¼in. tread — — — — 4/-
Do. Eglentine "Rustless," 4in., 4¼in. — — — — 18/6
No. 30.—BOY'S 3-BAR.—N.P. Iron — — — — 3/6
Do. Better Quality — — — — 4/9

Military Spurs

Straight Neck Jack Spur.

Swan Neck Jack Spur.

Also with Bottom Straps instead of Chains.

Nos. 40 and 41.—JACK SPURS.—With ½in. sides. 1¾in. to 2in. necks.
Solid Nickel Spurs, chains, straps and saves — — — — 11/3 pair
Leather Saves — — — — 1/3 pair
Chains alone — — — — 2/- pair
Straps — — — — 1/- pair

No. 33.

No. 33.—MILITARY BOX SPURS.—Solid nickel, correct dress weight, star dress rowels without points. 24/6 pair with boxes. The cost of fitting boxes into heels is 6/6 pair.

No. 43 Straight Neck.

THE "BOBS" SPUR

No. 42 Swan Neck.

No. 42 or 43.—THE "BOBS" SPUR is the style used at Duntroon College, and is one of the best military Spurs. Note that a single strap is used for top and bottom. Sizes of neck, 1¼, 1½, and 2in. long. In solid Nickel with Straps and Stirrup saves 11/6 pr.; without, saves 10/3 pr.

56

WALTHER & STEVENSON PTY. LTD., — 395 GEORGE STREET, SYDNEY

SPURS IN GREAT VARIETY.

ALL PRICES INCLUDE A SET OF SUITABLE STRAPS.

No. 28.—Straight Neck, swaged sides, ordinary rowels, 1in. to 2in. necks.
N.P. Iron, ⅜in. sides, 5/6.
Solid Nickel, ⅜in. sides. 7/6.
Do. ½in. sides. 8/6.
N.P. Steel, ⅜in. sides. 8/6.
Do. ½in. sides. 9/6.

No. 27.—CROSS ROWEL Straight Neck, Swaged Sides.—
Solid Nickel, ⅜in. sides. 7/6.
Do. ½in. sides. 8/6.
N.P. Steel, ⅜in. sides. 8/6.
Do. ½in. sides. 9/6.

No. 30.—BUSH SPURS, Flat Sides, straight necks, ordinary rowels.
Solid Nickel. 3/4in. sides. 12/6.
Do. 7/8in. sides. 14/6.
N.P. Steel, 7/8in. sides. [illegible]

No. 46.—CROSS ROWEL "BOBS" SPUR with Boss neck, loop and pin for single strap. In solid nickel, 10/3 pair, with straps.

No. 34.—LADY'S GUARD ROWEL SPURS, Solid Nickel. 19/6 per pair, with straps.

See page — and — for Boys' Spurs.

No. 29.—Swan Neck, swaged sides, ordinary rowels. 1in. to 2in. necks.
N.P. Iron, ⅜in. sides, 5/6.
Solid Nickel, 3/8in. sides. 7/6.
Do. 1/2in. sides. 8/6.
Do. 5/8in. sides. 9/6.
Do. 3/4in. sides. 9/6.
N.P. Steel 3/8in. sides 8/6.
Do. 1/2in. sides. 9/6.

No. 26.—DUMMY POLO SPUR.—
Solid Nickel, 3/8in. side. 8/6.
Do. 1/2in. side. 9/6.

No. 44 SWAN NECK Cross Rowels, Swaged Sides.—
Solid Nickel, ⅜in. sides. 7/6.
Do. ½in. sides. 8/6.
N.P. Steel, ⅜in. sides. 8/6.
Do. ½in. sides. 9/6.

No. 45.—BUSH SPUR, Flat Sides, straight necks, cross rowels.
Solid Nickel, 3/4in. sides. 12/6.
Do. 7/8in. sides. 14/6.
N.P. Steel, 3/4in. sides. 15/6.

No. 36.—LADY'S LOOP SIDE SPURS, Solid Nickel, 1in. or 1¼in. necks, ordinary rowels, 12/9 pr. with straps.

No. 36X as above, but Cross Rowels, 12/6 pair, with straps.

No. J80.—LADY'S LOOP SIDE SPURS.—Solid Nickel, 3/8in. side as illus., 1in. & 1-1/4in. 7/9 pair.

57

1932 Walther & Stevenson Catalogue, Sydney, New South Wales

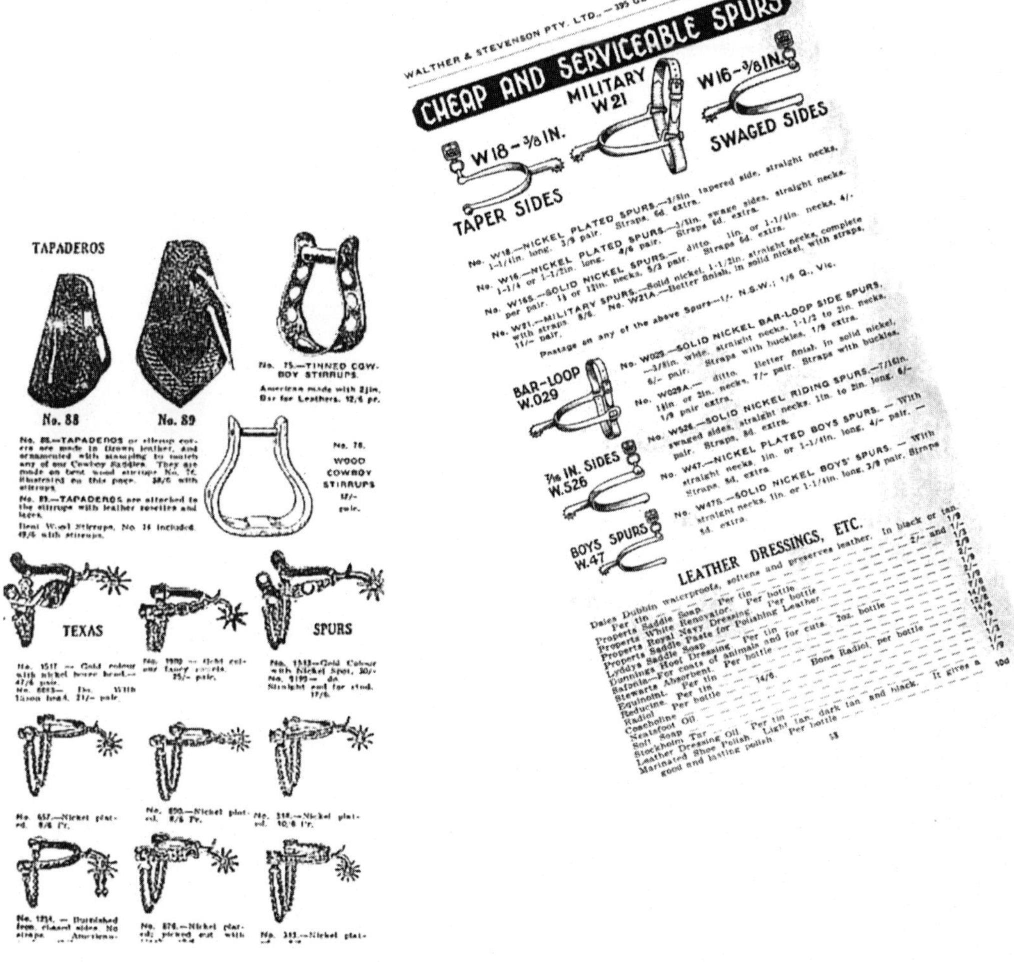

1929 John Wieneke Catalogue, Brisbane, Queensland

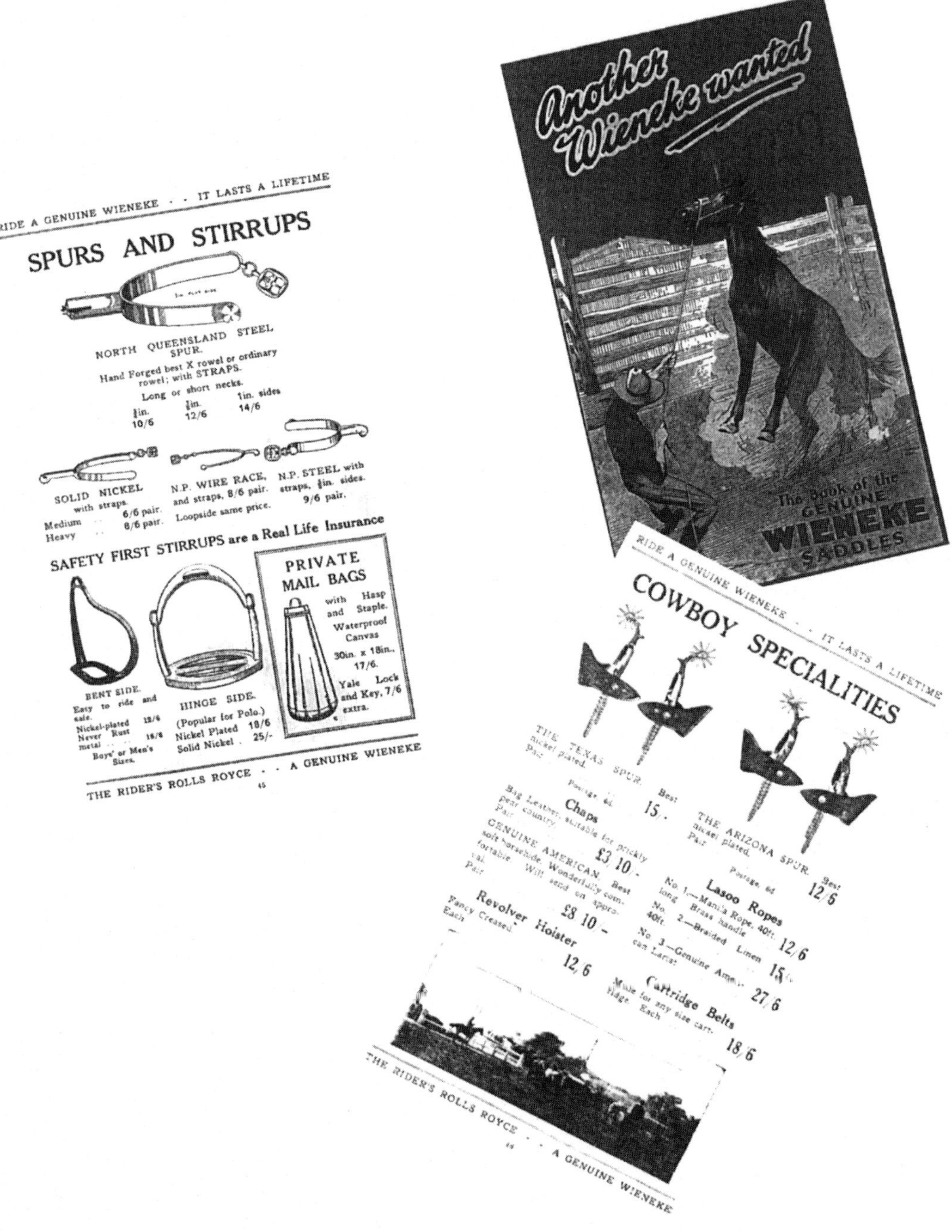

Advertisement from GRAZIERS' REVIEW, 1925

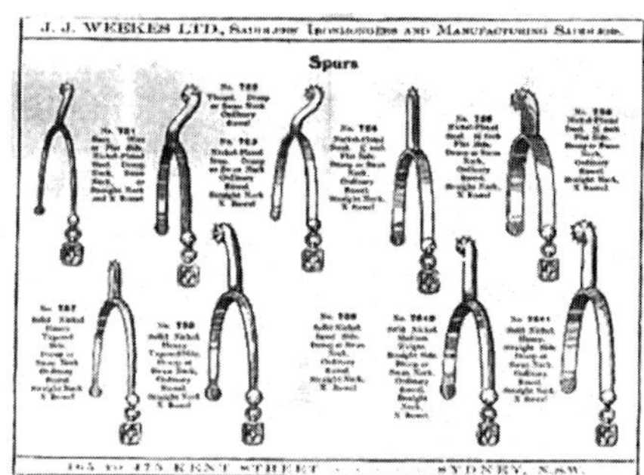

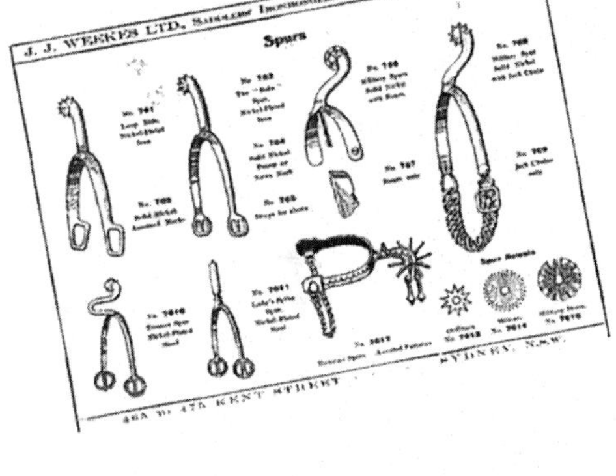

1920s – J. Weekes Catalogue, Sydney, New South Wales

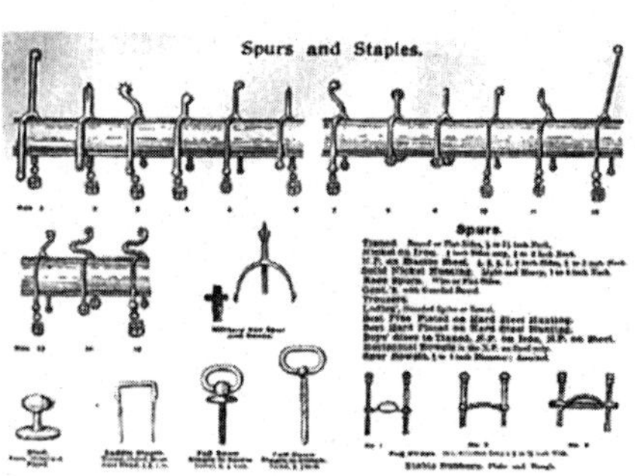

1902 Holdsworth, Macpherson Catalogue, Sydney, New South Wales

bibliography

Bowen, Jill. *Kidman The Forgotten King*, Angus & Robertson, Australia.

Coppock, Rose Rawlins. *Bush Tracks and Desert Horizons*, Outback Books, 1999.

Crosbie, Bill. *On a Good Horse in a Swinging Canter*, Bill Crosbie, 2008.

Donnellan, Teresa. *Tarcowie Place of Washaway Water 1873-1898*, Tarcowie Progress Association Book Committee, Tarcowie, South Australia.

Fogarty, Lloyd. *Not Without His Sons*, CQUP, 2008.

Gard E & R, Hewitt D, and Bamford M. *The Canning Stock Route*, Australian Geographic Pty Ltd., Terrey Hills, New South Wales, Australia.

Hammill, Bill. *Don't Trot the Bullocks*, Seaview Press, Adelaide, Australia.

Harbord, F. W., *The Metallurgy of Steel*, Charles Griffing & Company, Limited, London, U.K.

Hicks, Jenny. *Australian Cowboys Roughriders & Rodeos*, Central Queensland University Press, Australia.

Hill, Len. *Droving With Ben Taylor*, Hesperian Press, 2009.

Ingham, Anne Marie, *The Boss Drover and his Mates*, Halstead Press, Sydney, Australia.

Lewis, Darrell. *A Shared History, Aborigines and White Australians in the Victoria River District, Northern Territory*. Create-A-Card, Darwin, Australia.

Lewis, Darrell. *The Murranji Track*, CQUP, 2007.

McConville, Ray. *Thorpe McConville's Wild Australia*, Ray McConville, 1999.

McPhee, David R. *Snakes and Lizards of Australia*, Methuen of Australia, Sydney, Australia.

Macnamara, Ray. *The Way it Was*, Ray Macnamara, 2002.

Mannion, John and McKinnon, Malcolm. *No Place Like Pekina — A Story of Survival*, Pekina 125 Committee, Pekina, South Australia.

Makin, Jock. *The Big Run*, Rigby, Sydney, Australia.

Miller, Lilian Ada. *The Border and Beyond*, Lilian A. Miller, Mount Isa, Queensland, Australia.

Ogden, Pearl. *From Humpy to Homestead: The Biography of Sabu*, Pearl Odgen, Darwing, Australia.

Overton, Joice I, *Cowboy Bits and Spurs*, Schiffer Publishing, U.S.A.

Pattie, Jane. *Cowboy Spurs and Their Makers*, Texas A&M University Press, U.S.A.

Proctor, Ralph G. *Aim High – Proc's Journey*, Clare-Pear Publishing, 2005.

Schultz, Charlie and Lewis, Darrell. *Beyond the Big Run*, University of Queensland Press, Brisbane, Queensland, Australia.

Shannon, Alan. *Twentieth Century Profiles*, Boolarong Press, 1991.

Shaw, Bruce. *Banggaiyerri, The Story of Jack Sullivan, as told to Bruce Shaw*, Australian Institute of Aboriginal Studies, Canberra, Australian Capital Territory, Australia.

Simpson, Bruce. *In Leichhardt's Footsteps*, ABC Books, Sydney, Australia.

Simpson, Bruce. *Packhorse Drover*, ABC Books, Sydney, Australia.

Simpson, Bruce. Hell, *Highwater & Hard Cases*, ABC Books, Sydney, Australia.

Stone, George Cameron. *A Glossary of the Contruction, Decoration and Use of Arms and Armor, in all Countries and in all Times*, Jack Brussel, New York, U.S.A.

Webber, Ronald. *The Village Blacksmith*, David & Charles, Newton Abbot, Devon, U.K.

Weygers, Alexander G. *The Complete Modern Blacksmith*, Ten Speed Press, Berkeley, California, U.S.A.

Willetts, Pic and Briffa, Merice. *Wind On The Cattle, Recollections Of Fifty Years of Droving*, Auscribe Enterprises, Oxley, Queensland, Australia.

Williams, Reginald Murray and Ruhen, Olaf. *Beneath Whose Hand*, The MacMillan Company of Australia, South Melbourne, Australia.

Other Sources

Cattle Pads, The official newsletter of The Drover's Camp Association Inc. Camooweal, Queensland.

Stockman's Hall of Fame. The official publication of The Australian Stockman's Hall of Fame and Outback Heritage Centre, Longreach, Queensland, Australia.

R. M. Williams Outback Magazine. Netural Bay, Sydney, Australia.

index

Note: Stations are listed simply as places names

about the author

JOHN CORCORAN was born in Sydney, New South Wales, in 1936, and in his early teens worked in the North West of that state, as a station hand on Towri station, near Burren Junction, where the manager, Gerry Chapman, taught him the basics of riding and handling stock. Later, John and his mate, Mick Bower, were attracted to the Northern Territory by stories they had read, and in particular, accounts of the life there as depicted in *Hoofs and Horns* magazines of the 1950s.

They arrived in the Territory in 1954 and their first job was droving for Edna and John Jessop. This entailed taking a mob of cows from Helen Springs, near Renner Springs, to the rail head at Dajarra in Western Queensland, about three months on the road. It was Edna who decided that John would be called Don, (as there was already one John in the camp), a name that has stayed with him.

Don continued working in the bush for the next few years as a ringer in the Territory and Western Queensland, and as a station hand in New South Wales. He settled back in Sydney in 1956 and joined the New South Wales Police Force when he and Margaret Keenan, of Broken Hill, were married in 1957. After ten years as a policeman, six of those years as a Detective in the Criminal Investigation Branch, he resigned and joined the then fledgling computer industry, training as a salesman of mainframe computer systems.

Don has always maintained an interest in the outback and has been a collector of antique firearms since he was a boy. In 1975 he published a book, titled *The Target Rifle in Australia*, 1860 to 1900, regarded as the definitive work on the history of competitive rifle shooting in Australia up until Federation. This book was re-published in the U.S.A. in 1995.

In 1996 he decided to research the blacksmith spurmakers of Australia, believing that their stories, especially that of Fred Gutte of Wave Hill, needed to be recorded while there were still drovers and ringers alive who knew these craftsmen personally. While carrying out his research, Don found that the book was evolving into a collection of stories about people, rather than just about spurs and their makers.

Don and Margaret now live in North East Victoria where Don is continuing his research into antique firearms and the outback.

Photo courtesy The North West Star/Carpentaria Newspapers, Mount Isa, Queensland